TRIBE
OF **HACKERS**
BLUE TEAM

TRIBE OF HACKERS BLUE TEAM

TRIBAL KNOWLEDGE FROM THE BEST IN DEFENSIVE CYBERSECURITY

MARCUS J. CAREY & JENNIFER JIN

WILEY

Contents

Acknowledgments

I want to dedicate this to my family and all the people who have helped me over the years. You know who you are, and I love you.

—Marcus J. Carey

I would like to thank my friends and family for being my support system and the Tribe of Hackers community for supporting our mission. We had no idea what kind of reaction the first book would bring, and now here we are with an entire series. I am grateful for the team at Wiley for working with us to bring these books to life. Lastly, thank you, Marcus, for believing in my potential. I wouldn't be here without you!

—Jennifer Jin

Foreword

I'll be honest with you: I destroyed the first Tribe of Hackers book with my highlighting, dog ears, and pencil and pen markings. The 14 questions that interweaved career and personal lives sparked inspiring and thought-provoking concepts. I was thrilled to learn it was going to become a series. The Tribe of Hackers series is one that every person in the InfoSec community should read. It showcases red teamers, purple teamers, blue teamers, and veteran leaders who have participated in the InfoSec community. It is their lives, their stories. From hearing their stories, we learn more about the community and the importance of understanding the human element's role within security. Let's face it—it's one of the reasons why securing anything can be a challenge.

To secure anything, there needs to be a balance between offense and defense. We need both to keep us secure. Sometimes it seems blue teamers are not getting equal attention as red teamers, and this needs to change. So, *prepare* yourselves: I thought I should take the time to share why they need equal attention and praise.

It is the blue teamers who are *identifying* what lies ahead and what tools will assist them. Honestly, blue teamers have the uncanny ability to self-study to solve problems and know how to apply new skills and technology. They are the ones working with the end users and customers when receiving a security issue. They are the ones who know who to go to and create and run processes.

They know the ins and outs of different departments and the various roles to communicate and reduce risks across the organization. They become leaders to share security concepts and possible items that can impact business. At times, those individuals don't know much about security at all.

Being a good blue teamer sometimes requires a bit of patience and empathy when sharing risks and strengths within an organization's security. Blue teamers work with constructive communication; in other words, they try their best to build and have good relationships between team members. At the end of the day, we cannot fix or solve anything unless we work together and understand one another. There are times when they need to take a deep breath and try their best not to scream. Once they are done, they focus on the problem, discuss the issues, operate with facts, try their best to not point blame at someone or call them out if they don't understand, and, most importantly, listen actively.

Overall, there's never a break for a blue teamer. Once the *containment* of the security risk is assured, blue teamers still don't get to press pause. It is an ongoing battle to prevent breaches at all hours and to be on top of everything with the ability to predict.

I know that's not everything about a blue teamer, but I hope it paints a picture of why blue teamers deserve recognition, because let's be real—you never hear about the hack or breach that never happened. To be a good red teamer, you need to experience what it's like to be a blue teamer and vice versa. In the end, no matter if you are a blue teamer or a red teamer, you will never be perfect. What do I mean by this? Red teamers: You will never find every single vulnerability for a specific target. Blue teamers: You will never be 100 percent secure. The *eradication* of all vulnerabilities is what we all strive to achieve.

Many of us have experienced a breach in some way, shape, or form, or at least know someone who has. Those of us who have entered InfoSec to protect the world from malicious attacks and our loved ones' personal data know how bad the *recovery* can be. We all know that we cannot do what we do without the collaboration of red teamers, blue teamers, and purple teamers.

It is the Tribe of Hackers series that demonstrates why this community is wonderful, from how much we want to learn about the world to how we can protect it by using *lessons learned* by others.

Tribe of Hackers Blue Team provides stories of the everyday heroes who you may never hear about in the news. But they are *the* essence to keeping us secure every day. Their reflections are honest and true and have provided a deeper understanding of what it's like to be a blue teamer. I hope these interviews encourage you to understand their perspectives and have a deeper empathy for them. If you are a blue teamer, I'm incredibly grateful for your dedication in keeping us all safe. Thank you.

Chloé Messdaghi
Founder, WomenHackerz
May 2020

Introduction

There are two clichés that I think about when I think about cybersecurity, especially the blue team aspect of it. The first is, "The definition of insanity is doing the same thing over and over again and expecting a different result."

This has been so true over my 20+ years in cybersecurity. Some tools and practices are still in place even though they aren't effective risk countermeasures. If you asked about the effectiveness of certain tools to 100 cybersecurity professionals, you'd get about the same number of takes.

Without real testing and metrics, who knows what works? But regardless, we keep on keeping on with the same things.

Another cliché classic is from Otto von Bismarck, who said something like, "Only a fool learns from their own mistakes. The wise person learns from the mistakes of others." Most blue teamers are graduates of the School of Hard Knocks.

Many blue team careers have been built on using trial and error to create effective security models. The reason I started the Tribe of Hackers series is so that people can learn from other professionals' insights on how to optimize cybersecurity technology, processes, and personnel for optimal impact.

Just like the *Tribe of Hackers: Red Team* book, we took our questions from social media. We are pleased that the community came together once again to ask those questions. Our amazing contributors are leaders in cybersecurity who want to share their tribal knowledge.

Knowledge sharing is key to getting better at cybersecurity. Back in the day when I worked in the intelligence community, there was information sharing problems. This problem is still with us today, especially in the civilian sector.

I think we can learn a lesson from the medical profession on how they share new treatments. It helps out globally. In cybersecurity we do not share information globally. If any country, demographic, etc., is more vulnerable to easy-to-mitigate attacks, we all lose. We should treat vulnerabilities like infectious disease outbreaks.

Another thing that I'd like to emphasize is the need to practice our craft. We need to practice our craft as an organization and at a technical level. At a corporate and technical personal level, we have to stay sharp. There is an old saying that practice makes perfect. Organizations should use tabletop exercises to vet their cybersecurity and incident response capabilities. A tabletop can be done by picking a possible breach/incident scenario and walking through how the company would respond. From the executives to corporate communications to technical staff, the response should be known.

The other way technical first responders can keep sharp is by participating in training and capture-the-flag (CTFs) challenges. CTFs can be fun ways to learn topics such as network traffic analysis to reverse malware. These skills will translate to better defensive capabilities for the individuals and organizations.

So, my three calls to actions are as follows:

- Let's quit doing the same old things because that's how we always did it. Try things, measure them, and stop them if they don't work.
- Share more information because that makes the whole world more secure.
- Lastly, quit trying to reinvent the wheel. Find others that have executed the strategy that you are attempting and listen. Don't fall into no one trying to solve this or you have to roll your own death spiral.

Don't forget that most of the things that we do are not life or death (unless they actually are). Remember that we on the blue team are here to help mitigate risk. Give your best advice on how to do business in the safest way and keep it moving. Don't take it personally if people don't follow your advice. Imagine my doctor not talking to me because I won't stop eating my favorite dessert. Our doctors are still there when we need them.

Be vigilant, and be there when people need their security and privacy defended.

Marcus J. Carey

The Questions

Just like our *Tribe Hackers Red Team* book, we asked our colleagues questions gathered from the community. The following tweets, in no particular order, provided the inspiration:

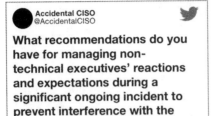

Accidental CISO
@AccidentalCISO

What recommendations do you have for managing non-technical executives' reactions and expectations during a significant ongoing incident to prevent interference with the team's response activities?

Oct 26, 2019

Andy Thompson, rainmaker
@R41nM4kr

What's your opinion on COMPLIANCE? Is it the catalyst for change, or is it the minimum viable product?

Oct 28, 2019

Bits & Digits
@bitsdigits

Is there a framework that aligns the activities or functions performed by a Blue Team with regulatory compliance requirements? Is it wise to do this, if not?

Oct 26, 2019

Bob Gourley
@bobgourley

How do blue teams establish trust with the many stakeholders they need to work with to be effective?

Oct 26, 2019

Damian
@decryptlyfe

How do you recognize blue teaming work, when in infosec red teaming is highly prized and glorified?

Oct 26, 2019

Duncan McAlynn
@infosecwar

What are some of the key strengths to an Incident Response Preparedness Program?

Oct 28, 2019

Jamy Casteel
@JamyCasteel

Where would you start if you were the only InfoSec staff member at a SMB with a primitive security infrastructure (perimeter firewall only)?

Oct 27, 2019

Kylie M(egatron)
@0xNBE1

What strategies do you use to communicate the threats you encounter to decision makers so they are aware of the risks?

Oct 26, 2019

Sahan
@SriLankanMonkey

How do you engage all the different units of an organization to maximize defense?

♡ ⬆ ♡ ✉   Oct 26, 2019

Sarah
@worldwise001

How do you define Blue Team? Especially when there are so many folks doing tangent work building secure systems or platforms but are not directly responsible for incident response?

♡ ⬆ ♡ ✉   Oct 26, 2019

Shawn Romines
@shawn_romines

What do you consider to be the one key foundational element in building a secure network from the ground up?

♡ ⬆ ♡ ✉   Oct 27, 2019

Thomas Pioreck
@TPioreck

How do you approach data governance and other methods of reducing your data footprint, restricting the scope of what needs absolute protection?

♡ ⬆ ♡ ✉   Oct 26, 2019

Tyler
@LonestarCyber

How do you continue to learn, practice, and grow as a blue teamer?

Oct 27, 2019

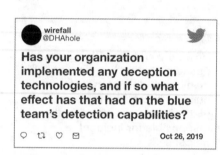

wirefall
@DHAhole

Has your organization implemented any deception technologies, and if so what effect has that had on the blue team's detection capabilities?

Oct 26, 2019

Andy Cooper
@integgroll

What is the least bang for your buck control you see implemented?

Apr 13, 2019

"At a micro level, the blue team consists of the individuals directly responsible for monitoring, defending, and responding to incidents."

Twitter: @marcusjcarey • **Website:** www.linkedin.com/in/marcuscarey

Marcus J. Carey

Marcus J. Carey is a cybersecurity community advocate and startup founder with more than 25 years of protecting sensitive government and commercial data. He started his cybersecurity career in U.S. Navy cryptology with further service in the National Security Agency (NSA).

1

How do you define a blue team?
At a macro level, the blue team is the entire organization, including the end users and customers. I say that because your end users and customers will be the first to notice when something goes wrong from a security perspective.

I know it's extremely awkward to have a customer let you know there is a security issue, but time and time again they end up saving us. Everyone is part of the team.

At a micro level, the blue team consists of the individuals directly responsible for monitoring, defending, and responding to incidents.

What are two core capabilities that a blue team should have?

I believe network visibility and log management are the two core capabilities every blue team should strive to master. In traditional infrastructures, network visibility allows organizations to understand what is happening on their network such as authentication, domain resolution, and all sorts of chatty protocols.

Network visibility goes hand in hand in the sense that not only do you have to ensure you can see what's going on the network, but you also need to make sure that information sources are logging events. They also need to ensure that the data is captured and can be analyzed (some in real time) for breaches.

This usually requires a log management system that requires enough storage to be useful for troubleshooting and forensic investigations.

TLDR: You have to make sure you are logging all the right stuff and that stuff can be retrieved for troubleshooting and incident response. Without those, you are probably playing security theater.

What are some of the key strengths of an incident response program?

I'm going to use the age-old concept of building a home-court advantage. You need to have a competent staff, which means you should invest in training and in hiring personnel hungry to learn and grow.

Solid incident response programs are built on top of knowing as much as possible about your system, software, and network infrastructure. You have to be able to ignore all normal activity as much as possible and zero in on the bad stuff.

Getting to zero is impossible because software will behave in weird ways, systems vary from organization, and users are going to do unexpected things. The key is to keep pushing, improving, and automating as much as possible.

How can blue teamers learn, practice, and grow?

I'm a big fan of the 80/20 model when it comes to learning and practicing your craft. Blue teamers should be able to spend 20 percent of their time on ongoing education and practicing new skills. It's a cycle in the sense that you learn first and then put those skills into practice, and the growth part is learning what works and what doesn't.

There are tons of free information sources that blue teamers can learn from. One of the traits of good blue teamers is their ability to self-study to solve problems. If you are hiring blue teamers, you should look for instances where they picked up new skills on their own.

If you are currently looking to get into a cybersecurity job, the most important trait that many hiring managers look for is your ability to self-study and learn new skills. You should "learn how to learn" and apply new skills. You'll drastically increase your value on the job market.

How do you reward good blue teaming work?

Compensate them properly and don't have them doing unnecessary security theater-type work. I personally make a promise to anyone who works with me that I'm going to ensure they are able to level up in their career. At some point in the future when they leave, their career will be on a higher plane. I sometimes see organizations stunt growth in order to retain personnel, which is wrong and always backfires.

What are some core metrics that a blue team can use to build, measure, and maintain a successful information security program?

When it comes down to it, blue teams will be measured ultimately in the mean time to detect breaches and mitigate the threats. To achieve this, the blue team is going to need to have the right people, processes, and technology to make it happen. The people need to be skilled, the processes have to be sharp, and the technology must be fully leveraged. Along the way, you have to continuously measure the mean time to detect along the way to improve and maintain those capabilities.

Where would you start if you were the only information security staff member at a small to medium-sized business with a primitive security infrastructure?

There are a ton of free resources from the National Institute of Standards and Technology (NIST). In particular, NIST's Cybersecurity Framework (CSF) is an amazing resource that any organization can pick up and start implementing.

In addition to the NIST CSF, there are several special publications (SPs) that they provide that I highly recommend for self-assessments, including these two:

- NIST SP 800-115: Technical Guide to Information Security Testing and Assessment
- NIST SP 800-37: Risk Management Framework for Information Systems and Organizations

What is the most bang-for-your-buck security control?

Limiting administrative privileges is the biggest bang-for-your-buck security control. Just by limiting these privileges you are going to reduce the number of intrusions on your network. It will keep people from installing unauthorized, bootlegged, or cracked software.

Attackers typically inherit the level of the user or service that they compromise. This means that they will not initially have privileges to do whatever they want on the system if they aren't administrators. If the attacker has to escalate privileges, it's another opportunity to catch them in their tracks.

Has your organization implemented any deception technologies?

No.

Where should an organization use cryptography?

The most effective places to use encryption are virtual private networks, web page logins, and full-disk encryption.

VPNs typically use encryption to keep the data private from end to end. Web page logins need to be encrypted so user-names, passwords, and all the other authentication data remain secret. Full-disk encryption is important in case a computer or laptop is stolen and the data on the disk is protected.

How do you approach data governance and other methods of reducing your data footprint?

I learned in the military that you always want to keep as little data as you can. Keep only what you are required by law or compliance. Don't keep unnecessary customer or employee data. Time and time again we see crazy stories of how organizations kept all their customer data around unencrypted on premises and in the cloud. The best way to avoid this is to not have the data in the first place.

What is your opinion on compliance?

I'm okay with compliance because it does set a bar and create a minimal threshold that organizations should adhere to. I hope that by now people realize that compliance is the absolute bare minimum and doesn't mean that they are secure by any means.

In addition, security leaders need to ensure they are communicating honestly.

Is there a framework that aligns the activities or functions performed by the blue team with regulatory compliance requirements?

I'm a huge fan of the NIST Cybersecurity Framework because it recommends continuous testing and evaluation of the security program at a higher level than most generic compliance standards.

How do you engage all the different units of an organization to maximize defense?

You have to work together to include all the different units of the organization as members of the blue team. Even if separated into different units, roles such as system administrator, network engineers, software developers, etc., need to be part of an internal cybersecurity review board that communicates and reduces risk across the organizations. That same team would be great in incident response when that eventual intrusion happens. When an incident happens, it shouldn't be the first time everyone is in a room together.

What strategies do you use to communicate the threats you encounter to nontechnical decision-makers?

I think security professionals need to speak more in terms of business risk and become educators to nontechnical decision-makers. The business should drive all security decisions. So, the security leaders need to be able to break down how security decisions impact the business in business lingo. Also, the blue team needs to help all members of the organization understand security concepts and how user decisions can impact the organization.

What recommendations do you have for managing nontechnical executives' expectations during a significant ongoing incident?

I recommend doing tabletop exercises with executives at least quarterly and going through the most likely incidents and responses. I mean everything—not just the technical, but also go through canned press statements, backup communications plans, incident response plans, disaster recovery plans, remote work plans, etc. Anything that is a part of the response should be covered so technical and nontechnical staff are on the same sheet of music.

Then when a significant ongoing incident happens, nontechnical executives have the proper expectations.

"We are all blue team."

Twitter: @DAkacki • **Website:** www.randoh.net

Danny Akacki

2

Who is Danny Akacki? He's just a storyteller perpetually looking for a stage. He loves nothing more than being able to attend conferences, give talks, write blogs, and find new ways to reach as many people as he can to educate them about security. For Danny, there is no greater satisfaction than community building.

He has been fortunate enough to spend his career in defense, learning from some of the best in the business, including teams at Mandiant, GE Capital, and most recently as a senior TAM with Gigamon. Danny loves what he does and the people he gets to do it with.

How do you define a blue team?

I define the blue team as every person in an organization. Everyone with a company login is inherently tasked with keeping the miscreants out. We are all blue team.

What are two core capabilities that a blue team should have?

A blue team should have an awareness of what data they have at their disposal and a way to look at it. Blinky boxes are nice, and vendor lunches are awesome, but if you don't know what data you have to begin with, or, more importantly, what data you're missing, you're dead in the water.

What are some of the key strengths of an incident response program?

- *Project management*: Making the trains run on time, or at least knowing where the fire extinguishers are when the engine is on fire.
- *Case management*: Where are you putting your team's findings and investigation notes? Is everyone on the same page?
- *Executive sponsorship and stakeholder buy-in*: IR doesn't live in a bubble. It needs to touch a lot of different areas guarded by a lot of different people with a lot of different goals.

How can blue teamers learn, practice, and grow?

- By studying the adversary.
- Threat emulation, programs like the Offensive Security certification track, reading every breach report that comes out, and studying attacker behavior.
- Getting to know their own network. Do you even know what you're protecting? Figure out what's important to your business and why/how someone would want to steal it.

How do you reward good blue teaming work?

Public acknowledgment and various treats of the jerky persuasion.

What are some core metrics that a blue team can use to build, measure, and maintain a successful information security program?

- Measure the percentage of increased incidents. Finding more stuff doesn't inherently mean your security is getting lax; it could very well be an indication of security process improvements. Things can appear worse while getting better.
- Applying employee training to actual business use cases. SANS courses aren't just expensive weeklong vacations. Make your people come back and debrief what they learned and then share that knowledge with the team.

Where would you start if you were the only information security staff member at a small to medium-sized business with a primitive security infrastructure?

Gather ye institutional knowledge. I'd find the person who's been there the longest and bribe them with treats to tell me everything they know about the company. Who owns what? Did we ever have a security incident? What happened? What exists where, and how can I get my eyes on it?

What is the most bang-for-your-buck security control?

The users. Every single person on the payroll is a member of the security team, and they are already getting paid to be there every day. They're also the most likely target for an adversary. Educate them and make them realize they have skin in the game.

Has your organization implemented any deception technologies?

Nice try, Fancy Bear.

Where should an organization use cryptography?

As the free square on a buzzword bingo card.

How do you engage all the different units of an organization to maximize defense?

By learning to speak their language. Translation is king, so find a way to translate security goals into business goals. Put a dollar amount on the damage of a breach. Better yet, put a news headline on it.

What strategies do you use to communicate the threats you encounter to nontechnical decision-makers?

Empathy. Find a way to care about what they care about and use that as a steppingstone toward mutual understanding.

What recommendations do you have for managing nontechnical executives' expectations during a significant ongoing incident?

Tell them Rome wasn't built in a day. Whatever happened, it took a while to happen, so it'll take a while to figure out. Help them understand that an IR team is a long-term investment, both in the longevity of the team and in the time it will take to understand what happened and why.

"A blue team at its core is an organization focused on defensive information security posture, analysis, investigation, and response."

Twitter: @teck923

Ricky Banda

Ricky Banda is a principal cybersecurity engineer at Blackbaud in Austin, Texas. With just over 10 years of experience in the field, he was recruited by the Air Force at age 16 as a government civilian to learn and support cyber operations around the world. Since then, he has worked in various organizations, from systems administration to hunting operations at an MSSP. While still young, Ricky is pressing forward to teach and open the door for those within his generation to follow similar paths to ensure growth within the information security sector.

3

How do you define a blue team?
A blue team at its core is an organization focused on defensive information security posture, analysis, investigation, and response. Dependent on the size of the organization, *blue team* may be the general term to reference a single department or multiple teams that make up defensive operations.

What are two core capabilities that a blue team should have?

Universally, the blue team should be able to perform the two following actions within an organization:

- **Consultation:** Educate, communicate, and assist stakeholders on the complexities of navigating the threat landscape, serve the organization as an area of expertise on risk mitigation, and build relationships to interweave security into various enterprise workflows.
- **Incident response:** Effectively respond rapidly to threats facing the enterprise to contain, eradicate, and enhance defensive posture for the organization.

What are some of the key strengths of an incident response program?

In my mind, the following items make up the strengths of an IR program; however, all are dependent on the documentation standards set forth by the organization.

- **Process:** The IR process should be clearly defined.
  - What is the IR process for the program?
  - Is an incident clearly defined?
  - What are the key areas of responsibilities between individual contributors and leaders?
- **Platforms:** Individuals who fall within the realm of executing tasks as part of the incident response program must have the correct tools to execute their tasks in a rapid manner.
- **Communications:** Clear lines of communications, standards, and SLAs (dependent on stakeholder) should be clearly defined. A strong incident response program will have effective manners of informal communications for rapid tasking and formal communications to inform affected users of an incident as well as leaders.
- **Actionable metrics:** A strong incident program will be able to communicate notables from incidents to leaders to make informed decisions on prioritizing and strategizing resource deliveries to enhance IR program capabilities.
- **Education:** The incident response program will be able to set standards of education and ongoing training for personnel to stay up-to-date on the changing threat landscape.

- **Relationships:** Most importantly, a strong incident response program will work extensively to build positive relationships with stakeholders to share information, concerns, and awareness to enhance defensive operations and maintain situational awareness.

How can blue teamers learn, practice, and grow?

Universally, it helps to have good use cases to model work around. In this case, the following example may be a good methodology to help in this practice as it's a model I follow for my growth:

- **Learn:** Create a hypothesis, and work through hypothetical but realistic situations in which blue team methodologies are put into practice.
  - Idea: Assume a threat actor has infiltrated the organization via a web application.
- **Practice:** Think of some questions to ask that relate to the idea.
  - Do I understand the underlying infrastructure that makes up the application?
    - The network infrastructure?
    - How the application is maintained?
    - The server infrastructure?
  - Can I re-create the attack method?
    - What does the network traffic look like?
    - What do the logs look like?
    - How was the application or infrastructure impacted?
- **Grow:** Can I reuse what I learned from this exercise for other attack vectors?

What are some core metrics that a blue team can use to build, measure, and maintain a successful information security program?

This is a difficult question to answer, as the typical response may be centered around alert closures or time to respond. However, as many are learning, these are not true metrics in which an InfoSec program may be effectively measured. Instead, such metrics should be centered on the following:

- Impact to stakeholders
- Impact to organizations
- Time spent on incident response procedures
- Risk mitigation measured via cost and/or hours

Where would you start if you were the only information security staff member at a small to medium-sized business with a primitive security infrastructure?
Understand the boundary. First, understand where the network begins and where it ends. Take an inventory of subnets, VLANs, and routing and switching standards implemented within the environment. Getting a feel and understanding ingress and egress within the environment helps when trying to build security controls in an organization with limited resources.

> Getting a feel and understanding ingress and egress within the environment helps when trying to build security controls in an organization with limited resources.

You won't be able to solve everything as single individual; however, in this use case, working from the network first does prioritize initial reconnaissance and sets the precedent for security controls within the rest of the enterprise.

What is the most bang-for-your-buck security control?
In my opinion, NetFlow and/or network intelligence–based solutions reviewing traffic to and from the boundary are the most bang-for-your-buck security controls. This type of visibility allows for further prioritization of work throughout the enterprise by informing the security organization of traffic coming in and out of the environment.

How do you engage all the different units of an organization to maximize defense?
Food. Seriously. The best way to maximize defense is to understand the stakeholders behind the products and processes you are defending. Take those individuals out to lunch, buy them coffee, and learn who they are and how their programs

> The best way to maximize defense is to understand the stakeholders behind the products and processes you are defending.

function. Oftentimes, blue teamers don't consider how their tools and visibility can help other departmental units with gathering information. As a force-multiplier for incident response, it's much easier to work with folks you know, and vice versa, when time is critical.

What strategies do you use to communicate the threats you encounter to nontechnical decision-makers?
Part of my strategy to build defense in depth is to educate decision-makers on the tools and workflows the blue team is utilizing to effectively respond to an incident.

For example, to a nontechnical manager who may be hesitant to install an EDR solution on their critical server, it's important to sit down and explain the use and purpose of the solution as well as the benefits, visibility, and awareness into how the tool will help during an incident or otherwise.

Explain the threat; teach, communicate, and collaborate; and do not mandate or expect nonsecurity folks to inherently follow your asks without justification. This only breeds resentment and raises barriers when incidents occur.

What recommendations do you have for managing nontechnical executives' expectations during a significant ongoing incident?
Educate the executive. Make time and ensure that the executive has clear expectations and deliverables for the incident. Establish SLAs, when they should expect to receive information, what actions they should follow, and what they need to do to support ICs during high-stress situations. Without educating the executive on incident response procedures, the incident program risks miscommunication and added stress that is otherwise not needed.

Executives are people too, with expectations on their shoulders during incidents; ensure that those needs are met along with the IR team.

> Without educating the executive on incident response procedures, the incident program risks miscommunication and added stress that is otherwise not needed.

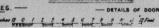

"To me, the idea of a blue team is a team that is protecting the company by building protections and putting them into practice."

Twitter: @__muscles • **Website:** www.linkedin.com/in/william-bengtson

William Bengtson

4

Will Bengtson is the director of threat detection and response at HashiCorp, focused on security operations and scaling security for the enterprise. Prior to HashiCorp, Bengtson worked at CapitalOne, Netflix, and Nuna, and spent many years consulting and working for the Department of Defense. Bengtson has experience in many areas of security and finds passion in infrastructure security, cloud security, and the detection space. Bengtson contributes to numerous open source projects and has spoken on topics of security across the world.

How do you define a blue team?

My definition of a blue team is any team that is not a red team or, in other words, any team whose job is not to continuously attack and try to find weaknesses in a company. This goes beyond the traditional threat detection or incident response team.

To me, the idea of a blue team is a team that is protecting the company by building protections and putting them into practice. If you stay within the confines of security, this is the team building detections, the team making sure infrastructure is secure by default, the team helping application owners secure their applications, the team helping secure corporate assets, and many others. Outside of security, this is the team that is developing an application securely, the users who are reporting suspicious emails and outreach, and many others.

What are two core capabilities that a blue team should have?

A blue team from within the security space should have the ability to automate and think clearly and outside the box when approaching tasks. With today's infrastructure and companies moving to the cloud, traditional ways of securing companies and responding to threats is forever changing. The need to automate exists to keep up and stay ahead with how fast companies are moving and growing in the cloud.

Keeping this in mind, having the ability to think clearly and outside the box will allow the individuals on the blue team to succeed in each task that they set out to accomplish. In the case of building new detections and automations, it allows them to think through each detection and determine gaps and what is needed when responding to them. It also allows them to come up with what should be detected in the first place. When responding to incidents, thinking clearly can be the difference of shutting an attack down successfully and missing something and allowing a threat to remain a threat.

What are some of the key strengths of an incident response program?

Key strengths of an incident response program are its capabilities and the ability to keep the noise of alerts near zero. The capabilities of a team will allow you to see the maturity in detections and response and directly relate to metrics around the team. These metrics can be number of alerts, false position, true positives, percentage of time spent responding to alerts versus developing new techniques, and automation.

Keeping the noise near zero is an indicator of how much time the team has to develop future alerts and tooling to continue to strengthen the team. It can also be an indicator of how happy the team is and whether you are at risk of losing team members. In my experience, a team member who is constantly responding to alerts and walking through a playbook is not going to stay happy for long.

How can blue teamers learn, practice, and grow?
Blue teamers have an advantage today in that there are numerous ways to continue to learn, practice, and grow. Some things that come to mind right away are pairing with the red team and application security teams to see what attacks look like and what techniques are being used. This can give them a new view on attacks and some runway to building new techniques for detections. There are numerous trainings that are available that can help the team members come up to speed and get some ideas to take back; one free one is OpenSoc.io.

Having the time to learn and play with the platforms that the company is using is another great way for the team to learn. They can also participate in CTFs or do a rotation in another area of security to learn and improve as a blue teamer.

How do you reward good blue teaming work?
I think a great way to reward good blue teamwork is recognizing the team for the great work that has been done. Oftentimes the blue team goes overlooked, and the countless hours of work to build and respond to detections go unnoticed.

Outside of public recognition at the company, some great rewards can also be conference attendance, trainings, tech books, or something outside of what they normally would be afforded to have/receive. You want to make sure their work is being seen as appreciated.

What are some core metrics that a blue team can use to build, measure, and maintain a successful information security program?
Some core metrics that a blue team can use to build, measure, and maintain a successful program are as follows:

- Number of detections in place
- Number of false positives
- Number of benign true positives (a true alert, but internal employee)
- Number of true positives

- Number of preventions in place
- Number of times preventions worked
- Amount of time spent responding to alerts manually

Where would you start if you were the only information security staff member at a small to medium-sized business with a primitive security infrastructure?
If I were to start at a business like this, I'd start with understanding what all exists and the current state of infrastructure and the environment. You can call this visibility and/or asset inventory, but having a true sense of the current state allows you to formulate where you should start from a security standpoint. Visibility is the number-one foundational element in building a secure network from the ground up. If you don't know what exists and what should be there, you will have a difficult time coming up with what a secure network should look like.

What is the most bang-for-your-buck security control?
The most bang-for-your-buck security control is a deception technique. Chances are the deception technique is not going to cost much from an implementation/maintenance perspective, and when it fires, it can provide you with incredible return on investment. Another one would be a security building block that allows teams to implement a security best practice for free. This is also known as a high-leverage solution to a problem and scales really well by enabling practitioners/developers.

Has your organization implemented any deception technologies?
Deception techniques have been very effective at my organizations. They have given incredibly high return on investment and have caught exploitations that would have been hard to detect otherwise.

Where should an organization use cryptography?
I think an organization should use cryptography anywhere that sensitive data needs to be protective. It depends on what we mean by cryptography here, but TLS should be used everywhere possible, and you should utilize encryption at rest, especially when it's free from a platform/cloud provider. When implementing cryptography, you should approach it by making it

easy for teams to take advantage of it and use it. You should not tell teams that they should use cryptography and leave it up to them to implement.

How do you approach data governance and other methods of reducing your data footprint?

When approaching data governance, the most important aspect is having a clear understanding and definition of the types of data you as a company may be holding/processing. Once you have the clear definitions, you can approach data governance through tagging/metadata. This will allow you to understand what data you have where and then start tackling security measures around the data. Depending upon what regulations you may need to consider, this will also help you in your architectures and approaches.

What is your opinion on compliance?

My opinion on compliance is that it is necessary and helps companies be more secure than they might normally be. In this same vein, I believe you should implement and do the right things at a company where compliance comes as a side benefit to the practices and processes you have in place.

Is there a framework that aligns the activities or functions performed by the blue team with regulatory compliance requirements?

The Center for Internet Security tends to be a framework that lots of tools have adopted to meet regulatory requirements. It is a great first start or scorecard for how you are doing from a security standpoint in the cloud. You might of course need to adjust it to fit your industry-specific/company-specific needs, but it will give you some great first things to consider when approaching security at a company today. A blue team will have many areas within these controls to claim ownership of and should have a good understanding of the remainder of the controls.

How do you engage all the different units of an organization to maximize defense?

I constantly engage all areas of the company to be aware of initiatives that are currently being worked or are on the roadmap. Normally this is done through weekly/biweekly/monthly syncs with leaders in the different areas of the company. The frequency is typically decided by how critical/frequent changes are that it is important to be aware and stay ahead of.

This is also an opportunity to talk about things that are coming from the blue team and areas of concern that need addressing throughout the organization/division/team. Another great way to engage is through all-hands demonstrations and communications around initiatives the teams are working on and planning to work on in the future.

What strategies do you use to communicate the threats you encounter to nontechnical decision-makers?
A strategy I've used to communicate threats to nontechnical decision-makers is to use an analogy that they would be familiar with that describes the impact and/or communicates it in a way that they will truly understand. Knowing your audience is the most important aspect in communications. If addressing execs, it might make sense to address a risk in terms of monetary losses/delays that would affect the company overall rather than the risk of exploitation of a particular vulnerability.

What recommendations do you have for managing nontechnical executives' expectations during a significant ongoing incident?
My recommendation for managing nontechnical executives' expectations during a significant ongoing incident is to check in continuously and assure them that things are under control and to instill confidence in the response.

Take time to sit with them and walk them through what happened until they understand it and can explain it in their own words. Discuss different ways of responding to the incident and the risks/confidence levels for each. The more they feel engaged and understand, the less anxiety they will have, the less they will misspeak to others, and the more trust they will have and bring you into top-level conversations with the board and/or other stakeholders, which will have priceless returns overall throughout the entire response time.

"Because we can't contain a blue team in a standard silo, it will ultimately consist of any member of an organization (or sometimes third parties) who contributes to the defensive security posture of an enterprise, software, or service specifically covering the CIA triad of confidentiality, integrity, and availability."

Twitter: @InfoSystir • **Website:** www.linkedin.com/in/amandaberlin and www.mentalhealthhackers.org

Amanda Berlin

5

Amanda Berlin is a senior security architect for Blumira and the CEO and owner of the nonprofit corporation Mental Health Hackers. She is the author of a blue team best practices book called *Defensive sSecurity Handbook: Best Practices for Securing Infrastructure* with Lee Brotherston (O'Reilly Media, 2017). She is a co-host of the Brakeing Down Security podcast and writes for several blogs. She has spent more than a decade in different areas of technology and sectors providing infrastructure support, triage, and design. She now spends her time creating as many meaningful alerts as possible. Amanda is an avid volunteer and mental health advocate. She has presented at a large number of conventions, meetings, and industry events. Some examples of these are DerbyCon, O'Reilly Security, GrrCon, and DEF CON. While she doesn't have the credentials or notoriety that others might have, she hopes to make up for it with her wit, sense of humor, and knack for catching on quick to new technologies.

How do you define a blue team?

If you look at the core of where the terminology came from in military exercises, it means defense plain and simple. I personally don't think you can limit a blue team to specific roles or job titles for several reasons. When a firewall administrator is configuring a next-gen firewall (NGFW) to have whitelist-only ACLs, they are performing a blue team function as it will be a portion of the overall enterprise defense. In contrast, when that same firewall admin is configuring a new route, that's a networking function.

Because we can't contain a blue team in a standard silo, it will ultimately consist of any member of an organization (or sometimes third parties) who contributes to the defensive security posture of an enterprise, software, or service specifically covering the CIA triad of confidentiality, integrity, and availability.

The blue team functions can incorporate many different sections in information security including engineers and architects who implement and design systems to be proactively more secure, managed service providers that spend their time threat hunting for malicious activity showing in their customer's logs, and penetration testers when they are writing recommendations into their reports.

What are two core capabilities that a blue team should have?

Generally defense and detection skills, which admittedly do cover a wide range of knowledge. If I were to choose the top capability from each of those categories, they would be a general understanding of how enterprise systems work and the ability to use that knowledge to identify what key actions should be monitored and deemed abnormal.

What are some of the key strengths of an incident response program?

Incident response processes are an integral component of being able to react quickly in the event of an incident, determine a nonincident, operate efficiently during an incident, and improve after an incident. Having processes in place before an incident begins will pay dividends in the long run. Key strengths to bring into the process portion of an IR program are standardized internal and external communication, high-level technology

processes, and the specifics of outsourcing to a third party if/
when needed.

The second half of this includes the tool and technology
strengths that are needed, including the ability to perform log
analysis and correlation, disk and file analysis, memory analysis,
and network traffic analysis. An IR program should cover analysis at each layer and step in the transmission of data.

The testing of these processes with tabletop exercises and
drills can serve as a proof of concept. A tabletop exercise is a
meeting of key stakeholders and staff who walk step-by-step
through the mitigation of some type of disaster, malfunction,
attack, or other emergency in a low-stress situation. During a
tabletop exercise, a moderator or facilitator will deliver a scenario to be played out. This moderator can answer "what if "
questions about the imaginary emergency, as well as lead
discussion, pull in additional resources, and control the pace of
the exercise.

How can blue teamers learn, practice, and grow?

The top four things are CTFs, podcasts, home labs, and books.

I recommend participating in capture-the-flag contests for
anyone in technology, not just in a blue team role. One of the
main aspects of performing blue team functions is the ability to
understand how attacks work, and CTFs do a great job of that
without you having to be a full-time red teamer. They also can
provide cross-training and team building, as well as increase
communication skills. Here are some CTF resources:

- Ctftime.org
- Ctf365.com
- Overthewire.org
- Hackthissite.org

Podcasts are a great source of information, from interviews to news.

- Brakeing Down Security
- Cyberwire
- Darknet Diaries
- Defensive Security Podcast
- Open Source Security Podcast
- SANS ISC Daily
- Security Weekly

Home labs when you're first starting out are a must. They allow you to understand basic networking, operating systems, and software, while also giving you the availability to try attacks and defense procedures without the hassles of change control or potentially harming a live environment. There are a massive number of resources out there for creating a home lab, but it will all depend on your current goal at the time. Your home lab might be better suited in a cloud environment as opposed to your office if the experience you're looking for is something like Azure or GCP.

There are a large number of books in the information security space. Hey, you're reading one of them right now! Here are my top recommendations for blue team–specific books:

Defensive Security Handbook: Best Practices for Securing Infrastructure by Amanda Berlin and Lee Brotherston
Blue Team Handbook: Incident Response Edition by Don Murdoch
Blue Team Field Manual by Alan J. White and Ben Clark
Intelligence-Driven Incident Response: *Outwitting the Adversary* by Scott Roberts and Rebekah Brown
Building an Information Security Awareness Program: Defending Against Social Engineering and Technical Threats by Bill Gardner and Valerie Thomas
How to Measure Anything in Cybersecurity Risk by Douglas Hubbard and Richard Seiersen

How do you reward good blue teaming work?

It's literally our job and what we're being paid to do. I suppose recognition and new job opportunities could possibly be part of that; however, that is just the nature of normally performing well in any function. It is super satisfying when penetration testers and red teamers are caught and/or stopped using defensive security tactics and even more so when it's a legitimate threat.

What are some core metrics that a blue team can use to build, measure, and maintain a successful information security program?

Depending on the portion of the information security program that is being measured, there are several different metrics that can be helpful. Applying these metrics consistently before a program is put into place, during implementation of new policies/procedures/technologies, and after improvements to the program will give a good idea about what is having a significant impact. Two beneficial resources for this are *How to Measure Anything in Cybersecurity Risk* by Douglas Hubbard and Richard Seiersen and *Building an Information Security Awareness Program: Defending Against Social Engineering and Technical Threats* by Bill Gardner and Valerie Thomas.

- **Number of overall security incidents:** As security posture gets better, this number should decrease.
- **% of out of date systems:** Firmware, software, and operating system patches should be tracked and part of the program requirements as they contribute to a large number of security incidents.

When implementing a security awareness program, an example is the average time it takes for an employee to report malicious activity. If there are no or a low number of reports prior to training, and the reporting becomes more frequent and quicker after the initial malicious activity, it stands to reason that the education method and materials are working as intended.

Where would you start if you were the only information security staff member at a small to medium-sized business with a primitive security infrastructure?

Asset management hands down. It is one of the most difficult verticals to cover. Without proper asset management, an environment cannot be protected to its full potential. There is no way to craft a complete defensive strategy without knowing what is being defended. One of the first things an attacker or red teamer does during an attack or engagement is discovery. In larger networks, it is next to impossible to completely be aware of each and every device that is connected or every piece of software the users may have installed. However, with the correct security controls in place, it becomes much easier.

Classify, organize, automate, define, gather, track, monitor, report, document, rinse, lather, repeat.

What is the most bang-for-your-buck security control?

A majority of enterprises have a vastly underused resource at their fingertips with Windows Group Policy. Group Policy objects

(GPOs) are used to centrally manage hardware and software settings in a domain configuration. They are broken up into both local and domain policies and can be applied to specific accounts or containers in a certain order to see differing results. Instead of starting from scratch attempting to build a secure GPO by going through each individual setting, there are fully configured templates available for use. The National Institute of Science and Technology (NIST) has a secure base set of GPOs that can be downloaded from its website.

The NIST GPOs contain settings such as meeting standard password security requirements, disabling LM hashes for domain account passwords, disabling the local guest account, and preventing cached user credentials, as well as hundreds of other user and computer settings. They can be found well laid out and documented on the website, along with the downloads and revision history.

Has your organization implemented any deception technologies?

Yes! I currently work for a software-as-a-service provider called Blumira. Our main goal is to collect the logs from customers and provide actionable alerts tied to playbooks for smaller security teams to follow and receive step-by-step instructions on what incident response or remediation procedures should accompany each finding. Many times, especially at smaller organizations without full security teams, deploying any type of deception technology can be extremely daunting. A part of the service we provide is a honeypot deployment automatically built in to the solution inside the organization.

Where should an organization use cryptography?

Everywhere! I can't think of any data in motion or at rest that wouldn't benefit from being encrypted. One of the issues seen in software, however, is when companies attempt to create their own cryptography standard as opposed to using one of the common versions already available. Unless they are an expert in security/cryptography or have had the scheme analyzed by multiple experts, it's rarely a good idea. Instead, follow the OWASP Cryptography Cheat Sheet or NIST recommendations.

- owasp.org/www-project-cheat-sheets/cheatsheets/ Cryptographic_Storage_Cheat_Sheet
- csrc.nist.gov/projects/block-cipher-techniques/bcm/ current-modes

What is your opinion on compliance?

There is definitely a right and wrong way to go about compliance. Compliance can be obtained without security in mind; however, most of the time if you have a secure mindset going into an enterprise design, compliance will likely follow. These standards are a minimum, not a complete security program. It is easy and lazy to be just a "checkbox checker" when going through implementing controls in a compliance list, and it's possible to technically be compliant with a standard and still not have a secured environment. Many standards leave room for the imagination and can be interpreted in different ways. For example, HIPAA is focused on the safety of patients and patient records, no matter if it is on a piece of paper or a piece of technology.

How do you engage all the different units of an organization to maximize defense?

Working in tabletops with different members of the organization can show how poorly things can go for the entire business when security isn't taken seriously. Having upper-level champions or advocates in the C-level who understand why certain defensive security measures must be implemented will help get engagement and traction when needed. A member of the blue team who is able to speak to groups in engaging ways to educate them without talking down to them can also be a beneficial step to maximizing the security efforts.

What recommendations do you have for managing nontechnical executives' expectations during a significant ongoing incident?

If they ask, which can be rare, providing clear and concise information about the plan of attack, potential outcomes, and potential repercussions in regular updates is usually satisfactory.

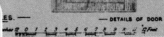

"A blue team is defined by offensive and defensive security capabilities."

Twitter: @sirmudbl00d and @hatnull • **Website:** www.linkedin.com/in/
o-shea-bowens-52344915 and nullhatsecurity.org

O'Shea Bowens

6

O'Shea Bowens is a 12-year cybersecurity enthusiast. He's the founder of Null Hat Security, which focuses on the areas of incident response, threat hunting, SOC operations, and cloud security. Null Hat Security also addresses workforce issues with skills and gap assessments via cybersecurity training.

His background is in incident response, security architecture, and security analytics. He's an international speaker and has presented at conferences such as DEF CON, ITWeb Security Summit, Qubit-Prague, Texas Cyber Summit, and SANS Blue Team Summit.

O'Shea is also the cofounder of the Intrusion Diversity System Podcast, founder of the SkiCon Conference, board member of ISSA – New England, board member for Cyber Security Non Profit (CSNP), advisor to SANS Blue Team Summit, and advisor to the Layer8 Conference.

How do you define a blue team?

A blue team can be defined in two distinct buckets: industry collaboration and offensive and defensive security capabilities.

- **Bucket 1:** A blue team is a global effort for cybersecurity defense practitioners across the industry to collaborate. If a company is breached by an attacker, anywhere in the world, that's unfortunate. If another company is breached in the same manner, it's a lack of effective information sharing and lessons learned assessments. Attackers think globally when picking targets, find allies to aid in their mission, and execute. It's that simple. As blue teamers, we must enact the same line of thinking and "big picture" approach to put a dent in attackers' plans.
- **Bucket 2:** A blue team is defined by offensive and defensive security capabilities. These capabilities are strengthened through the collaboration of different minds to respond to attackers and stop future attacks. In this game, we can't win playing behind the opposition. Take a step back and think about what the traditional aspects of digital forensics and incident response (DFIR) have done for the industry; we have positioned ourselves to shrink the time to respond to attacks and kick them out of our environments. Now add cyber-threat intelligence, cloud security, and threat-hunting capabilities; we're slowly taking the offensive to prevent future attacks while maintaining the capability to respond and detect threats. That's what blue team means to me.

What are two core capabilities that a blue team should have?

Visibility and response capabilities. It's difficult to fight blind, which is essentially what you're doing if you have no methods of visibility across networks and systems. Ensuring you have the capability to respond to attacks is vital, whether that's memory artifacts collection, the ability to block layer 3 traffic on the fly, or tearing down systems and replacing with backups.

What are some of the key strengths of an incident response program?

Patience. In my experience, the story of an attacker is pieced together, clue by clue. If you aren't a patient person and are under the thumb of management for a quick answer, you're going to miss something.

Flexibility. I've personally fell victim to this in my career. When your firm spends and spends to incorporate tools into your environment, you're operating under the assumption that they will always be available or the entire team has a deep under-standing of them. What happens in cases of employee turnover and new folks not being acclimated yet? Better yet, the tool experiences errors and can't perform. What do you do then? Having a plan that's flexible enough that you can leverage open source tools is huge for me.

How can blue teamers learn, practice, and grow?

Work on a breach investigation. Seriously. The work is not over once you kick the attackers out; it's actually just beginning. You're looking at an overhaul and thorough review of your tools, process, and procedures.

Listen to the gray beards. If you want to get philosophical, mind your elders. There are so many people with 30 to 40 years of experience in security, and they perhaps aren't on Twitter. Find those folks and try to form a relationship with them. Soak up all the knowledge they're willing to share.

How do you reward good blue teaming work?

This is an interesting question as businesses don't apply that mindset to defense. Think about uptime and the average number of days there isn't an incident at your company. This likely outweighs the alternative. Recognition is a great start. After that, the team functions on the company's dime. Or maybe, just maybe, they pay for more than one conference annually for the team to attend.

What are some core metrics that a blue team can use to build, measure, and maintain a successful information security program?

- Time to respond
- Incident time to closure
- Vulnerability remediation median time

Where would you start if you were the only information security staff member at a small to medium-sized business with a primitive security infrastructure?

Know thy network. Understanding the current ingress and egress points is always a good start. After that, a focus on protocols and encryption schemes should be up for review. Once I understand these areas, I can begin to plan for implementing a solution to aid with monitoring and detection.

What is the most bang-for-your-buck security control?

Least privilege controls. Everyone doesn't need administrative rights.

Where should an organization use cryptography?
Storage and transmission of mission-critical data.

How do you approach data governance and other methods of reducing your data footprint?
I have a pretty open mind when it comes to working with governance, risks, compliance (GRC) professionals. I try to follow their lead as that's not my strongest area of practice. Know your limits.

What is your opinion on compliance?
Long story short, if you're in a vector where noncompliance may affect the bottom line, do what you have to.

Is there a framework that aligns the activities or functions performed by the blue team with regulatory compliance requirements?
NIST CSF is a great reference not only when building out blue team functions but when creating a security operations program. I think it's a place to start and judge the strength of the security program.

What strategies do you use to communicate the threats you encounter to nontechnical decision-makers?
I try to not operate in a fear, uncertainty, doubt (FUD) capacity, but rather provide real-world examples of how attackers obtain access, pivot inside an environment, and ultimately exfiltrate data. The hard work, in a sense, has already been done via yearly reports like Verizon DBIR.

I try to relate security requests back to the bottom line. For example, "I need money for a SIEM" is a broad statement. However, "I need $60,000 for a SIEM, and here's how I can protect us against these top ten threats and ultimately save the company $200,000 to $500,000" is a much better approach.

What recommendations do you have for managing nontechnical executives' expectations during a significant ongoing incident?
Have a game plan before you jump on a call or walk into a meeting with an executive because if you veer from your original statement, they'll pounce on it. That's not to say they're out to get you, but one must keep in mind that at the end of the day, someone has to eat the blame.

Try to communicate milestones versus end goals. For example, "Within seven days we'll have more answers of how we were attacked and next steps" works better than "We'll have this resolved in seven days." Don't over-promise. Refer to my first answer as to why.

"Everyone working in IT has a responsibility to build, operate, and maintain their systems in a secure manner."

Twitter: @jbizzle703 • **Website:** www.linkedin.com/in/john-breth-730b7755 and www.youtube.com/channel/UCmJJUewPWfnyzvZRrFHlykA

John Breth

7

John Breth is the founder/managing principal of JBC (jbcsec.com) and is an experienced architect and author with 17 years' experience helping the nation's federal agencies, defense and intelligence agencies, and critical infrastructure companies identify, implement, and protect against cyber threats. John has designed and implemented mission-critical systems to support a Tier 1 ISP's cyber protections for the federal government, numerous DoD joint networks, and Air Force One's secure network. John has earned multiple high-level certifications from (ISC)^2, Cisco, and CompTIA, as well as having earned an MS degree with a focus on information technology from Johns Hopkins University.

How do you define a blue team?

There are two answers here, with one that is the generally accepted answer that we use when trying to conceptualize things for management, especially when dealing with funding and resources. That's the default blue team definition of a team of people (or defenders if you come from a DoD background) who monitor and respond to potential incidents.

My more holistic answer is that everyone working in IT has a responsibility to build, operate, and maintain their systems in a secure manner. That makes every one of us in IT a member of the blue team. I think it is disingenuous to not be fostering this mindset in new folks who want to be administrators and engineers. It might not be your job to tune, watch, and respond to alerts, but you should be cognizant of implementing best security practices and understanding your role in increasing the safety of your environment and its users.

I also think there can and should be a lot of overlap between the actions of impactful red and blue teams. For instance, a good blue team member or even IT person should verify and test the mitigations they put in place (i.e., something akin to red team activities). Likewise, a good red team person should provide actionable information on ways to improve the defense and alerting of the organizations they test (i.e., something that blue team folks should be doing continuously as well).

What are two core capabilities that a blue team should have?

Technical capabilities are going to be dependent on the budgets for resources (technology and qualified team members). This is always going to be working against the reality of always having less time than desired to implement the next tool, augment the team, etc. So, I think the most important capabilities that are independent of technological ones deal with mindset. We need folks who operate in an impactful manner given those challenges. To me, these are having the ability to look at and process information from multiple viewpoints and the ability to be tenacious in their actions.

Looking at things from multiple perspectives allows team members to identify threats, weakness, develop countermeasures, create impactful alerts, and define and implement usable and repeatable processes. It involves looking at things from the perspective of outside threats, inside threats, users, other IT staff, and other members of their team. A tenacious mindset is what drives team members to go the extra mile in thinking through adversarial scenarios; spend a little bit more time on that event that seems a little off; and continue to learn more about the tools, technologies, and infrastructure that they are responsible for protecting.

What are some of the key strengths of an incident response program?

A successful IR program is one that is in a continual state of improvement and adjustment. Threats change, technologies change, and regulations and policies change, as do teams and responsibilities. Having the ability to not only modify the scope and policies of the program but also test the procedures for technical and programmatic effectiveness is critical. This involves bringing together all the interrelated touchpoints in an organization and actively seeking their input and participation. You can't create an effective IR program in a black box.

How can blue teamers learn, practice, and grow?

A work culture that values both the accumulation *and* sharing of knowledge is important. This means supporting learning opportunities within the organization (brown bags, vendor training, and on-the-job training) and externally (conferences, boot camps, college classes). An emphasis should be placed on sharing the knowledge that others already have, and pathways should be put in place for learning more. This takes active participation from both junior folks, senior folks, and management.

On a more granular level, there are three things that I think prove beneficial. First, an often-underappreciated area is documentation. Writing down procedures is useful to the folks writing them and expediates the knowledge transfer to junior staff when used for training purposes. Second, external training can be expensive as you normally must have someone travel far away, and the course can be very pricey.

A great way for an organization to foster knowledge sharing is by supporting their staff to go to their local security conferences, such as the BSides cybersecurity conferences. These are near most major cities, last anywhere from one to three days over the weekend, and cost very little (normally less than $50 for a ticket). It's a cost-effective way for an organization to support a culture that values knowledge. Lastly, most vendors are willing to throw in some type of training (often on-site) when you purchase equipment/software from them. This is no skin lost to a salesperson trying to close a deal. As potential customers, we get hounded enough throughout the year by sales folks. When it comes time to buy, make sure you fight to get free training thrown in with your purchases. This can pay off tremendously for your team members.

How do you reward good blue teaming work?

This depends on the person, their career, and their technical pursuits. However, before we even go there, let's start with this: *Pay folks like you appreciate their work!* I say this as a small business owner. Take care of your people. The first and foremost way to do this (especially for folks who excel in their role) is pay them in a way that makes them feel respected and appreciated. That is the baseline.

After that, we get into understanding the specifics of the individuals. Rewarding good work could include allowing them to pursue training on things they enjoy, giving them responsibilities within the organization that align with their goals, and promoting them into positions that reflect their growth. These things differ, though, depending on the person. It's imperative to have the conversations to determine these things and is so important to a healthy team. It comes back to positive acknowledgment and respect, both in private and in public, along with communication and support of the individual. And while this was a question about blue teams, this is applicable to all staff independent of their role in the organization.

Where would you start if you were the only information security staff member at a small to medium-sized business with a primitive security infrastructure?

The first step is understanding what you have and what you need to protect. So, I'd want to know what assets exist, what are their business/mission functions, what are the crown jewels in the environment, and what tools are in place for monitoring, management, logging, scanning, and patching. Proper documentation is the key underlying function. If we all can't agree on what's here, what's important/needs to be protected, what tools are in place, and what are our primary threats, we're just going to be spinning in circles.

Once information starts to be discovered and verified, we can then determine where to start putting our effort. Do we need logging and monitoring tools? Do we need to implement network segmentation/restrict data flows? Do we need to focus on patching because nothing has been patched in two years? But those decision can't be made until we get a decent grip on the current state and gaps in the environment.

What is the most bang-for-your-buck security control?

I love this question, because my answer for it is one of my favorite things to talk and write about. I'm a big proponent for network security basics, and the primary one that can really have an impact in an environment is network segmentation. It's something that if done from the beginning in an environment can dramatically limit the ability for lateral movement. I can attest from having hosted a decent amount of assessments; it can really frustrate red teams. I have a three-phased approach when implementing this in environments.

The first step is breaking up the network in separate VLANs/subnets/security zones for each unique function and sometimes even subfunctions. At a high level, that means domain controllers go in their own VLAN, printers in their own VLAN, and monitoring tools in another VLAN. Just imagine how Oprah likes to give out cars to her fans; that's how I like to give out VLANs. This can obviously grow quite a bit, and in larger environments, automation is going to be your friend here.

Second, I then like to take those VLANs/subnets/security zones and implement private VLANs within them. This is a VLAN technology that allows you more granularly determine which hosts can communicate with each other inside the VLAN. For instance, there is no need for workstation-to-workstation communication. So, within the private VLAN they reside in, you place them in isolated mode. Now, the only other device in that VLAN they can talk to (even though they are all on the same subnet) is what you have configured as their gateway. No lateral communication between the hosts!

Lastly, I like to implement access control lists at three levels. At the gateway/firewall level, I implement the specific rules for the data flows that go between different VLANs/security zones (i.e., inter-VLAN ACLs). At the switch level, I then implement intra-VLAN ACLs to control all the data flows between hosts in the same VLAN that the private VLAN configuration is allowing to communicate. Then as a final protection, I make sure that ACLs are implemented at the host level. There's no real magic with these steps, and if you are being very specific with your ACLs, you can really provide a strong foundation for network defense with this type of segmentation.

Has your organization implemented any deception technologies?

I've really gotten into reading up on the deception technologies in the past year or two. Shout-out to John Strand at Black Hills Information Security. The information they put out on this topic has been fantastic, and I'm grateful I got to take his Active

Defense class at Black Hat last year. I've started implementing some of the methodologies and tools that align with this in some of my clients' environments.

Some simple things like honey accounts were really an easy solution that I'm surprised more places don't implement. I've been toying around and testing honey ports (and obviously honeypots), as well as canary tokens.

One other toolset that I have worked with aligns more with the Active Defense class (not necessarily deception but more attribution) is beaconing detection with Bro/Zeek/Corelight and Active Countermeasures AI Hunter/Rita.

Lastly, for one of the security services that I support, we do have a DNS sinkhole service with redirection to a honeypot for our clients' infected hosts. So, alerts based on that are quite useful.

What is your opinion on compliance?

Compliance is important and can be used to validate that you are doing the baseline level of things that you should be doing in your environment for safety and hygiene. There was a great quote that I saw on Twitter that I couldn't verify who originally said it, but it perfectly sums up my opinion on compliance. "Good security practices is [sic] like washing hands; you should take time to do it thoroughly. But if all you're doing is washing your hands, you can't use them as hands."

I've seen it be a challenge to maintain the ever-growing list of compliance demands just for the sake of a checkbox. There should be a happy medium somewhere, but the process itself of verification and reporting shouldn't take more effort than the actual securing and monitoring.

Is there a framework that aligns the activities or functions performed by the blue team with regulatory compliance requirements?

This is a tricky question, so I'm going to say it depends. My opinion is that frameworks can be helpful as a guide or starting point to get a person/team/organization pointed in the right direction. But they aren't a one-size-fits-all solution, and you need to take a holistic approach with what works or doesn't work for your team and organization (unless it is something that you are legally bound to do; then you need to bite the bullet).

From an overall IT perspective (including blue team activities), I find the NIST 800-53 Security Controls and Traceability Matrix

(SCTM) to be a useful starting point. Again, there is a lot of nuance here, and I'm by no means saying it is perfect. I do feel that if you are starting from scratch and looking for some guidance on what you should be implementing from a controls perspective, this is a pretty decent shove in the right direction.

How do you engage all the different units of an organization to maximize defense?

I've always found structured and efficiently managed weekly/biweekly meetings that bring together key members of the various groups that need to interact with each other are beneficial. At least in this manner, there is a certain amount of situational awareness. It helps building relationships with members in other groups, and I'm lucky in my current organization, there is a lot of cross-pollination between teams. I've worked previous places where one group goes and implements something, without talking to other teams. Then this causes a chain reaction of spun-up responses to what very few folks know is an approved implementation. So, communication from a planning and awareness perspective is key.

What strategies do you use to communicate the threats you encounter to nontechnical decision-makers?

This can be a challenge for folks who are strictly technically minded. This also ties back to understanding what your organization's mission is, what are their drivers, and what are the potential negative impacts to their mission if there is some type of threat that comes to fruition. If you have quantitative data about the potential loss (hours/dollars/resources), that is an understandable story to explain to nontechnical people, although that type of data is often harder to gather and formulate.

It can be beneficial to get an outside point of view and recommendations. For some reason, sometimes leadership (sadly) responds more enthusiastically to an outside consultant or assessment team by giving recommendations on what the threats are and how to respond and protect against them. One thing I like to do when doing assessments is ask the IT/cyber teams if there are things they have been requesting and not getting from management. If it seems like it makes sense, I'm more than happy to put something in my recommendations write-up that the team mentioned needing X and that I agree with them based on reasons A through D.

"I would classify blue team as anyone whose primary focus is defensive practices."

Twitter: @synackpse • **Website:** linkedin.com/in/leebrotherston and squarelemon.com

Lee Brotherston

8

Lee has spent the majority of his career in blue team roles including engineer, incident response, consultant, forensics, and leadership positions. These roles have spanned many industries such as telecommunications, finance, hospitality, transport, and IoT. He is the co-author of *The Defensive Security Handbook* (O'Reilly), and he regularly speaks at conferences on a number of information security–related topics.

How do you define a blue team?

This definition is actually harder than I thought. Every time I start with something like "improving the security posture of an organization," the definition falls apart because a red team also attempts to do this via other means. So, in the broadest sense, I would classify blue team as anyone whose primary focus is defensive practices.

What are two core capabilities that a blue team should have?

Communication is a core capability. If a blue team cannot speak to people in other areas of the business effectively, then their ability to effect change will be severely impacted. This is true in the cases of both strategic initiatives and operational tactical decisions. Ultimately the security team probably doesn't wield ultimate power and so will rely on the support of other teams to be able to ensure that the right changes happen, and these other teams need to be on board to be able to do that. To illustrate, if you need to disable a public API because of a vulnerability, the blue team will need the support of management, particularly if it is customer-facing. To support this move, the development team will most likely need to spend time writing a fix, the comms team will probably have to craft an announcement, etc. Being able to accurately articulate the problem, in language that each of these teams understands, will lead to better outcomes and higher efficiency.

Pragmatism is also a really strong capability to have. If the blue team attempts to die on every hill in pursuit of security utopia, then they will probably achieve nothing and alienate themselves from the rest of the organization in the process. Picking your battles is an underestimated skill. By fighting every fight, you spend a lot of the social capital that you have built up, and people will find ways to sidestep you if they perceive that they know what the answer will be. Whereas if you are pragmatic in your approach, on the occasion that you do really have to provide a strong "no," then people will take you much more seriously as your word carries more weight. Similarly, you are expending less energy and resources fighting battles within your organization that are really bringing minimal benefit. To bring it down to a simple way of considering this, if you fight for perfection and lose, you have achieved 0 percent of your goals; if you fight for 60 percent of the way there and let the other 40 percent slide, you're still 60 percent ahead of the perfectionist.

> If the blue team attempts to die on every hill in pursuit of security utopia, then they will probably achieve nothing and alienate themselves from the rest of the organization in the process.

What are some of the key strengths of an incident response program?

My experience with incident response has been that you absolutely cannot account for all eventualities. If you could, then response would have been automated already. Thus, a plan that attempts to enumerate all the possible incidents that we face is doomed to have omissions, so I believe that a plan that is flexible is a key strength. Certain things should be fixed, of course, such as escalation paths, communications plans, roles and responsibilities, SLAs, etc. But a click-by-click playbook for each and every malware combination, for example, is simply not possible.

How can blue teamers learn, practice, and grow?

I think that the best way to learn is first to work out how you learn best. Some people learn by reading and listening, in which case there is an abundance of books, podcasts, blog posts, conference talks, etc., available. If you are happy to spend some money on this, various companies run training courses on a range of topics.

> I think that the best way to learn is first to work out how you learn best.

Some people learn by doing, in which case defending your own network can be a great learning ground. Configure your own firewall and IDS for your home network, or run a cheap virtual server somewhere and learn to harden the OS, detect and alert on attacks, etc.

Growth also comes in the form of growing your experiences and understanding outside the traditional realms of security. This growth is not only great from a personal perspective but is incredibly marketable when seeking out new employment opportunities. For example, being able to understand budgets and legal documents will pay dividends when talking to leadership and more business-oriented people, which could help with those who seek to move into a security leadership position. Learning skills such as programming or network management will give you a greater understanding and the vocabulary to talk to developers and network engineers whose support you need to get security work done.

Finally, make use of both the community and your personal network. Either in terms of mentoring or ad hoc advice, there are a number of people who are willing to step in and help. People are more than happy to offer advice on technical decisions, sharing experiences, résumé review, career advice, etc., and you can often find your answers this way.

How do you reward good blue teaming work?

Choosing how to reward blue team work is difficult as it can easily introduce perverse incentives. For example, if you choose to provide some kind of bonus to those who spot vulnerabilities and close them, it could incentivize people to surreptitiously introduce vulnerabilities that they can later "find" to claim their bonus. If you introduce safeguards to prevent people from finding vulnerabilities in their own code, then they may partner with someone else so that one can introduce and one can discover.

> Choosing how to reward blue team work is difficult as it can easily introduce perverse incentives.

I think that rewards should be metric based but by using a metric that is more tightly aligned with quality of work.

With regard to the reward itself, that very much depends on the individual. Of course, most people like to get more money or vacation, but many also look for career progression, learning opportunities, preferred assignments, training, etc.

What are some core metrics that a blue team can use to build, measure, and maintain a successful information security program?

Metrics are hard. There are many terrible metrics that we could choose and that I have seen people choose, but they're meaningless really. These are things like number of viruses stopped, spam filtered, port scans blocked, etc. To choose good metrics, we should really first ask ourselves, what is it that we want

> There are many terrible metrics that we could choose and that I have seen people choose, but they're meaningless really.

from our metrics? With regard to the security program, I would probably want to focus more attention on overall improvements in the security posture of our organizations than an arbitrary metric around number of prevented attacks, which can vary wildly irrespective of the level of security maturity.

So, what should we measure? I would say that we focus more on things like reduction in risk, for example. A simple proxy for this may be something like the number of high- and critical-level vulnerabilities in the environment or the mean time to patch these vulnerabilities from discovery. This sort of metric will provide a more meaningful insight into improvements in the security posture of the organization that blocks attacks.

Depending on the organization, there are a number of other metrics that may or may not be useful. For example, in a development organization, we may want to use metrics such as the output of static code analysis tools, checks on vulnerable dependencies, bug bounty submissions, or other proxies for code quality.

Where would you start if you were the only information security staff member at a small to medium-sized business with a primitive security infrastructure?

Given the case of a primitive security infrastructure in a small to medium enterprise, my experience is that it is unlikely that the company will have remained on top of tasks such as patching operating systems, deleting old accounts, enforcing 2FA, etc. Ensuring that these fundamental-level practices are in place is key to success; otherwise, you can start rolling out more complex countermeasures only to be undone by a run-of-the-mill piece of malware. Next I would use one of the red team tactics: live off the land.

> Next I would use one of the red team tactics: live off the land.

A red teamer will often repurpose pre-existing tooling in an environment to avoid detection; we can repurpose existing tools to be able to make improvements without the disruption, cost, and resources of having to deploy new infrastructure or software.

For example, many monitoring and health tools for servers and networks gather a number of metrics from hosts to determine when they are not performing properly. Many of these metrics can be repurposed to detect potential security issues too. This will of course be dependent on the specifics of different environments; however, any deviations from the norm can be useful signals.

Tools that monitor web logs for statistical and analytical purposes can also be repurposed to alert on potential attacks. For example, a higher than usual number of 3XX or 4XX errors is often indicative of someone who is attacking a server, enumerating endpoints, brute-forcing something, etc.

If your organization uses internal DNS caches, proxies, or firewalls, then it is typically simple to use these existing tools to extract lists of visited domain names and IP addresses. There are many resources available to check these for connections to known command-and-control networks, phishing sites, etc.

Has your organization implemented any deception technologies?

Personally, I have mixed feelings with regard to deception technologies. Many of the technologies that get deployed can have a higher than desired false positive rate and in fact themselves introduce vulnerabilities and weaknesses into an environment via growing the attack surface.

However, there can be a lot of value in canary tokens such as creating API keys or access tokens that have no access to anything but that generate an alert when used. You can then place these keys on developer laptops, for example, and if an alert comes in, you can assume that a developer laptop has been compromised. Similarly, dummy customer accounts, which generate an alert when accessed (or when seen in a data dump), can be a good indicator of a compromised customer database.

By carefully using canary tokens, it is easy to create a high-signal, low-risk method of deploying tripwires around your infrastructure for attackers to trip over.

What is your opinion on compliance?

My opinion on compliance really depends on your environment and can be both a negative and a positive. Compliance for compliance's sake alone can be costly, in terms of finances, time, and social capital.

In these cases, it can be true that the security team has used up all of these valuable resources on compliance and thus has none left to expend elsewhere. This can be

> Compliance for compliance's sake alone can be costly, in terms of finances, time, and social capital.

exacerbated by compliance programs that force the adoption of technologies or processes that are really not applicable to the environment.

The counter to this is that if an organization is averse to undertaking security initiatives, compliance can be a really good lever or forcing function. Typically, legal and finance departments are likely to have your back. They want to see regulatory compliance achieved, and they can help solicit executive sponsorship, ensure that funds are made available, and such. Additionally, the business case for compliance is often easier to demonstrate to leadership. Lack of compliance = a monetary fine per customer. This is easy math and makes it relatively simple to put a dollar value on noncompliance; therefore, so long as the cost of meeting compliance is less than this, then it's effectively a return on investment calculation.

Is there a framework that aligns the activities or functions performed by the blue team with regulatory compliance requirements?

As compliance often includes many activities for which responsibility lies outside of the blue team, it makes sense to have someone else "own" regulatory compliance and ensure that the blue team takes ownership only of the portion that they can and should deliver.

At this point, the scope of work by the blue team should be formalized and, in my opinion, captured in whatever planning/performance framework the organization uses. Many organizations can only prioritize work that is in their official plan, because they are incentivized (often financially) to perform against that, so other work can fall by the wayside. By making regulatory compliance work part of the plan that the department is measured on, compliance becomes incentivized.

How do you engage all the different units of an organization to maximize defense?

Having as many people aware of security issues as possible, having as many eyes on things as possible, can be advantageous. My preferred method is to deploy a blend of different techniques to achieve this.

- First is incentivizing people to take notice and report things in the first place. And by this I do not necessarily mean a financial incentive; it could simply be in terms of recognition or ensuring that this sort of activity forms part of their OKRs, KPIs, or whatever performance metrics are used within your organization. By making it in their interest to help, you make it more likely that they will!
- Making security something that people find either fun or important (or both) can also help to inspire people to help. Often, I find that there is a lack of engagement because

people believe that they do not possess the necessary knowledge or the barrier to entry is too high. Taking developers through performing a SQL injection or XSS attack, through to something like credential theft, can be powerful and make them realize that they do not know more than they realize. Or taking a customer service agent through a voice phishing exercise can show them what to look for and more importantly how to think about these topics.

- Finally, next is making reporting of issues simple, easy, and stress-free. People may not report things for fear of being mocked for flagging something that is not a concern or being burdened with follow-up paperwork. If the process for reporting is made simple and people can feel confident that it will be dealt with appropriately, via a team that is more "here to help" than the big bad department of "no," I believe that engagement will grow significantly.

> People may not report things for fear of being mocked for flagging something that is not a concern or being burdened with follow-up paperwork.

What strategies do you use to communicate the threats you encounter to nontechnical decision-makers?

I find that the best approach is to understand the motivations and language of decision-makers. For example, decision-makers do not necessarily understand this: "We should enforce 2FA on customer accounts because credential stuffing from outside breaches is a really effective way of gaining access to their accounts."

However, what they may understand is this: "One of our corporate goals is to reduce our high customer churn. One of the stated reasons for customers leaving us is lack of trust in us as a company. If we provide them with 2FA on their accounts, then we can visibly demonstrate that we are acting in their best interests and increase trust levels. This in turn can contribute to reducing churn."

This has been framed in a way that meets both their and the company's objectives. This can be measured with metrics that they are comfortable with (e.g., churn rate, customer ratings,

2FA adoption rate) instead of what appears to them to be an arbitrary "We won't get credential stuffed" and is worded in a way that is more customer focused and marketable, even though the end result is exactly the same.

What recommendations do you have for managing nontechnical executives' expectations during a significant ongoing incident?

I am a strong believer that open communication with executives is key to both keeping them happy and preventing those directly involved with incident response from being interrupted by being asked for updates.

My preferred method to achieving this includes the following:

- Send regular update communications to executives. This should include when they can expect the next communication. If you don't set the expectation on the next communication, you are almost guaranteed to get an "any updates?" email at some point.
- If there is no update, communicate that there is no update. Doing this prevents the "tap, tap, tap, is this thing on?" response.

Communications should include the information that they are interested in. This is likely to include very little technical detail, and it is much more likely to focus on whether SLAs are likely to be in jeopardy, whether customer-facing communication is required, whether regulatory compliance is at risk, how long until estimated resolution, how many people are affected, and what they can do to support those who are responding. Ensure that communications is a defined role as part of the incident response plan.

> # Ensure that communications is a defined role as part of the incident response plan.

This ensures that someone is tasked with ensuring that the updates happen and ensures consistency between different communications. Provide a single point of contact for executives if they have questions about the incident; this is probably the communications person. This allows them to reduce interruptions to people who are heads-down on the incident and let the executives feel that they are getting the feedback that they expect.

> "The blue team are the 'soldiers' employing the equipment (weapons/tools), training, and organizational principles to defend against the aggressor or adversary."

Twitter: @Cobrakaii • **Website:** www.linkedin.com/in/rbushar

Ronald Bushar

9

Ronald Bushar began his career in the U.S. Air Force serving as an officer in the Information Warfare Aggressor Squadron. Mr. Bushar is a seasoned, highly effective, and innovative cybersecurity leader with more than 20 years of experience in cyber-defense operations, cybersecurity consulting, and incident response services in both the government and commercial sectors. Mr. Bushar has a track record of successfully building strategic programs and dynamic teams that deliver innovative cyber solutions, ensure effective security, and minimize organizational risk.

Currently, Mr. Bushar serves as senior vice president and chief technology officer for government solutions at FireEye. In this role, he leads a global team of cyber experts who deliver FireEye's unique platform of innovative security program capabilities and solutions to protect critical missions, infrastructure, and national security interests worldwide.

Prior to his work at FireEye, Mr. Bushar served as the director of the Department of Justice Security Operations Center (JSOC), where he led transformative efforts to redefine and restructure key information security and cyber-defense operation capabilities. Mr. Bushar also served as the department's Insider Threat Program manager and liaison to the National Insider Threat Task Force. In previous roles, Mr. Bushar built and led expert teams of cyber-defense operators, incident responders, and red teams at several U.S. intelligence and defense department agencies.

How do you define a blue team?

To me, a blue team has always adhered to the original military definition used in exercises and operations planning. Simply, the blue team consists of the defenders. They protect against the adversary, the aggressor, the red team, or the "opposing forces" in an exercise context. This definition cuts across all domains/dimensions of human-driven conflict (land, sea, air, space, cyber, espionage, etc.).

Again, probably because of my military training, I tend to align these team definitions fairly strictly to operations and operational functions. Specifically related to cyber, I don't tend to link in security engineering, tooling, platforms, applications, or design/maintenance of security infrastructure with my definition of blue team. Those functions are enabling, or "organize, train, and equip" type, features. The blue team are the "soldiers" employing the equipment (weapons/tools), training, and organizational principles to defend against the aggressor or adversary. Under this framework, a blue team can include the following: SOC analysts, incident responders, threat hunters, threat intelligence analysts, and forensic/malware analysts.

What are two core capabilities that a blue team should have?

Blue teams should be able to do two things extremely well.

- Find and fix *any* adversary in the designated environment that is being defended. This is traditional alert/detection, review, analysis, identification, and coordinated/cross-functional communications.
- Maneuver against the adversary to achieve one or more of the following outcomes, depending on the risk posture and functions of the organization:
  - **Deny:** Prevent the intruder from gaining initial access (after detection of reconnaissance) or further access into the environment after initial compromise. Patch systems, implement firewall/proxy/DNS blocks, etc.

- **Degrade:** Implement additional measures or controls to slow an attack or make attack actions more difficult/visible to the defenders. Deploy additional IOCs, expose malware, C2, TTPs, internally and/or externally, etc.
- **Disrupt:** Try to stop at least some attack actions somewhere in the lifecycle. Block C2, remove backdoors, etc.
- **Deceive:** This is usually a more advanced function but is the ability to steer or contain an attacker to portions of the infrastructure that are under strict control and observation. This enables the defenders to buy time and learn more about the attackers, TTPs, motivations, and intent while formulating a response plan.
- **Destroy/remediate:** In this context, we mean to fully stop and remediate an attack. Kick the attacker out and ideally prevent or minimize any damage they might have imparted on the organization.

In addition to having the knowledge, skills, abilities, and tools to perform these functions at a high level, the blue team must also be able to function, coordinate, and communicate across other IT and security teams, as well as the key organizational stakeholders (usually defined as business-line leaders and other core business functions such as finance, legal, HR, communications, etc.). The best blue teams function as the incident "commander" or "quarterback" during significant breaches and provide key nontechnical incident handling functions while also actioning the technical response.

> The best blue teams function as the incident "commander" or "quarterback" during significant breaches and provide key nontechnical incident handling functions while also actioning the technical response.

What are some of the key strengths of an incident response program?

Key technical strengths should include the following (not all in one person, but across the team):

- Network security monitoring and analysis
- Threat hunting
- Cyber-threat intel analysis
- Live host analysis
- Malware analysis

- Disk forensic analysis
- Security log analysis
- Security event coordination/analysis
- Key management/leadership/"soft" skills
- Written communications
- Verbal communications/briefing skills
- Planning/coordination skills
- Critical thinking/analysis

How can blue teamers learn, practice, and grow?
People who are passionate about honing blue team skills and growing in the career path should focus on technical depth in one or more key functional areas and gaining broad exposure to both simulated (exercise) and real-world attacks. The simplest starting point is setting up a network defense/security operations center at home, using open source tools (Security Onion is a great starting point). Practicing and learning at home is cheap and easy.

Formal training, such as SANs and Black Hat, can be useful in accelerating specific technical skills and learning and making industry and peer connections. Many blue teamers get their first job as a level 1 SOC analyst. While these positions can be grueling, you have the opportunity to see and work on a ton of real-world systems, data, and attacks. They often offer the opportunity to learn basic networking and system administration skills as well.

Finally, spending time on an IR team, at a company, at a consulting firm, or independently will offer you the most intense and high-pressure experience you are likely to ever see. This "in the trenches" expertise will sharpen both your technical skills and your ability to think, analyze, and communicate effectively under pressure.

How do you reward good blue teaming work?
In the simplest terms, getting to work on interesting cases, solving challenging problems, and catching (or at least thwarting) bad guys is usually the first and best reward for someone who is passionate about blue teaming. Beyond that, public recognition, even if it stays within the organization, is hugely valuable. Security organizations tend to want to stay close-lipped about attacks and the response to those attacks. This is a huge mistake. Every day an attack is prevented, mitigated, or

remediated; it should be tracked, reported, and exposed all the way up to the executive team and the board.

If the blue team actions result in an arrest/persecution, that should be big news, and everyone involved should be publicly recognized. Another reward can be allowing/encouraging blue teamers to work on pet projects, functional improvements, code, tools, etc., as part of their daily job function, and not just in their free time.

Allowing team members to innovate and create is hugely empowering and rewarding for the individual and the company.

Finally, of course, there are financial rewards. Bonuses or bounties for great work or for stopping an attack can have a meaningful impact and demonstrate the value the organization places on the team.

What are some core metrics that a blue team can use to build, measure, and maintain a successful information security program?

I helped to define and implement this security metrics white paper: www.nist.gov/system/files/documents/2016/09/16/mandiant_rfi_response.pdf

This is a great foundational framework for key blue team and security organization metrics that are applicable across almost any organization.

What is the most bang-for-your-buck security control?

To me, the most impactful security control isn't really a security function by most definitions; it's asset management. Understanding and managing *all* of an organization's systems (including data) creates the foundation for almost all other security controls and blue team functions.

- Ability to deploy proper endpoint controls and detection response capabilities
- Ability to understand critical assets and proper segmentation strategies
- Ability for the blue team to understand and monitor "normal," which makes finding anomalies so much easier
- Ability to properly control access to systems and data
- Ability to rapidly and effectively patch and remediate vulnerabilities in a prioritized process

- Ability to understand the business owners/impacts/risks to systems and data
- Ability to understand the effects and criticality of attacker access, actions, and tools in the environment to design and implement an effective incident response plan

None of these things is possible or can be done efficiently and effectively if you don't have the basic asset controls and management in the organization.

Has your organization implemented any deception technologies?

I have not had much practice with deception systems since my military days. They tend to be fairly specialized and/or not particularly useful for organizations until and unless they are fairly mature in the primary areas of network defense and security operations.

Where should an organization use cryptography?

Everywhere! Of course, this sometimes makes the defender's job more difficult, but protection of data both at rest and in motion is paramount in today's threat landscape. In addition, more consumers and regulations are demanding strong data protections and encryption of any sensitive or privacy-related information.

How do you approach data governance and other methods of reducing your data footprint?

Data governance is critically important and works in concert with asset management and risk management. An organization has to understand what data is important to the business and why. Once that is understood and properly modeled, smart decisions can be made related to business risks and planning, additional security controls, reduction and protection strategies, and overall impacts. It's also critically important to understand what data is actually regulated and what is assumed to be regulated but in fact isn't.

With the advent of GDPR and other similar protection regimens, we see many organizations over-classifying information and spending tremendous amounts of time and effort securing data and systems that aren't actually required. Similarly, without a thorough accounting of all data, important systems may be missed and exposed to attack as well as fines due to lack of proper controls.

What is your opinion on compliance?

The often-quoted perspective on compliance is that it is the floor, not the ceiling, of a good security program. In many industries, compliance regimes are the primary, or only, means of compelling the implementation and oversight of security capabilities. I often find that organizations struggle to determine where to start or what to prioritize when they start thinking holistically about a security program and controls. A compliance framework has the benefit of providing a solid roadmap of *minimum* capabilities and controls.

> The often-quoted perspective on compliance is that it is the floor, not the ceiling, of a good security program.

It must be understood, however, that just implementing a compliance program, with minimum controls, and focusing on audit findings and remediations will never result in a robust and mature security capability. In fact, most compliance programs do not even mandate a blue team function at all! I view compliance as the foundational elements that will keep an organization out of regulatory and legal trouble and can provide a starting point for more effective security capabilities. Checkbox security, by itself, will never stop the attackers.

Is there a framework that aligns the activities or functions performed by the blue team with regulatory compliance requirements?

The NIST Cybersecurity Framework tends to align well to blue team functions, especially the detect and respond domains. It's now being used as the basis for several government compliance requirements such as CUI protections and CMMC in the Department of Defense. Other regulatory and compliance regimes are starting to align to NIST or similar frameworks that account for detection and response, not just preventative controls, as keys to enable a robust defensive capability. The New York DFS cybersecurity regulation is a recent example.

How do you engage all the different units of an organization to maximize defense?

Cybersecurity is a team sport. The reason we pivoted from the term *information security* to *cyber* years ago was in part to

> Cyber risks cut across and influence every other risk an organization thinks about and plans for in most industries and most parts of the world today.

acknowledge that this domain is no longer confined to an IT function. There are real-world physical, privacy, financial, safety, and operational risks and impacts when an attack occurs. Cyber risks cut across and influence every other risk an organization thinks about and plans for in most industries and most parts of the world today. Cyber defenders and blue teams are reacting to real people who think and respond to what they are doing as fast or faster. An organization has to understand these realities and make sure that every leader in the business supports key decisions and actions or ultimately the defenders will lose and the bad guys win.

The best way I've found to engage non-cyber-stakeholders is to clearly explain the risks and potential impacts in terms they understand (legal, finance, privacy, client satisfaction, etc.). This is an ongoing effort as the business and the threats constantly change. Once you have that engagement, you must show value to each of these stakeholders. You cannot simply ask for money or IT changes (that slow them down or are a pain) or compliance without showing a return for that investment. That return has to be tailored to each key stakeholder and can include risk reduction (in terms they understand), speed to market with security confidence, added agility in their IT or application planning, costs savings or avoidance (fines, loses, breach costs), etc.

What strategies do you use to communicate the threats you encounter to nontechnical decision-makers?
I love to use analogies that the decision-maker understands because of either their current role or their past experience. Simple physical criminal analogies (e.g., bank robbers) tend to work well. It is also important to clearly articulate what is reality and what is TV/movie fiction. Yes, attackers can really gain a remote shell on an application server in a few seconds. No, they can't "take down" the firewall and hack your key servers in a matter of minutes. Yes, we can block C2 traffic quickly (ideally), but no, we can't collect and analyze telemetry from 100,000 systems in 2 hours.

What recommendations do you have for managing nontechnical executives' expectations during a significant ongoing incident?

There are some simple rules I live by during any incident, but especially those breaches that are high impact and in the public or media sphere.

- **Stick to the facts:** Making assumptions or speculating without accurate information to support the analysis will almost always result in mistakes and may have huge consequences for the credibility of the team as well as the organization.

- **Move quickly but think and analyze methodically:** There is a tendency in all crises, and especially cyber where the enemy is invisible, to demand immediate answers and to focus on too many things at once. Many organizations quickly overwhelm their IT teams with competing or contradictory requests or guidance. Prioritize data collection, deployments, blocking, system and account changes, and every other activity in a way that maximizes resources and minimizes delays. Planning and practicing before an event are key here.

- **Try not to react/respond until you understand the full scope of the issue:** Knee-jerk reactions based on the first bits of analysis are like trying to land a plane in dense fog with no instruments; you are likely to miss the runway. Allow time for further data collection, analysis, and validation before deciding on a full course of action. Ideally, your blue team has developed a robust IR plan that anticipates this gut reaction and has mitigations preplanned to further isolate/protect the organization's most sensitive systems and assets while the full investigation is conducted.

Not every decision can be what's best from a pure security perspective. Business operations are a reality. The security team may have to accept less than ideal operational restrictions, and the business may accept some level of ongoing compromise to continue or restore operations. These trade-offs and risks should be war gamed, analyzed, documented, and tested on a regular basis.

> Not every decision can be what's best from a pure security perspective. Business operations are a reality.

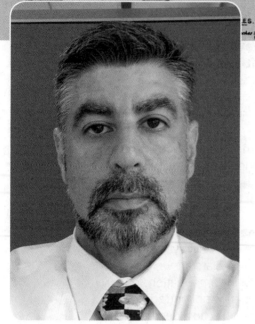

"So, how do I define a blue team? Expertise and vigilance. Commitment to an everlasting onslaught. Unlike Sisyphus, we aren't pushing a boulder up a hill every day; we are holding back the sea."

Website: www.linkedin.com/in/christopher-caruso-cissp-4a318177

Christopher Caruso

10

Chris has been in the civilian IT/OT cybersecurity/infrastructure industry for more than 30 years. He has held several certifications over the years, most recently CISSP, and has completed his Military Emergency Management Specialist training and accrued more than 90 hours of IT/OT cybersecurity training with DHS and the federal government.

Over his professional career, Chris has worked with 4 of the top 10 companies in the United States with various facilities on almost every continent and in 45 countries. He has IT/OT cybersecurity management experience in many areas and has managed teams ranging from 3 to 24 staff members with opex budgets as large as $2 million per year. He currently works for 1337 Defense out of Austin and also has his own cybersecurity firm called Houston Auditing and Compliance, based out of Houston, that performs cybersecurity compliance audits and provides reports.

Chris has a degree in engineering but believes that nothing beats keeping abreast of both new technology and emerging threats.

How do you define a blue team?

The analogy I use for blue team is to think of someone who designs a castle. The castle architect has to know how high and thick the walls should be, how deep and wide the moat should be, how many turrets, how many guards, what type of locks, what type of gates on all the entrances, and who manages the keys. How is threat intelligence against the fortress digested and disseminated? Pretty quickly you start to draw the direct references to a blue team.

The problem is that the red team or the enemy has to find only one open gate and sneak past one guard. So, how do I define a blue team? Expertise and vigilance. Commitment to an everlasting onslaught. Unlike Sisyphus, we aren't pushing a boulder up a hill every day; we are holding back the sea.

What are two core capabilities that a blue team should have?

On a personal level, blue team members should have commitment and vigilance. On a technical level, they should have the ability to visualize their digital terrain much the way game players visualize their digital realms so that they can "see" the porosity. They need to know where to set monitors and be ready to react to alerts, but just following one-size-fits-all best practices or compliance may not be a perfect fit for your unique environment, so they need to see the gaps like loose mortar in a castle wall.

In most network diagrams, we refer to various segments with different industry-standard names, such as intranet, DMZ, etc. The reality is 100 percent of everything inside the dirty firewall, or inside the corporate boundaries, is one thing—"adversarial space"—because this is the area that you will contend with when dealing with an attacker. As long as you keep that mind-set, you are in the blue team frame of mind.

What are some of the key strengths of an incident response program?

Like the rest of a good security program, the strengths are people, processes, and tools. When it comes to people, assuming they have the right core traits, it's training. When an incident occurs, there will be stress. At that point, people need to be highly trained—trained to read their SEIMs, to interpret the alerts, to tell when it really is a false positive or when an attacker is trying to get them to desensitize or misdirect their attention. Training comes in when situations get really tense. Servers might be going down, or managers might be screaming about service delivery. First responders (and make no mistake they are very much like first responders) are trained to "disconnect" and compartmentalize and let their training kick in.

Processes are next, and they need to be designed and refined using lessons learned during training. The processes need to be in place to investigate, formulate, strategize, and mitigate in real time in a close working relationship with management to get approvals and handle communications.

Lastly are the tools. If an analyst doesn't have alerting because the HIDS reports only to the end user or there is no NIDS, the best IR will be left deactivated.

How can blue teamers learn, practice, and grow?

As I've mentioned, training. That means staying current with emerging threat intelligence and staying current on the latest trends and improvements in the tools in their industry.

They need to continually challenge themselves to learn. Just because you have a Security+ certification doesn't mean you shouldn't stop trying for the CISSP. Just because you're a CISSP doesn't mean you shouldn't go for CISSP-ISSEP.

> Just because you have a Security+ certification doesn't mean you shouldn't stop trying for the CISSP.

Literally challenge them. Mock exercises and penetration tests that simulate intrusion and persistence will help them hone their skills and give them training to fall back on when things do go bad.

How do you reward good blue teaming work?

Putting aside all of the management accolades and possible bonuses for meeting KPIs, I believe one of the biggest rewards for good blue team work is a lower-stress work environment. When the blue team does their job, true positives should be zero, false positives should be as low as possible, sensitive data stays confidential, and their contribution to availability remains high. Job satisfaction always rates as one of the key factors in employee retention, along with pay, respect, working conditions, and benefits. But the reality is bonuses are consumables, accepted, spent, forgotten. Awards just gather dust.

> # When the blue team does their job, true positives should be zero, false positives should be as low as possible, sensitive data stays confidential, and their contribution to availability remains high.

An employee who comes in every day to a well-run, secure environment and receives the recognition and is respected, in addition to being compensated at an industry-standard rate, is most likely to stay and put in the effort to continue to improve themselves and the environment.

What are some core metrics that a blue team can use to build, measure, and maintain a successful information security program?

True positives, false positives, breaches, incidents responded to, threats mitigated.

- If an attacker makes it past all of the defenses and is not detected, that is a true positive. As far as metrics go, those need to trend as closely to zero as is possible.
- False positives are an indicator that monitoring is either too sensitive or not monitoring the correct indicators. Post any new implementation, there should be *some* false positives as heuristics learn the environment, but that should be a trend line that continually goes down as well.
- Breaches, due to either true positives or failures in processes, also needs to trend toward zero.
- The one metric that is likely to continually go up is threats detected and threats stopped. Whether it's visitors stopped for not having a badge or being escorted, or malicious web traffic halted, real-time threat indicators are most likely to trend upward and good for demonstrating to management the nature of the challenge we are facing.

As long as the other metrics trend toward zero, the only other metric is cost. As a security program becomes more successful, the tendency is to assume the threat either is no longer present or has been mitigated, which is why it is important to demonstrate the rising threats mitigated by either malicious traffic halted, phishing emails thwarted, or viruses caught to demonstrate the ongoing effectiveness in comparison to budget dollars requested.

Where would you start if you were the only information security staff member at a small to medium-sized business with a primitive security infrastructure?
Training the end users. In a small environment, you probably will not have the money or the infrastructure for monitoring or sandboxing attachments, so you are virtually 100 percent dependent on your last line of the defense, the end user. Security is a lot like HS&E; having a well-trained user community that takes preventatives measures and precautions seriously goes a long way.

> An end-user community with a blue team frame of mind can thwart most attempts in a small environment.

An end-user community with a blue team frame of mind can thwart most attempts in a small environment. Ideally, they will refrain from dangerous surfing behavior, safeguard BYOD and physical assets, recognize intruders on-premises, and be able to recognize phishing and malicious emails. The reality is that even in a well-funded environment every end user still needs to be a sensor of sorts and part of the security program.

What is the most bang-for-your-buck security control?
When you're talking about ROI, free security controls are hard to beat. Passwords, user access controls, Group Policy, and security groups are all configurable at the sunk cost of the employee performing the configuration, so it's hard to imagine a greater bang for your buck.

If I were to pick a close second, I would say an end-user device AV/firewall that acts like a good HIDS. They can be as inexpensive as $15/device, and some MSPs will throw in HIDS and asset inventory including hardware and software and monitoring for less than $10/endpoint. These are great examples of how to spend very little per unit and get truly great results.

Has your organization implemented any deception technologies?

We've enabled honeypots in the DMZ. Some honeypots are easy to detect and bypass if they are improperly configured or improperly placed. Configuring a server named Finance located in the DMZ or on the user VLAN should get bypassed by any self-respecting pentester or real hacker who made it past your firewall or physical barriers, so we configure them with web or FTP and name them something that actually can resolve via reverse DNS even if they aren't NAT'd through the firewall.

As for our detection, honeypots really do serve as an early warning system that "something" scanned and then ran enumeration against it. This provides us with a cross-check that confirms the effectiveness of the NIDS in the DMZ. For example, if an attacker is fragmenting packets or sending them out of order, they might be able to bypass triggering a NIDS, but because the honeypot is basically a HIDS that reassembles the packet as the target, what was missed by the network intrusion detection will trigger the host intrusion detection technology on the honeypot. The trick is to have a honeypot, which in effect is a lure or decoy, that looks and behaves like a real high-value target. Too many common off-the-shelf (COTS) products are easily identified as decoys and quickly bypassed by attackers.

Where should an organization use cryptography?

The correct answer to such a question is you should use cryptography where you are required to from a compliance standpoint. This is one of the areas where meeting compliance does a good job of achieving a good security posture.

The reality is that encryption is ubiquitous today and virtually free of licensing costs, so it's almost better to ask when and where encryption should *not* be used. A sales laptop can use BitLocker for endpoint encryption at rest. Most AV clients have built VPN tunneling, and most small SOHO routers have VPN clients, so even casual encryption in transit for everyday surfing is available. Obviously, anywhere sensitive authentication data, account numbers, or personally identifiable data or HIPAA data resides is automatically encrypted at rest and probably in transit as well.

All of the tunnels to any corporate-delivered web interfaces for customer service delivery should be encrypted with strong ciphers.

Aside from a few low-risk file shares, the only place within a corporate environment that encryption really cannot currently be used is in an industrial control environment. As of this writing, the closest we have to protocol security is DLP3, and that still doesn't give us encryption, only cyclical redundancy checking.

How do you approach data governance and other methods of reducing your data footprint?

The data retention policy is the most important document in the policy arsenal for reducing a data footprint. It is virtually impossible to expect or rely on the end-user community to police their own data.

> It is virtually impossible to expect or rely on the end-user community to police their own data.

Most end users are digital hoarders. If given the opportunity, most would save every sent email from the dawn of time "just in case." We all know that we have to balance the potential cost of a discovery motion versus being able to provide a demonstrable defense via a trail of electronic communications.

The flipside of that coin is knowing what needs to be saved, and that takes input from the various department heads and stakeholders. If, for example, there is an application that was originally compiled in FoxPro that has some particular business logic that no one has been able to reverse engineer and it represents a significant revenue stream, that must be considered and taken as an exemption until a more suitable and perhaps more secure replacement can be found.

What is your opinion on compliance?

Compliance is a fact of life. I do believe that just because you are compliant does not mean you are

Compliance is a fact of life.

secure, and vice versa, but compliance is the cattle prod that forces management to engage in cybersecurity even when breaches continue to trend at or around zero for long periods of time. So, while most people think of compliance as a hassle, I believe it has matured and see it as an ally in the ever-ongoing battle for budget dollars.

Is there a framework that aligns the activities or functions performed by the blue team with regulatory compliance requirements?

The NIST CSF and specifically NIST 800/30 and NIST 800/53 are examples of frameworks that will help guide the implementation of good security practices within any typical significant to large corporate business environment. The new NISTIR 8183 CSF for manufacturing is another. For small businesses, even here in the United States, an excellent short read is the British "Minimum Cyber Security Standard" or for medium-sized businesses the Canadian "Cyber Security Self-Assessment." It was written for federally regulated financial institutions, but it's a great guide for any manager of any medium business. (It's interesting to note that *cyber security* is still two words in Canada and the UK versus having become its own noun here.)

How do you engage all the different units of an organization to maximize defense?

I am a big believer in communication. "Security gets in the way," and it costs money, so it's both unpopular and competes for budget scraps, so communicating and making allies are key for a good InfoSec manager or CISO to achieve. I start by including stakeholders in steering committees, both so they have a say and so that they have visibility. Participating in any security implementation helps them to understand "why" because even if only through osmosis, they learn the topography of the threat landscape and are more amenable to cooperating and understanding why budget dollars are going toward cybersecurity. Cybersecurity executives need to have a seat on all of the various governance committees that touch IT or affect continuity, such as change management, patch management, and business continuity committees. You can act as an SME and also be there to help guide corporate policy while you mentor your colleagues and help validate that security will be served during any new implementation.

One part of communication is often the most overlooked, and that is communicating not just your yearly agenda but what your department is doing right now, especially if there is any possibility it may have impact on any other business sector. Examples are vulnerability scanning or deploying new badge readers or implementing a new data retention policy or DLP rule in Exchange. Let people know *what* you are doing, *why* you are doing it, *when* you are starting, how *long* it will take, and what the *impact* will be both by doing it and by choosing not to take action. An informed user base is less likely to become an angry mob when unforeseen consequences occur and you have to initiate your fallback procedures.

Another example of communication is sharing relevant threat information. In the OT sector, sharing information about smart-RTUs helps bridge the gap between OT and cybersecurity by opening a dialogue about a particular threat and how you will work together to mitigate it.

What strategies do you use to communicate the threats you encounter to nontechnical decision-makers?

I use analogies and share the risk of inaction. Any report I write has recommended courses of action (COAs). A COA could be ripped out and replace every switch in the building or do nothing and accept the risk. If you want them to not choose to accept the risk, it is up to the writer to explain the risk in simple terms, such as with the following:

"There is an unresolvable fatal flaw in the software of our firewall that would allow a hacker to connect to our network, as if they were standing in our office, and we would have no way to detect it. The risk of doing nothing is HIGH, because our firewall version can be easily enumerated remotely, this vulnerability is well-known, it is easily implemented remotely by unsophisticated threat actors, and it cannot be stopped by our current detection technology."

What recommendations do you have for managing nontechnical executives' expectations during a significant ongoing incident?

Clearly it is up to the incident commander to maintain their own situational awareness and to convey succinct, regular, and honest reports about the ongoing incident. Nontechnical managers are less likely to panic and decide that they are going to go see what the heck is going on for themselves if they are receiving regular updates about the event.

For the truly irate manager, explain to them that you need to let the team do their job. What's done is done; onlookers standing over the firefighter and telling them where to direct their hose probably won't get the fire out more quickly, and laying blame before an investigation only causes more stress. Assure them that you, as the manager, are also engaged and helping guide and direct resources and efforts so they under-stand that you understand the sense of urgency. Remind them that your staff has trained for situations like this and that they are working the problem. Stress is normal, and it is expected, but it should be redirected into something positive like asking them to begin communicating calm to their staff and to the service delivery recipients that the internal staff is aware of the issue and is engaged in resolving the matter as quickly as possible. There will be time in the after-action review to discuss continuous improvement, later, should they feel that the issue could have been handled differently.

Managing nontechnical executives' expectations during a crisis reminds me of a joke, which is how I will end my interview.

A new CISO comes on board and finds two envelopes in the desk. The envelope on top says, "Open me now," so the CISO opens the envelope and finds a note inside that says, "Blame whatever goes wrong on the previous CISO."

A month goes by and there is a ransomware attack, so the CISO does exactly that, blames their lack of preparedness on the previous CISO. The board accepts that excuse, and all goes well for a few months, and suddenly there is a massive data breach. The CISO, fretting about what to do, runs and rips open the second envelope, hoping for another nugget of wisdom, but instead this note reads: "Prepare two envelopes."

"The way that I define blue team is essentially anyone who is responsible for defending an organization, its people, and its data."

Twitter: @bucfoo

Eddie Clark

11

Eddie Clark has been in technology for more than 20 years, with about half of that time in security. He started in structured cabling and networking, spending lots of time in Pacific Bell and AT&T phone offices in the 1990s. He can still stitch cable with the best of them—just need to find some nine cord and a sewing needle! He has worked in security for the local and federal government as well the private sector. Throughout his career, he has been a system admin, network admin, and security analyst, and he has participated and led cyber-incident response team (CIRT) engagements. He was fortunate enough to have the opportunity to build a security program from the ground up.

He has served on the Phoenix ISSA board for four years as well as run a local security meetup (EVSec) and run the local Spicecorps in Arizona for the past couple of years. Currently, he is a security solutions architect helping organizations in their efforts to become more secure. He spends a lot of his free time learning from others in the InfoSec community and spends some of it mixing cocktails on his small YouTube channel and hanging out with the family as much as possible.

How do you define a blue team?

The way that I define blue team is essentially anyone who is responsible for defending an organization, its people, and its data. For a blue team to perform their job, many people need to be involved prior to the actual defense of an organization. Risk, security and operations architecture, and engineers are all crucial in this process. But ultimately, the blue team is responsible for the action of defense.

What are two core capabilities that a blue team should have?

Tenacity and aptitude. The tenacity and will of the team are important to keep pressing on to resolve an incident regardless of how difficult it is and how tired they become. The aptitude of a team is key as things always are changing and the team will need to learn constantly.

If the members on the team are not motivated to learn, this will greatly reduce the efficiency of the team as a whole.

> If the members on the team are not motivated to learn, this will greatly reduce the efficiency of the team as a whole.

What are some of the key strengths of an incident response program?

One of my biggest frustrations from my time in incident response was lack of visibility. I remember in one of my past roles in SecOps, I would often get asked by my CISO, "Are we good?" If we had visibility into the correct logs, I could give him reassurance that we were good (assuming we were). Few things feel as bad as coming back with the answer, "From what we can see, yes." That didn't help him sleep better at night. Of course, people and tools are important (especially the people), but without the proper visibility, you may miss what you need to see.

The ability to effectively communicate to other teams is absolutely essential in order to have the technology and processes in place to run your incident response program. If you need an agent installed on the company's DCs to have logs sent to your SIEM, you better make sure that you are on good terms with the sys admin. This holds true regardless of the team that you are working with.

Another great example of the importance of building solid relationships would be with the DevOps team. I guarantee that if you come to the DevOps team with all the things they need to fix in their application after many iterations of code have been refined, it will not go well. It is essential to work with them to build security into the beginning stages of the SDLC. This security also needs to not inhibit them meeting their deadlines that have been imposed on them or they will find ways around it. Also, take time to sit down with the DevOps team outside of work. Buy them a beer or coffee and talk about security and how it can help and not hinder. Developing that relationship will prove to be extremely valuable in the long run.

Another key strength that an incident response program needs to have is investment in its people. This goes a long way in retaining your talent. Just like any team, if you can have a team that works together consistently, they tend to perform better. Think of an offensive line in football. There are five different positions, and each has a specific job. If that unit has worked together for a while, they know that they only have to focus on their singular job, and the other four will take care of theirs. This is similar to an incident response team and their level of trust in their teammates.

> Just like any team, if you can have a team that works together consistently, they tend to perform better.

Emphasis on employee development is important to improving the incident response program. Each member of the team needs to constantly work on growing and getting better. As the saying goes, you are only as strong as your weakest link. This employee development needs to be done both professionally and personally.

> Each member of the team needs to constantly work on growing and getting better.

For professional development, it is essential for the blue team to stay informed as the attackers and the threat landscape are constantly evolving. This can come in the form of formal training, learning materials including access to cyber ranges, or just the encouragement to have "heads down" time to learn on their own. It is important for an incident response program to not only allow this but encourage and reward this.

For personal development, it is important to allow for recharge time. Working on an incident, especially one that is critical, does not allow for much sleep or time to take care of yourself. Creating some sort of "mandatory" time off after incidents can go a long way in helping to prevent burnout. Recognition of the team members as they do a good job is also key to keeping the morale of the individual up, and it creates a sense of loyalty, which helps for talent retention as well.

How can blue teamers learn, practice, and grow?

Getting involved in a local security group is a great way to learn more from other blue teamers. One afternoon I started to write down all the local groups in Arizona, and I stopped at 20. The groups are out there, but the key is to make an effort to network even if it means stepping out of your comfort zone to do this. I stepped out of my comfort zone a few years back at a Phoenix ISSA meeting and ended up volunteering to be part of the board to help manage their website. I developed some friendships and great networking contacts while volunteering for four years.

I also received some great advice in 2016 at CactusCon in Arizona. Grifter was giving the keynote, and he said something to the effect of, "To grow in the security community, you need to become a high-functioning introvert." I have made that my mindset ever since.

There are also a lot of resources online that can help. There are people like IronGeek who put conference videos online. I can't tell you how many times that when I have a hard time sleeping at night, I have browsed to his YouTube channel and watched conference talks by some very smart people. Getting other people's perspective is a great way to add to your knowledge. There are resources by great organizations out there like Black Hills Information Security (BHIS) and TrustedSec that are very involved in providing not only security content but security tools that can help blue teamers learn. I look forward to every week (or so) when BHIS puts out another great webcast. I never hesitate to point people who are new to or want to start a career in InfoSec to "Your 5 Year Plan into InfoSec" by

> It never ceases to amaze me how helpful people in the InfoSec community can be.

BHIS, which is a webcast and list of resources. It never ceases to amaze me how helpful people in the InfoSec community can be. You just need to know where to look and be intentional in your efforts to learn.

One of the best ways to practice your blue team skills is to secure your home environment. While there is some investment, a lot of what you can do at home can come from open source or at a very small cost. There are a number of webcasts and resources that can guide you through defending your home network. Grab a low-cost managed switch; create a few virtual machines for log management, intrusion detection, and network monitoring, as well as a few other tools; or grab a copy of *Security Onion* by Doug Burks, which has most if not all the tools you need to protect your home network. You will break stuff and that's okay. Since it is your network, you will have extra incentive to fix it and make things work right. The process of working through the problem will give you a very thorough understanding of how the solution works. This is without question the most effective way to learn, and the more you add on to your defenses, the more you learn.

You will break stuff and that's okay.

How do you reward good blue teaming work?

Recognition and training. Most security professionals, blue or red, have an innate curiosity that makes them good at their job as they won't give up easily without solving a problem. Even though their drive comes from inside, recognition is still important. An important part of recognition is to try to understand how people want to be recognized. Yes, this requires more effort. An example would be if you choose to recognize the blue team by inviting them in front of the room for a round of applause. Some would love this and thrive. Others would be mortified by this, and it would have a negative effect on them. Be intentional and know your people and it will pay off in the end.

The other reward for great work by the blue team would be training. If possible, let them choose the training. There should be some guidelines as you don't want to pay for your blue teamer to get their realtor license, for example. But if you have a blue teamer who wants to learn about red team tactics for attacking the cloud, let them. It will both make them happy and provide them with a better perspective from the attacker's eyes, which will make them better as a blue teamer.

Where would you start if you were the only information security staff member at a small to medium-sized business with a primitive security infrastructure?

My first step would be to create a plan to increase visibility to the environment. The first two controls of the CIS top 20 are inventory of assets and software. It is hard to defend something if you don't know what or where it is. On most networks, scanning can be done for free with things like Nmap and other scripts/tools without negative effects, depending on the type of equipment that is on the network. The other part of the plan would be to create a log management strategy. Most technologies that you will want to implement into your security program will require logs. If you can get a handle on this prior to implementing other solutions/processes, it will make you more efficient in the future and create a solid foundation to build from.

What is the most bang-for-your-buck security control?

This is a tough one. Each organization and what matters the most to it is different. As an example, in one organization that I use to work for, intellectual property was incredibly important to protect as this is what distinguished them from the competition. For others, it could be patient or financial data. But, if I have to choose one, I'd say email protection. The number-one attack method against organizations is phishing. Having solid email protection in place can help to prevent or respond to phishing attacks when, not if, they happen. Even the most security-aware employee can fall to a phishing attack for any number of reasons, including the timing and quality of the phish.

> The number-one attack method against organizations is phishing.

What is your opinion on compliance?

For so many, compliance is required to allow their organization to do business in their respective industry. In this way, opinion doesn't matter a whole lot.

Having said that, like so many things, it depends on the intent of the action. If compliance is sought after only to check a box, this is the wrong mindset. Terms like *best effort* and *reasonable effort* can be used in a way that allows the organization to only check a box. This also allows for a false sense of security for the business. Many executives have sat in a board room and asked the question, "How can we have been hacked? We are compliant." If compliance is all that is being sought after, at some point, this will fail.

If you are using compliance as part of your overall security strategy to help the organization become more secure, it can be a great tool. The time spent on creating these standards is definitely important to each industry as there are some controls geared specifically toward the type of business. Each organization needs to understand that compliance is a key component of a security strategy. Additionally, the organization needs to understand where the gaps are to what is not covered by the compliance standards and then develop a prioritized plan to close those gaps. While the closing of those gaps is separate from the compliance efforts, this can and should be done in parallel when possible.

Compliance is important, but it isn't the end all be all. The key for organizations is to become compliant *and* become secure.

How do you engage all the different units of an organization to maximize defense?

This sounds like the easy answer, but it is key to start the conversations early on with the other teams to truly open the lines of communication. It is also essential to make sure that when those early conversations start, the tone is one of collaboration and not confrontation. So many times security is seen as the team that is telling everyone no. If the blue team can show the other teams in the organization that the goal is to help the business and not hinder the business, the adoption rate will be much higher.

Lastly, it is important to communicate often. The sooner a team hears about a control that needs to be addressed, the better chance that team can resolve it. Keeping everyone informed along the process of maximizing defense will allow everyone to succeed, the organization will be better defended, and everyone will look better. That is a true win for everyone.

What strategies do you use to communicate the threats you encounter to nontechnical decision-makers?

The nontechnical decision-makers need to understand how the threats can affect them and the business. I have always used a format where the top part of the email/memo is one to two sentences each for what the threat is, who and what is/can be impacted, what is the method and ETA of remediation, and what a workaround is in the meantime. It is important to have this information succinct and at the top of the email because with management and the C-suite, the more efficient you can be, the better. The bottom half of the memo is where you put more detail regarding the threat for those who may want to dig in a bit deeper.

While informing decision-makers of threats is important, letting them know when the threat has been mitigated is also crucial. This information not only helps them sleep better at night but allows them to move their attention and efforts on to the next important item at hand.

What recommendations do you have for managing nontechnical executives' expectations during a significant ongoing incident?

Practice, are we talking practice? Yes, practicing an incident in the form of a tabletop exercise is a great way to prepare both the technical team and the nontechnical executives. During this exercise, the expectation

> Yes, practicing an incident in the form of a tabletop exercise is a great way to prepare both the technical team and the nontechnical executives.

of communication will be set for all parties. Providing nontechnical executives with expectations of who will be their point of contact, how often they will receive updates, and what is expected of them is a great way to help for a smoother incident.

The team working the incident also needs to have proactive communication in the form of regular updates. If the team can provide the information that the nontechnical executives need before they ask for it, there will be no need to cause any interruptions during the incident.

> "If you aren't assessing an organization's defensive capabilities from an operational perspective, you are not likely on a blue team."

Twitter: @bullz3ye

Mark Clayton

12

Mark Clayton is a former red teamer turned detection engineer. Additionally, he does security engineering and application development. Professionally he is all security, and at night it is all web and mobile application development. Having an earlier focus on DevSecOps to blend both his security and development experience, he recently focused on applying his previous experience to detection and response. At a young age, he was under the mentorship of a Cult of the Dead Cow (cDc) member, who showed him the ropes and taught him the security ecosystem, and he's stayed true to those lessons.

How do you define a blue team?

The blue team shares the responsibility alongside a red team of assessing an organization's operational security posture and identifying network, application, and outer-space vulnerabilities (outer space is a joke by the way. . .or is it?). At the highest level, the red team attacks, while the blue team defends.

Recognize that as a blue teamer your job is to not only defend but to continuously find ways of improving your defensive (detection) and reactionary (response) capabilities, tactics, and methodologies. It is a practice and continual process of improvement between both teams to make the organization resilient to more and more advanced attacks. As a result, the blue team is then trained and capable of responding to real attacks that happen within the organization. If that feels like what you do at work, then you are likely on a blue team. If you aren't assessing an organization's defensive capabilities from an operational perspective, you are not likely on a blue team.

What are two core capabilities that a blue team should have?

In my opinion, the two core capabilities are an ability to detect and an ability to respond. These are two core/umbrella disciplines that carry a ton of weight, and the mature interoperability between the two can result in high visibility into attacks against your environment and the capability to perform rapid and thorough incident response, remediation, and forensics.

As a former red teamer and previous penetration tester, I know that an organization with a lack of detection capabilities can be a literal playground. This means that I can enter, sit, and traverse the network while barely being noticed. It's not because I'm particularly stealthy; it's just because they don't have the detection capability to know I'm there. A lack of detection ultimately reduces the risks of exposure that the offensive actor considers during the engagement, which results in confident attackers.

A lack of response increases the length of time in which an attacker will confidently stay on the network, which results in persistent attackers. The entire incident response program is predicated on these two core capabilities and sets the foundation for additional disciplines like threat hunting and incident response automation.

What are some of the key strengths of an incident response program?

- **The plan:** A mature incident response program should have a well-defined and comprehensive incident response plan that can be carried out at the time of the incident to identify, contain, eradicate, and recover. This plan is a result of industry standards, tribal knowledge, and most importantly lessons learned. Over time, the plan continues to mature and mold within an organization as post-mortem communication occurs to identify areas of improvement and feed this information back into the plan. This should reduce your mean time to detection and response (MTTD/MTTR) as your plan matures.

- **The team:** At the time an incident is declared, the ability to rapidly assemble a centralized incident response team with predefined roles is a key strength of a maturing program. Roles such as the incident response manager, communication lead, threat researchers, and subject-matter expert should be assumed by team members without dispute over who should take what responsibility. Additionally, the team should be able to act on established goals that align with the incident response plan with effective communication and discipline.

- **The tools:** Effectively tooling is critical to a team's ability to alert, contextualize, communicate, and respond in a well-orchestrated and often automated fashion. The tool selection is a result of your team's method of communication, culture, methodology of gathering contextual information, and overall process of handling an incident.

- **The mentality:** The final strength is the ability to remain grounded in the workflow and confident in the team's process. A team that freaks out and frantically attempts to individually put the fires out without sticking to the plan is a team that will not recover well. This causes coverage gaps to occur, as well as communication and visibility breakdowns to arise, throughout the process. Keep calm and trust your team's plan.

How can blue teamers learn, practice, and grow?

Blue teamers are not nearly as effective without a red team; otherwise, your "team" is just securing systems. It is like training for a fight without an opponent. How do you know what a real fight looks and feels like if you don't spar? How do you perform under pressure, when you are deep in the trenches? The point I'm trying to make is, you have to train and practice like it's real every time. This results in a breeding ground of gaining knowledge, experience, and confidence as a blue teamer. Each scenario that the blue team and red team decide to carry out needs to be as close to reality as possible. As blue teamers look to improve their detection and response posture, the red team should continuously improve their attack methodology.

Through this collaboration, blue teamers learn both new attacks and corresponding defensive capabilities. As red teams become aware of new threats and test for them, the blue team is now aware of the threat and must create corresponding detection and response capabilities. The most important factor for improvement as a blue teamer is communication with your team and the red team. Both teams mature each other by planning and developing new capabilities to outperform each other and then come together afterward to implement more mature security controls and respond to real-world threat actors.

How do you reward good blue teaming work?
I believe recognition and positive empowerment to be effective rewards for good blue teaming work. Give credit where it is due, and keep the morale high within the team so people are motivated to continue to improve their capabilities. At the end of the day, each blue teamer wants to know that what they are doing and training for will be effective in responding to real attacks that occur. Providing recognition when such attacks are prevented skillfully in an exercise instills that confidence in each team member. Long story short, do not be short of positive feedback, and ensure that criticism is constructive and not belittling.

What are some core metrics that a blue team can use to build, measure, and maintain a successful information security program?
This was mentioned previously, but the three core metrics that I think help to measure the overall maturity of a security program are the following. I think the ways in which a team answers the following "how" questions are key indicators of a security program's overall success.

- **Mean time to detection (MTTD):** How well does your detection solution work? Where do your alerts come from? Is it users, administrators, or your detection solution? How long does it take your solution to detect something that should be an immediate actionable alert?
- **False positive rates:** How well can you trust your alerts? Are you being flooded with meaningless signals, or are you alerting on the events that align with your organization's incident criteria?
- **Mean time to response/remediate (MTTR):** How long does it take to go from alerting/detection to response and remediation?

Where would you start if you were the only information security staff member at a small to medium-sized business with a primitive security infrastructure?

The first thing I would do is implement a vulnerability and patch management process. If anything, I want to first eliminate low-hanging fruit and reduce the overall attack surface to recent vulnerabilities. A successful implementation of this would ideally keep the organization from getting breached by remote code execution issues from 2008. This includes improving system designs and architecture to consider associated security risks. Alongside this, ensure sufficient logging is in place to eventually alert on. At a high level, my two main objectives would be to build an initial detection capability and also enforce secure infrastructure through communication and support.

I would try my best to promote a culture of security being a forethought as opposed to an afterthought. I'm not here to be a gatekeeper but to help other teams succeed while providing a secure baseline environment for teams to operate and deploy in. Lastly, educate team members about security considerations and available risks that are present to the infrastructure or development process currently in place. Security is everyone's responsibility, and promoting that mentality may help them to be aware and motivate how they engineer their solution.

What is the most bang-for-your-buck security control?

Firewalls. Just kidding. Logging. Without logging, I do not have a foundation to detect, alert, hunt, contextualize, and respond to events that occur throughout an organization.

Where should an organization use cryptography?

This is a huge question. I love it. Cryptography should be used to encrypt data in motion such as mutual TLS, VPN, SSH, email (PKI), and lovely Wi-Fi. It should also be used to encrypt data at rest, such as full disk encryption, encrypted file systems, or hardware security modules (HSMs). If you want to get really sexy, you use fully homomorphic encryption to address data in use. At a high level, cryptography should be used to enforce data integrity, privacy, confidentiality, and nonrepudiation where needed. For any area that needs one of the aforementioned aspects, it's probably a good idea to use cryptography. This question is very large, and each subject opens a rabbit hole consisting of several books and whitepapers. Lastly, we can't forget about blockchain. . .but I digress.

What is your opinion on compliance?

I tend to stay away from conversations around compliance and regulatory frameworks. However, I wholeheartedly recognize their importance to an organization and how security controls and policies are defined within an organization. I oftentimes find that the controls that are being implemented align somewhat with policy and compliance to some degree. Without compliance, how can another organization ever be deterministic in your organization's security posture? There has to be an agreed upon standard for an organization to adhere to for others to be confident in engaging with them.

How do you engage all the different units of an organization to maximize defense?

Traditionally, security teams have been known to try to "enforce" security controls throughout different units without true consideration of the unit's current workload and of the impact on velocity that the control may cause. "You need to enforce X to comply with industry best practices," they said. This has left a negative perspective of security teams when they attempt to communicate their wishes and are often not seriously considered or blatantly ignored in a worst scenario.

The way to fix this stigma is to work alongside different units to engineer secure solutions instead of telling them that they need to adhere to a standard that may or may not consider the current business requirements. Be part of the solution, understand the current work and business requirements, and then provide guidance that helps the teams continue to perform both effectively and securely.

What strategies do you use to communicate the threats you encounter to nontechnical decision-makers?

Focus on the risk likelihood and real and financial impact that the threat presents to business operations. It's not about the technical intricacies of what can happen to the infrastructure; it is about what damage can happen to the business, what recovery looks like, and how your team has addressed the situation.

What recommendations do you have for managing nontechnical executives' expectations during a significant ongoing incident?

Bottom line up front: Keep the nontechnical executive informed on the absolute reality of the situation and how the incident is being managed without going into the technical weeds.

> "Whether you are a SOC analyst, security architect/engineer, compliance manager, or CISO, you're on the inside defending."

Twitter: @coffeewithayman • **Website:** www.linkedin.com/in/infosecleader, cloudsecuritylabs.io/about, and gettingintoinfosec.com

Ayman Elsawah

13

Ayman Elsawah is a vCISO who helps high-growth companies get their security in order, with a technical focus on AWS security. He loves educating, whether it's helping CTOs start with their security program or helping engineers understand the complexities of AWS security. His passion for giving back led him to teaching at bootcamps and local colleges. He is the author of *Breaking IN: A Practical Guide to Starting a Career in Information Security* and host of the *Getting Into Infosec Podcast*, a Fresh Air–style podcast walking through the career transitions of those new and old in the industry.

How do you define a blue team?
Blue team to me means any team internally focused on detecting, preventing, and stopping security incidents. Keep in mind security incidents (attacks, misconfigurations, data mishandling, etc.) can be malicious or accidental, internal or external. Whether you are a SOC analyst, security architect/engineer, compliance manager, or CISO, you're on the inside defending. If you are none of those, guess what—security is still your responsibility!

Blue teamers are inherently builders, whereas red teamers are known to be breakers. This is not black-and-white, but you get the idea.

Before "security" I started off in the networking space, building and designing Cisco Networks with some sys admin work here and there. Then I became a SOC analyst and eventually a security engineer at a corporation deploying and managing security tooling like DASTs and SIEMs. It was awesome and rewarding work. At some point, the allure of being a pentester caught my attention. I had some pentest certs (not the OSCP) and would get rejected in interviews, but I would learn something new along the way. Then I finally got a job at a pentesting company! I took a huge pay cut (50 percent), but figured I could work my way up. I learned a lot—not just about pentesting but about that industry.

At one point I was placed on a three-month project building an SSO helper application, and I was in heaven! I would stay late to work on it and would think about the code on my way home. I even discovered some bugs in the AWS metadata API, particular to STS. After this project I came to a realization: I am a builder. I was not a "breaker." I've been a builder my whole life, and that's not a bad thing. When I went to a pentest project afterward, I was not as happy. I wanted to build things. I got assigned another project to build something, and I shined so well there. It was awesome. After a year, I went back to security engineering and architecture and knew that blue team was the life for me. I don't regret my decision to be a pentester, but it *was* an expensive learning experience; however, it only made me stronger, and the experience was valuable. I met some awesome people along the way too.

Many of us are attracted to the red team side of the house, but the majority of jobs out there are on the blue team. Blue teaming if at the right organization and with the right people can be very rewarding, dynamic, and exciting.

> Many of us are attracted to the red team side of the house, but the majority of jobs out there are on the blue team.

What are two core capabilities that a blue team should have?

- **Good situational awareness:** As a blue team member, knowledge is key. You can't defend a system if you don't know what's going on with it or what's broken with it.

Excellent logging is foundational. Being involved in the planning of new projects early on is also key. I don't know how many times I've been asked to do a security assessment of something that's going live tomorrow—as if I'm going to wave my hand and give it a security blessing and we're good. Or worse, I find out an app was built and went live a month ago without any security review.

- **Having a lack of complacency:** Some of the biggest threats I've seen out there are good security people and teams stuck/happy with their level of security. They feel like they have a good handle on things and have lost that curious mindset or the ability to question the status quo. I've come into environments where I asked several questions and was told "We've done that already" by security, but when I go check or ask an engineer, I found out it's not in place at all.

My favorite is asking new clients, "Are we storing passwords in our logs?" I'm always told no. Believing in "trust but verify," I will often search for *password=* or *secret=* and lo and behold find a web application leaking passwords into logs.

What are some of the key strengths of an incident response program?

Testing, testing, testing.

Planning, execution, and testing are the key strengths of a good incident response program. Dust that incident response program (IRP) off and do a tabletop exercise ASAP. It's the most efficient way of finding flaws in your IRP and improving it. Have the right people involved in the plan from the beginning, including HR, legal, and engineering. I've seen plans created in a bubble without the involvement of engineers even. In other cases, I've seen IRPs tucked away on the intranet somewhere not being updated for years—don't do that. Testing often will keep your IRP healthy and up-to-date.

> Dust that incident response program (IRP) off and do a tabletop exercise ASAP.

How can blue teamers learn, practice, and grow?

Training and cross-team participation/rotation is a great way. It's easy to get siloed, especially in a large organization, so encouraging cross-team communication and rotation is essential. Have your blue teams work closely with your red teamers or outside your security organization with developers and product managers. Not only will they build relationships, which is *essential* in security, but they will learn more about different aspects of the company, which will help them do their job better. They'll know what to look for internally, and it will promote ideation.

> It's easy to get siloed, especially in a large organization, so encouraging cross-team communication and rotation is essential.

How do you reward good blue teaming work?
Give credit where it's due and often. Blue teaming can be unglamorous and difficult at times. Put your blue team on a pedestal periodically and showcase the good work they've done to other groups in the company. Have them do presentations to the larger organization, or maybe host a lunch-and-learn session with engineers and product managers. Be aware of burnout and preemptively give them time off to recharge. Send them on training often. Encourage them to work on security projects not directly related to their job if they want. Open source any tooling they create so they can have recognition in the industry.

> Put your blue team on a pedestal periodically and showcase the good work they've done to other groups in the company.

This last point is super important. Many engineers will want to open source their work so they can showcase but also receive help on their projects. A lot of companies have an "allergic" mentality toward this, which results in the projects not being open sourced and security engineers disappointed and resentful. Be an advocate for open sourcing their work; it's essential in the security community.

What are some core metrics that a blue team can use to build, measure, and maintain a successful information security program?
The number of false positives is an important one to help reduce alert fatigue and burnout within the blue team. Tune

your system constantly to improve the signal-to-noise ratio so that anything you are being alerted on is high signal and actionable.

Time to detect and remediate are other good indicators. How long did it take for your team to detect an issue and remediate it? Leveraging automation here is going to be key, for detective and corrective actions.

One thing to note, having more *preventative* controls in place, so that we are not relying so heavily on detective and corrective controls, is key. Time spent on preventative controls will pay dividends later.

Where would you start if you were the only information security staff member at a small to medium-sized business with a primitive security infrastructure?
Working with high-growth startups, this question comes up often. Identity and logging are the two places I usually recommend starting with.

Authentication is a great place to start because in a growing business, onboarding and offboarding are usually not very smooth or streamlined (I see it happen at large enterprises as well). If onboarding/offboarding is not automated or followed through, you are likely to find former employees with access to systems or longtime employees with too much access (access creep). I recommend gradual adoption of a zero-trust model, which will force/guide concepts such as least privilege access

> I recommend gradual adoption of a zero-trust model, which will force/guide concepts such as least privilege access throughout your company.

throughout your company. This will have a multiplier effect for your security.

Logging is also really essential, because you need to know what's going on in your environment before you can fix it! If you're security engineer #1 and are focused on security awareness training or employee password strength but your SaaS application's admin portal is open to the web and getting brute-forced all day long, or you have engineers opening up 0.0.0.0/0 security groups in AWS exposing your Jenkins server (yes, I see this often), then how are you really working on what's important? Every security project is important, but is it priority #1? Having excellent logs will enable you to make the best use of your time, effort, and resources. Through good logging, you might actually find systematic issues throughout your company that with a simple process modification can completely improve your security

> Through good logging, you might actually find systematic issues throughout your company that with a simple process modification can completely improve your security.

What is the most bang-for-your-buck security control?

Single sign-on plus MFA hands-down. Not only does it allow you to take control of your sprawling applications, but you're actually making people's lives easier overall! When I come into an organization, I'm looking for MFA first but advocating for SSO. Why? Because I want a win and a solid handle on authentication to all apps. Oftentimes, MFA is not set up or at least not enforced, which is bad, especially for admin accounts and execs. Also, onboarding and offboarding are a mess, so I often find old employee or contractor accounts that haven't been deactivated or, worse, new accounts with default passwords, not to mention the sprawling list of shadow IT applications.

The short answer to the question is MFA. However, instead of rolling out just MFA, which is a high-touch process, and then eventually rolling out SSO sometime later (it's bound to happen), then why not roll out SSO + MFA? Listen, if you're going to have an impact on the user, you better 1) not mess it up and 2) not disrupt them as much as possible with multiple changes. The latter will get security in the doghouse.

As a security professional, be cognizant of your impact on the user and the frequency of high-touch projects. *High touch* means something that will dramatically change the user experience or require a high level of intervention to deploy.

So, when I come into an organization, I'm going to want a "win" under my belt, because at some point I'm going to ask people to do something

> It's rare that a security control wins favors, but trust me, they will love you for rolling out SSO!

that they might not necessarily want to do. Yes, I'm asking them to do MFA now, but I *am* making their lives easier by rolling out SSO, which is something they will all buy into, especially if you educate them and prepare it well. It's rare that a security control wins favors, but trust me, they will love you for rolling out SSO!

Has your organization implemented any deception technologies?

Many of the companies I work with now barely have a handle on their actual data and don't have large security teams to deploy honeypots and honeynets. I do often put honey tokens, like AWS keys, in my presentations, though, to see whether anyone thinks it was a real token.

Where should an organization use cryptography?

Everywhere possible! At one point I thought encrypting everything was not necessary, but with a zero-trust model, the idea of defense in depth, and the plethora of tools available now, it makes sense. For example, AWS S3 bucket leaks have been, and will continue to be, an issue. So, my recommendation is to encrypt those objects with KMS keys. There are a bunch of key management tools now, which makes them easier to deploy than before. The reason to encrypt with a KMS key, though, is that should that object be publicly accessible for *whatever* reason (accidental or malicious), access to the KMS key would also be needed to access the data, rendering the object useless and unreadable.

I used to not like encrypting everything, especially with logs, because my downstream SIEM was not able to ingest the data easily. Work with your teams on what should be encrypted, at a minimal level and in phases. You should have a data classification and handling standard that defines the different pieces of data and how they should be handled or if they should be encrypted. Don't just come in yelling to encrypt all the things but have no good reason. Give your people clarity and documentation to educate them but also listen to their needs and adapt. Encrypting data for new projects will also be easier for teams to adopt.

How do you approach data governance and other methods of reducing your data footprint?

If I don't have it in the first place, then I don't have to worry about dealing with it. As a modern security professional, you don't want more privileges or data than necessary. That's a lot of responsibility. So if the business doesn't need the data, then it's less of a

> As a modern security professional, you don't want more privileges or data than necessary.

liability for you. If you can anonymize the data before it's stored, that's also good. Just make sure you're actually doing what you say you're doing.

However, not capturing sensitive data is not always possible. Some companies have data engineering teams, and they are sometimes the de facto data owners or at least the ones who know what data there is. I recommend actually coming up with a Data Owners group and documenting who owns what, so when a decision has to be made on what to do with that data, it's clear who to ask and how it will affect them.

What is your opinion on compliance?

My opinion? It doesn't matter my opinion! If you're subject to PCI, then that's life. If your enterprise customers are asking for SOC2 compliance, that's the reality we live in.

I see this all the time.

The problem is that these compliance frameworks are not built for that 50-person or 100-person successful SaaS startup that's got an awesome product. They don't have $50,000 to spend on getting an audit, let alone having the additional head count to maintain logging and alerting. What ends up happening is companies outsource some of the components to merely satisfy a checkbox. They can also automate it but would need someone to build it, and they're often deciding between allocating resources for building a feature or fixing a bug for a customer.

On the other side, I am unfortunately still seeing the old mindset of security and compliance folks who sit behind "policy" and do not engage the small SaaS vendor in meeting or negotiating some of their compliance requirements. Deals are lost because the enterprise compliance team is not willing to meet halfway on security needs, or even listen.

In one engagement I was involved in, the potential customer's security team didn't even show up to a meeting to simply discuss the requirements. The business was there and the vendor was there, but they refused to engage until all requirements were met. This was for a demo environment!

Is there a framework that aligns the activities or functions performed by the blue team with regulatory compliance requirements?

This is tricky. Regulatory compliance means I *must* comply. For example, if I am a public company, then I must comply with SOX-404 laws, which may align you with COBIT or COSO. If I take credit cards, then I'm subject to PCI standards, which are private standards enforced by Visa, Mastercard, Amex, and Discover. If I am a SaaS provider, then my customers *expect* me to comply with SOC2 standards, also a private standard. If I deal with the government, then I have to be FedRamp compliant. Then you have ISO, NIST, CAIQ, and CIS Benchmarks, as well as a plethora of vendor security questionnaires, not to mention GDPR and CCPA, which are regulated.

So, it's complicated.

I have helped companies achieve SOC2, PCI, and SOX-404, but I am *not* a compliance expert. I do believe in using common sense, though. A lot of people take comfort with compliance frameworks because it's prescriptive and gives them definition, which is totally okay. If you can pick a framework and run with it, then by all means do! The problem, in my opinion, is relying on them too much, giving a bit of false comfort or, worse, rigidity in working with other teams. Sometimes it leads to a lack of creativity or technical awareness to come up with a compensating control if you can't meet a specific requirement, which you are allowed to do. A square peg not fitting into a round hole isn't always the end of the world, but many people panic.

> A lot of people take comfort with compliance frameworks because it's prescriptive and gives them definition, which is totally okay.

I'm going to be controversial here, but if you're not subject to any of this, I want to let you know you are allowed to come up with your own framework. Many people don't know this. Then you can align or map it to one or more of these for credibility. Just document it well (half of compliance is documentation) and be sure to follow it, continuously, and not just during an audit once a year.

Oh, and compliance does not always equal security. There are also so many gray areas, such as the auditor's mood that day, their technical awareness, or their ability to understand the rules.

I guess it's a long answer, but it's better than me pigeonholing you into one framework and walking away.

How do you engage all the different units of an organization to maximize defense?

War stories! I love this part of my job: working with all the different departments, including the nontechnical ones; introducing them to the security team; and also educating them why we're here, what we're working on, and how to engage us. Creating an inviting environment and letting them know security is a service to help them and the company.

Lunch and learns are a great way. A monthly newsletter is another way. Video messages can work too. It's a lot of marketing and engagement really.

Listen, a lot of folks are scared when they hear about the security team. Really. I've been told several times that there was a level of apprehension when they see an email from the security team, but when they opened it, they felt better.

I once came into an organization where the security team had a bad rap. Various units didn't want to engage with the security team and in fact listed them as a "risk" in a project kickoff meeting! Keeping this mind, I made sure to be extra consultative with various teams when I engaged them, walking over instead of hiding behind an email, or scheduling a coffee if it's a little complicated.

In the end they would say things like "We didn't think you would agree" or "Okay, that was easy" after meetings, thinking they would have a difficult case presenting their challenges. It helped that I was technical and offered a technical or phased solution that would work with them yet didn't compromise security, but it was about approach. After a couple years at this organization, I had PMs and engineers coming to me in the hallway saying things like "Hey, Ayman, did you hear about Project XYZ? They're working on something, and you should probably take a look." *I had my own whistleblowers inside the company!* It was awesome! I was the first person in a 40-person security organization to know about upcoming projects, but more importantly I had people helping me get a handle on projects early on. As we all know, involving security early in the process pays dividends and is way cheaper (in time, energy, and resources) to bake in earlier than later.

Get involved early on in projects. Be approachable. Get out of your comfort zone, and go meet other teams. The "donut" app in Slack is great for this. I had many security wins meeting random groups and individuals at companies, from CS reps to engineers to project managers.

What strategies do you use to communicate the threats you encounter to nontechnical decision-makers?
Storytelling, good (and relatable) analogies, staying brief and to the point, empathy, and speaking their language.

Decision-makers need enough of the right information to make a decision. They are relying on our expertise, opinion, and understanding of impact and consequences for the choices they have in front of them. Our job is to give the information to make a sound decision, especially if it involves them accepting a level of risk for the department or company.

> Decision-makers need enough of the right information to make a decision.

They also have many things on their head, so being cognizant of their time is important. Don't make a decision for them, but do your research and be well prepared. Anticipate their questions and don't waste their time on small items. Explain things and avoid jargon. Don't BS either; be honest if you don't fully know the answer to something.

Of course, you need to be in front of the *right* decision-maker. Some organizations bury security so low down the totem pole that risk and consequences are not factored into business decisions. That's why having the CISO or security reporting high up is important; sometimes we don't have that luxury, though.

What recommendations do you have for managing nontechnical executives' expectations during a significant ongoing incident?
Make sure you have the right people in the room for an incident. Don't sugarcoat anything, state the facts and the unknowns, and communicate what you are doing to remediate the incident and inform them if you need a decision, action performed, or support from them/others or not.

Executives have a nature to. . .execute and get things done. They can also handle bad news, but don't make them fill in the blanks with their imagination. Update them hourly or every half-hour, make sure your facts are absolutely confirmed, and let them know any things that are not confirmed. Unknowns are never good in an incident, so get those squared away.

"A blue teamer is someone who is committed to the defense of systems."

Twitter: @SriLankanMonkey

Sahan Fernando

Sahan has nearly a decade of experience architecting, testing, and defending systems and networks of all sizes. Sahan utilizes his background in business information to ensure that IT and InfoSec programs are available, scalable, and secure while aligning with business objectives and needs. Sahan has assisted and led the creation of programs at organizations of all sizes. Sahan oversees all of Intrinium's managed and engineering services, which include the 24/7 SOC/NOC. Sahan is a graduate of Gonzaga University, obtaining a BBA and MA. Outside of the office, he enjoys rowing, music, food, and spending time with his dog.

14

How do you define a blue team?
To me, a true blue team is anyone involved in information security defenses, whether directly or indirectly. The SOC is obviously critical, but the system administrators and service desk people who are involved in building secure systems contribute significantly as well. A blue teamer is someone who is committed to the defense of systems.

What are two core capabilities that a blue team should have?

Two core capabilities that a blue team should have are the ability to detect and respond to a security event (identify, detect, triage, respond, review) and the ability to provide input on how to secure business objectives and processes without disrupting them.

What are some of the key strengths of an incident response program?

Having a clear set of roles, responsibilities, and accountabilities is number one in my mind after having an incident response policy. From there, the policy can dictate the response playbook for identified risks/threats to the organization. You can then identify the resources you need to be successful in detecting, triaging and responding, and eradicating threats while also tracking the risks that you need to accept and still be ready to address.

How can blue teamers learn, practice, and grow?

I have found this to be an effort on multiple fronts. I encourage all of my staff to develop relationships and learn not just from one another but from other teams as well (like service desk, red team, engineering, etc.). I believe it is important to be open to trying a lot of different things and figuring out what you like and want to go deeper from there.

How do you reward good blue teaming work?

Public praise is the first step! I call it out in all company chats/emails and occasionally will throw in other rewards (monetary, conference attendance, etc.).

What are some core metrics that a blue team can use to build, measure, and maintain a successful information security program?

This is always so difficult! Your audience is going to be really the key here—are they technical or the executive? For the latter, you have to phrase the data in business terms (and ideally link back to risk related to business objectives). Technical metrics that seem to provide true value are alerts by criticality, classification of alerts, average time to response, and average time to remediation. You can also do things like patch compliance level, time to remediate critical risk items, social engineering test statistics, and policy violations detected.

Where would you start if you were the only information security staff member at a small to medium-sized business with a primitive security infrastructure?

I would start with understanding the business. That will inform every action from there—what I am trying to protect, what governance and compliance I am dealing with, what the culture is, who the stakeholders are, and so much more. The foundational element of building a secure network from the ground up is knowledge around what you are protecting.

What is the most bang-for-your-buck security control?

I am pretty simple. I like a great firewall that has AV, web filtering, application control, IPS, and other functionality like a wireless controller built-in. While this is not nearly enough, it's an achievable and relatively inexpensive first step for organizations that are just starting to worry about their security and the impact of breach events.

Has your organization implemented any deception technologies?

In general, my opinion on deception technologies is that they have their place, but most security teams have other priorities to handle first. There are some great tools that are free and easy to implement.

Where should an organization use cryptography?

I am a big fan of encrypting everything. Rarely is the cost of encryption greater than the value of the information, and the industry has done a great job of pushing to encryption by default. Unencrypted communications like HTTP, Telnet, etc., should be the exception, not the norm.

How do you approach data governance and other methods of reducing your data footprint?

Beyond the simple "what we are required to do legally," I believe that organizations should put forth as much effort as is feasible to understand where their data is stored, the classification of the data, which people/applications have access, and the flow of data through business processes. From there you can make continuously informed decisions about changing processes, opportunities, and what you want your overall footprint to be.

What is your opinion on compliance?

It is an incredibly powerful tool, and some fantastic people have a very difficult job in enforcing it. At the end of the day, an organization chooses to engage in business practices that might result in compliance and regulation, and it is our job to support that decision. Compliance should be viewed as a leverage point toward greater information security, but not the end state or goal. In most cases, compliance is barely a baseline of security, but the fact that many compliance frameworks focus on risk management is an actionable way to link your broader risk management back to the legal requirement of compliance and therefore get funding.

> Compliance should be viewed as a leverage point toward greater information security, but not the end state or goal.

Is there a framework that aligns the activities or functions performed by the blue team with regulatory compliance requirements?

NIST CSF is a popular choice, and I find that it has value beyond just the alignment. It makes it easier to convey to executives where the organization stands and compare against peer institutions as well. No framework will be a perfect fit for an organization, but it'll give you most of what you need, and then you can adapt it to your organizational needs. NIST CSF also has the benefit of being easily mapped to from other compliance regulations, so you don't have to duplicate efforts.

How do you engage all the different units of an organization to maximize defense?

I start with working to understand what each unit performs for the business. From IT to HR to accounting, it is that much harder to be effective in defense if you do not understand the business processes and what assets/tools are involved in those processes. It is genuinely interesting to hear what they do in their own words—and shows you care.

> From IT to HR to accounting, it is that much harder to be effective in defense if you do not understand the business processes and what assets/tools are involved in those processes.

From there, you can start building the relationship and soliciting their input on how to make any security improvements and collaborate. For the technical staff in a SOC, the same approach works—show that you just care about what they do and that you are there to support the organization's mission and vision, and don't be the security person who just says no.

What strategies do you use to communicate the threats you encounter to nontechnical decision-makers?

I always phrase the threat in terms of the risk it presents to the organization. Talking to them in relatable terms is the only way to be truly effective; otherwise, it is white noise and results in the inevitable "How much is the final cost?" question. When it is shown in terms of financial loss, downtime, reputational harm, and other undesirable outcomes, decision-makers are much more engaged in the conversation and the solution.

What recommendations do you have for managing nontechnical executives' expectations during a significant ongoing incident?

Be honest. Don't try to scare them or hide anything, but just convey, ideally proactively and regularly, the current status, objectives, and next steps. Don't try to explain, in this moment, what "should have happened" or have any "I-told-you-so moments." Focus on restoring business operations. Your root-cause analysis post-event (because you're doing these, right?) can highlight the should've/could've. Show that you are working to address their concerns as best as possible (i.e., "We are working to validate there is no attacker presence so we can resume normal business operations").

"Those who are working to build, maintain, and grow not only security but computer systems within an organization are blue teams."

Twitter: @tothehilt

Stephen Hilt

15

Stephen Hilt is a senior threat researcher at Trend Micro. Stephen focuses on general security research, threat actors, malware behind attacks, and industrial control system security. Stephen enjoys breaking things and putting them back together with a few extra parts to spare. Stephen is a world-renowned researcher, having spoken at Blackhat US, RSA, HITB, and many more. His research has gained him Dark Reading top hacks of the year twice. Stephen is an Nmap contributor, and he has written some Nmap scripts for ICS and other mainstream protocols. This work took him into becoming an expert on ICS protocols and coauthoring the book *Hacking Exposed Industrial Control Systems: ICS and SCADA Security Secrets & Solutions*.

How do you define a blue team?
A blue team is the team that counters the red team, which is the "attacker." The blue team is the "defense." Those who are working to build, maintain, and grow not only security but computer systems within an organization are blue teams.

One of the best examples I have of this idea is the DHS training that they put on at Idaho National Labs for Control Systems. At INL, the blue team is trying to prevent attacks by patching systems, working on figuring out critical information flows, and directly making changes to network infrastructure to stop attacks, as well as everyone's favorite part, putting in tickets to document the changes.

What are two core capabilities that a blue team should have?

Detection and response are the two core capabilities that a blue team at a minimum should have. Most blue teams deal with many different types of incidents and alerts and figure out which ones to prioritize and respond to first. Response depends on the type of incident and the priority of the system to fix.

What are some of the key strengths of an incident response program?

The ability to detect, categorize, prioritize, and respond to incidents with business impact kept to a minimum. To detect an incident, an IR program should have the proper tools to detect incidents in near real time and should have the ability to store valuable information that is needed to perform analysis of the event. Once an alert has come into the process, they should categorize the event. This could include looking into the source and the validity of the information, including if it could be a false positive. Then based on the impact to the business, the incident needs to be prioritized. Response to the incident of course is one of the most important because how you respond can define how your team is viewed internally as well as externally. Let's just say no one remembers the properly done IR and disclosures, but the ones that are done wrong are remembered for a long time.

How can blue teamers learn, practice, and grow?

The top things I recommend based on things that I did to help myself grow are as follows:

- **Learn:** Read blogs, listen to podcasts, take training, and follow people on social media who have good content that keeps you up-to-date on the newest trends.
- **Practice:** Home labs, work labs, labs, labs, labs. You'll learn the tools and techniques better if you are using them, install IDS software at your house, respond to your own incidents, and defend your family like it's your company. Of course,

your spouse might not like being blocked from sites they frequent, but then again that goes back to knowing the organization. As someone who is a big proponent of and has developed multiple capture the flags (CTFs), one of the best ways to learn how to defend attacks is to learn the tools and techniques that attackers use, which can be found in a lot of the CTFs. CTFTime.org has a good list of CTFs that you can participate in. Hackthebox.eu is a resource that is a paid-for CTF that is really good for learning.

- **Grow:** Have goals for yourself and your employees. If someone wants to learn new tasks to put them on a track to do another aspect of the job, then that should be supported if it also benefits the organization. Personal development is one of the keys to making sure you are growing the way you feel that you should to achieve what you want to do with your career.

How do you reward good blue teaming work?
Use the normal corporate structure for rewards. Any employee going above and beyond in performance should be rewarded.

What are some core metrics that a blue team can use to build, measure, and maintain a successful information security program?
Key metrics are something many organizations are trying to track and figure out what matters to them. One of the most important metrics is the incident rate over time. Meaning, the number of incidents you see over time should go down as the organization matures and gets better. The number of vulnerabilities seen during passive and active scanning activities should be also going down as the organization gets more mature. Also, internal user awareness training should be considered as should the rate of success of, say, phishing tests to help bring the awareness levels up to make not only the security and blue team a success, but the organization as a whole a success.

Where would you start if you were the only information security staff member at a small to medium-sized business with a primitive security infrastructure?
Knowing what's on your network. Asset management is one of the biggest hurdles of medium-sized businesses, and even larger businesses, to tackle as assets are always coming and going in and out of the network. Without knowing what is on

your network, or even what is yours but off your network, you won't get a good picture of what you are supposed to be defending and where the priorities should be.

What is the most bang-for-your-buck security control?

Principle of least privilege (PoLP). This is something that all pentesters will exploit and find where this fails. If you have a sound PoLP setup, you will find that attackers will have a more difficult time gaining access to, maintaining it, and moving within your networks. While this is one of the more difficult things to achieve, you'll get the most out of it, in my opinion.

Has your organization implemented any deception technologies?

I work for Trend Micro, and we deploy honeypots all the time. I myself have run multiple honeypot projects that research has been published on. With that said, there are of course risks to running honeypots within your own network infrastructure if your organization is not mature enough in security to handle the incidents that might come from the honeypot.

Where should an organization use cryptography?

While there are a few different approaches here when it comes to when to encrypt data in motion versus data at rest, it comes down to the sensitivity of the data itself. I believe that data should be encrypted anywhere it is if it's sensitive to the function of the business. One downside to this is that you cannot control where people store information and you are chasing down where they stored it unencrypted a lot of the time.

The other option is to encrypt data everywhere. However, if you are doing this, ensure that all encryption standards are in use. This means looking for phrases such as *custom encryption*. In my experience, when you see this, it's usually XOR, which isn't encryption at all but encoding.

What is your opinion on compliance?

Compliance is a step in the right direction but always is what the organization feels is the bare minimum of what they should do. In many cases, they feel that if they do more, it's sometimes worse than not doing the minimum as it could expose other issues that the regulators will pick apart. Multiple standards should be unified to have a standard set of common criteria so that one could meet NIST, NERC, HIPPA, and PCI all at the same time without jumping through hoops to make sure they are compliant on each.

Is there a framework that aligns the activities or functions performed by the blue team with regulatory compliance requirements?

NIST 800-53 is a good start of what needs to be documented as security controls. These are what the government uses to help create, run, and audit a security program. They allow for the flexibility for you to define your own controls that are reasonable for your organization.

How do you engage all the different units of an organization to maximize defense?

Tabletop exercises. Companies should be practicing what they would do in the case of a cyber event. This is because if they don't practice, some of the business units might not know what is expected of them and will have a slower response time for an event. In the energy sector in the United States, NERC puts on a cyber exercise that helps companies do this. The U.S. government puts on tabletop exercises in many federal agencies each year.

What strategies do you use to communicate the threats you encounter to nontechnical decision-makers?

Speak the language of the business. When you explain to someone working in a factory or a power plant the importance of security, you can't get into the technical weeds and have anecdotes that don't relate back to computers.

What recommendations do you have for managing nontechnical executives' expectations during a significant ongoing incident?

Regularly update the executives if they ask for them. This would include where you are in the incident response phase, the potential outcomes you see currently, and the risks you see to the organization. This should be clearly given to the executives if they ask it of the incident commander. They should not be talking to the technical staff as this distracts them from working the incident. I've been in incidents where we had to provide hourly updates to the executives. This was funneled through the incident commander, who then had quick calls with the executives. Executives should be made aware of any major incidents that could impact business, reputation, or any other factors that they need to be aware of due to business impacts.

"Given that red team is somewhere between 'someone who cosplays a hacker but without any of the risks' to 'internal recovering penetration tester,' a blue team, as I see it, is anyone who works on defensive security."

Twitter: @beajammingh **Website:** www.linkedin.com/in/beayeah, mumble.org.uk, speakerdeck.com/barnbarn, and www.instagram.com/fredandlillers

Bea Hughes

Bea came to security the way many did, by using all the kindly offered free equipment available for learning supplied by companies that didn't have firewalls on the 1990s Internet. After dropping out of high school to pursue a career at an ISP and not, thankfully, at the piercing studio she was working in at the time, Bea discovered that the skills acquired in her poorly assembled home network were actually useful in the alleged real world. Bea has spoken at numerous conferences the world over but mostly likes to be at home snuggling cats, who are better at Instagram than she is.

16

How do you define a blue team?
I was never sure when teams became color coded. I doubt this helps the color blind. I've never knowingly worked on a blue team, at least not one that self-identifies as one, so I don't feel all that qualified to define it. Given that red team is somewhere between "someone who cosplays a hacker but without any of

the risks" to "internal recovering penetration tester," a blue team, as I see it, is anyone who works on defensive security.

A much quicker way of defining a blue team is "the collection of people who argue you don't need to hire a red team as we have X, Y, and Zed or Zee to fix long before we go looking for more vulnerabilities."

What are two core capabilities that a blue team should have?

Patience and optimism! Those are much more important than any product, tool, or process.

- Patience because defense feels like an extension of Hofstadter's law and always takes longer than you imagine.
- Optimism because it's so easy to get burned out, especially because as a defender, you can see so many ways something can (and sometimes will) go wrong and overlook all the ways that your defenses will actually work.

You only see the ways into the castle and never the effectiveness of the moat or the success of the battlements. The reality that an attacker would have to walk this maze and get everything right without tripping a single alert has often been the furthest thought from my mind, so maintaining perspective, optimistically, is very much core to staying energized.

What are some of the key strengths of an incident response program?

"You know what kind of plan never fails? No plan. No plan at all."

—Ki-taek, *Parasite (2019)*

In incident response, not having a plan rarely succeeds, but by their very nature, you're already responding to something that has failed. Something failed to keep the intruder out or the data in, the encryption was more of a suggestion than a promise, etc. So, having a process takes a lot of the guesswork out of what to do next. PagerDuty has an extensive process documented at response.pagerduty.com/ that borrows heavily from the National Incident Management System (NIMS), and while it was primarily created to focus on the systems side of things, the hard parts of incident response are communication and coordination and not necessarily the area it's applied to.

Where would you start if you were the only information security staff member at a small to medium-sized business with a primitive security infrastructure?

Hiring. Pretty much the single biggest force multiplier is to just multiply your force.

Assuming one doesn't have that option, I will delve in to one of my favorite topics—threat modeling! Threat modeling is a pretty big topic, and there are few ways to do it, but the angle I go for most is working out what we have or do that is of value to people, and to whom, and then how they would most likely attack that.

By way of exemplum, over the years I've worked for financial services companies such as Stripe and everyone's favorite knitting and homecrafts website, Etsy. While similar in that they both deal with services and money, Stripe is far more likely to be targeted by higher-end hackers and even something approaching some nation-states (a lot of the SWIFT hacks of 2018 were performed by APT38 for North Korea). Etsy, on the other hand, mostly being a website for selling macaroni art and deer hoof ornaments, was largely left alone by GCHQ and the NSA, we believe.

If you're building a new platform, know that someone will try to use it for harm, sadly. Any platform used to host images will be used to host images you don't want to see on there. Anything that can be used for good, like, say, Firefox, Let's Encrypt, or CDNs to prevent DDoS, will be used by attackers and general bad people. Knowing this and planning for this in the beginning will save a lot of pain later.

Isolation of systems and ownership helps too. Every startup has gone through a period where a key large service was tied to some former engineer's credit card and account. Your AWS root account owner will almost certainly be someone who joined so early that their name has entered lore, regardless of whether they still work there. Fix these things before they cause panicked incident response calls at 2 a.m. to try to get access to that account or to quickly turn it off.

What is the most bang-for-your-buck security control?

Multifactor authentication. It can be free, and the amount of security it adds to your accounts and authentication is immense. There's a current vogue of dismissing SMS-based two-factor authentication (2FA), due to insecurities with the aging SMS and telecoms infrastructure, but I would take it in a heartbeat over having single factor.

Ideally, one would use something stronger than SMS, such as time-based one-time password (TOTP), which I'm sure many people have experienced in terms of having to scan a QR code on their phone in an app and then entering a six-digit code that changes at regular intervals. If you have between $20 and $50 per person to spend as part of your IT budget, then getting a USB "security key" such as a Yubikey and using FIDO/U2F as a second factor increases your multifactor security to include digital signatures completely transparently to the user and means you don't have to worry about whether your smartphone or classic Nokia 7110 gets compromised!

Has your organization implemented any deception technologies? If so, what effect has that had on the blue team's detection capabilities?

If I tell you, then it wouldn't be a secret.

In the past, certainly. Way back in the distant land of the early 2000s I used LaBrea (wow, it's still up on SourceForge!) to set up tarpits. This was around the time of delights such as the SQL Slammer and Code Red. Generally, SMTP open relay scanning meant it generated a lot of traffic, and the tarpit would happily accept connections from anyone and then ever so slowly respond, keeping whatever it was on the other end on the line waiting. From the logs, I would cross-reference that with the networks that our customers had to helpfully inform them that they may have a compromised machine out there that they might want to look at.

Fast-forwarding about 15 years through my so-called career, I've used the excellently innovative Thinkst Canary at a number of places and in a number of places. It is kind of an homage to UNIX in a "do one job and do it very well" sense in that their only job is to sit there and "be vewy quiet" all the while looking like an interesting or unguarded target, until someone finds them, and then to alert that someone is poking around.

I think one of the reasons that these canaries are so loved by those who use them is the low false positive rate on them. Everyone who's ever gotten an alert has gotten more alerts than they wanted. I'm not selling PagerDuty perfectly here; we are but the messenger. But reducing false positives and having your alerts be actionable and not noise is so critical to the efficiency of incident response. As an example, in the Target breach of 2014, one of the largest in history, its FireEye malware detection tool actually caught the initial intrusion and alerted on it, but no one acted on the alert because they got so many.

Where should an organization use cryptography?

As the esteemed cryptographer Adi Shamir's (the S in RSA) law states, "Crypto is bypassed, not penetrated," so feel free to add it, but understand why you're adding it and what it does. The delightful Peter Gutmann of the University of Auckland has a whole talk entitled "Crypto Won't Save You Either" about ways crypto is avoided rather than broken.

This doesn't mean crypto is useless—quite the opposite—but it is not a silver bullet. It's often not even a shiny chrome bullet. Cryptography is useful in raising a bar or forcing an attacker to do something different. For example, I've heard of many security consultants say that as soon as they uncover anything involving encryption, they go attack somewhere else because trying to work out a bunch of encryption things will take ages, and as real-world attackers are under not dissimilar time and financial pressures, the same applies for them.

Conversely, when the loving NSA attacked Google's servers, rather than some groundbreaking new cryptanalysis against TLS, they just tapped the fiber connections after the decryption had been performed. Google employs some pretty amazing cryptographers, and the cryptography was sound, but the architecture was not, so that's where they attacked.

If you go around blindly encrypting everything, then you now have a key management problem. To be fair, you almost certainly had one of those before; it was just less unmanageable (which is why services such as Amazon's KMS and Google's Cloud Key Management Service are such lifesavers). Encrypting backups is always a great move; when I play attacker, I love going after much less defended backups than the main systems. Encrypting them makes them much less useful for an attacker, unless the key is laying there right next to them, which is why we need key management.

Knowing limitations of encryption is also important. Yes, you have full-disk encryption enabled on your servers, which means when you SSH or whatever into them, all the files are accessible as they normally are, and it's completely transparent. Wait, why did we do this if all the files can just be copied off exactly as they were? I occasionally like to ask how we know that cloud services that say they're encrypted are. It's not like AWS is going to mail you an old hard drive as way of proof. There's no useful way to see what's written to disk, so we just all merrily go about our day safe in the knowledge that the thing no one had access to anyway is encrypted. So in short, encrypt everything you can.

What is your opinion on compliance?

Compliance is a "necessary (not quite) evil," but not good. Without things like PCI, we would have a lot more credit card numbers in the clear, as it is a useful stick to making sure at least some things are in a reasonable secure shape, even if that shape is 10 years old and designed around how it would look for Windows NT. Compliance is in a hard place. Move too slowly and you may as well not exist; move too quickly and no one becomes compliant, and it becomes a full-time job for everyone.

Compliance also feels like exams from school days. You don't have to get the answer right all the time. You just have to show your work to get most of the marks, and you always have to answer the question the examiner gives you, not the correct answer for reality. Every Mac and Linux host in PCI scopes runs ClamAV because it has to run an antivirus, because computers used to get viruses when we blindly copied floppy disks.

Antivirus has "evolved." The virus scene is now tiny (and largely replaced by other things such as malware—sorry, I mean "advanced persistent threats"), but everything still has to have an antivirus solution, and ClamAV is free: box ticked. Has ClamAV ever saved any credit card data from landing on a Ukrainian carding forum? No. Has anyone ever read the output of ClamAV in their PCI environment? Also no. Is this a useful and sensible security control? You've earned yourself a third no! Should it go away? I doubt it. The same with IDSs, which perhaps would have saved Target if they had read the logs, but if you've ever turned Snort on with the default rules, you know the best place those alerts can live is /dev/null because it alerts on things that haven't existed since Windows competed with OS/2 (probably).

The best way to solve compliance at an organization is to work with a company and auditor you like, and then, when they eventually get burned out on being an auditor, and they will, hire them to be on the other side and give them a better life.

They will thank you for saving them, and they will reward you with all your audits passing from that point on.

Is there a framework that aligns the activities or functions performed by the blue team with regulatory compliance requirements?
I think the MITRE ATT&CK framework is currently in fashion. It has a cool name where they've changed the second A to be an & to appeal to the youth market. The competing one is the Cyber Kill Chain framework, which is from Lockheed Martin, which is why it sounds like it's from a *Call of Duty* video game.

How do you engage all the different units of an organization to maximize defense?
Maximize relatively or absolutely? You will never have an absolute maximum, 100 percent security defense. What you should strive for is to be as secure as possible while still enabling the business to function. If you want your website to be as secure as absolutely possible, take it off the Internet. You don't want that, as you will go out of business very quickly if you only do online sales. So, the question could become, "How can you secure all the elements of an organization while still facilitating them all to perform their function?"

In my own world, few things distress me more than telling "users" (people) not to open attachments from people they don't know. That's a core functionality of email. If your company has recruiters, one of the key parts of their job is to open attachments from people they don't know. So, do they listen to the security team members, who just appear to shout nonsensical orders at them, or do they do the thing they were hired to do, such as "use email"? Ideally they do what they were hired to do and help hire you a new security team, because this one ain't cutting it. Email attachments being dangerous is not the user's fault. People opening attachments is not something that they should be in trouble for. Technology has failed them in failing to make safe standards and safe systems to do their job. Security's job here should be to make their opening of emails safer, whether that be PDFs going through a product to scan them or résumés going directly to an applicant tracking system to be parsed and not the recruiter left worrying.

No one likes *that* security team. Don't be that security team. Don't work with that security team.

Also, treats/snacks are a powerful ally in getting people to talk to you! Never underestimate the power of jelly beans.

What strategies do you use to communicate the threats you encounter to nontechnical decision-makers?

As security professionals, we have a habit of over-hyping bugs, and I'm not just talking about the latest, coolest named attack, but findings or reports that say the sky is falling. I am super guilty of this throughout my career (sorry if you're reading this), so try to temper my excitement upon finding something to actually fully understand its impact and risk.

You only get a number of "the sky *is* actually falling" warnings before management thinks you're starting to cry wolf, so double-check you weren't actually coming from an internal IP or that you do actually run that vulnerable version in production. If the version of Apache you're running had to worry about the millennium bug, then taking another five minutes to check that something isn't lying about its version isn't going to increase its overall exposure a whole lot more.

What recommendations do you have for managing nontechnical executives' expectations during a significant ongoing incident?

I'd start with calling them something other than "nontechnical" as they're executives, and that's a pretty technical business function.

The NIMS framework for incident response has a lot on communication and expectation setting. It relies on your organization understanding that during incident response the responder's (okay, incident commander's) word is kind of final, so they've already bought into this.

Though, as with much of incident response, you won't really know how everyone reacts until they react, which is why practicing this process with simulated attacks or tabletop exercises can be supremely beneficial, but don't underestimate just how stressful they can be on the people involved and adjacent, often near as stressful as a genuine attack. It's a path that I wouldn't exactly recommend, but if you inherit a company that has had a breach in the past, this unsurprisingly does wonders for helping set expectations going forward.

"The blue team first proactively defends our systems, responds to threats and incidents, and looks for areas of improvements within our security posture to close gaps."

Twitter: @tjackson78 • **Website:** www.terence-jackson.com and www.linkedin.com/in/terencejackson

Terence Jackson

Terence Jackson is currently the chief information security officer at Thycotic Software. His responsibilities include protecting the organization's information assets and managing the risk and information technology programs. Terence is an industry-acknowledged expert and public speaker and is regularly invited to speak and share his insights by some of the largest and most respected organizations in the world, including Forbes, Dark Reading, BrightTalk, Cloud Security Alliance, SC Magazine, InfoSec Magazine, Tech News World, The Guardian Hedge Fund Monthly, and Spectrum News. When not working, he enjoys spending time with his wife and two children.

17

How do you define a blue team?

I define the blue team as my internal SWAT team. The blue team first proactively defends our systems, responds to threats and incidents, and looks for areas of improvements within our security posture to close gaps.

What are two core capabilities that a blue team should have?

I would say detection and response are two core capabilities that every blue team should have. They are fundamental tenants. Without them the blue team falls flat. Without detection there is no response; similarly, if you don't know what you're protecting, there is little chance at detecting when it is under attack.

What are some of the key strengths of an incident response program?

The first strength of the program or team is to be able minimize dwell time or plainly detect incidents quickly.

The second is acting without thinking. During an incident, the response team needs be able to act as one and communicate effectively, so having playbooks that have been practiced and expertise in the respective aspects of IR will minimize the damage that is done by the adversary and reputationally.

Lastly, I would say preparation. They have to always be ready.

How can blue teamers learn, practice, and grow?

By participating in tabletop exercises, participating in CTF events, attending industry conferences such as RSA, Black Hat, and local BSides events. They must also continuously stay up-to-date on new tactics the adversary is leveraging, so education is a huge part of staying relevant.

How do you reward good blue teaming work?

I reward my team with monthly lunches, competitive salaries, leadership opportunities, awards, training, fun, and flexible work environments and trust. I also allow my team to think freely on how we can solve interesting problems, which allows them to explore alternative ways of problem-solving. This comes in handy during those budget crunches.

What are some core metrics that a blue team can use to build, measure, and maintain a successful information security program?

I like to look at dwell time and mean time to detection (MTTD). Being able to minimize the time an attacker can lay dormant in your environment and perform reconnaissance is a key capability. I also like to look at the number of tickets that are generated on phishing emails from end users. That lets me know how well we are doing at educating our end users.

Where would you start if you were the only information security staff member at a small to medium-sized business with a primitive security infrastructure?

Implement a zero-trust architecture by segmenting the network using VLANs. I would then isolate my most critical assets such as domain controllers and file servers as a red forest architecture to minimize the potential of lateral movement. Lastly, I would use privilege access management solution to protect our crown jewels.

What is the most bang-for-your-buck security control?

Application whitelisting and removal of local admin rights. If you only allow a handful of applications to run and your users don't have administrative controls, you have greatly reduced your attack surface.

Has your organization implemented any deception technologies?

We have, and it has helped us analyze the TTPs of the adversary. Obviously, I can't go into too much detail, but we did go beyond the typical honeypot. This has helped my team observe how quickly assets are scanned when they are deployed to the internet.

Where should an organization use cryptography?

Being able to protect the confidentiality and integrity of data, communications, and identities is two-thirds of the familiar CIA triad.

Everywhere possible: network communications, file and database servers, endpoints, mobile devices. Being able to protect the confidentiality and integrity of data, communications, and identities is two-thirds of the familiar CIA triad.

How do you approach data governance and other methods of reducing your data footprint?

First by going through data mapping and data classification exercises. Then by implementing appropriate IAM controls along with DLP. Finally, I would not hold on to data longer than we need to. Oftentimes enterprises don't set retention policies appropriately. The more data you unnecessarily hold on to, the more risk you have.

Is there a framework that aligns the activities or functions performed by the blue team with regulatory compliance requirements?

There are different thoughts on this, but I am a big believer in the NIST Cybersecurity Framework and ISO 27001. Both of these give a blueprint for controls, policies, and procedures for a solid security program.

What recommendations do you have for managing nontechnical executives' expectations during a significant ongoing incident?

Tie the incident to quantitative outcomes and potential loss expectancy. They may not understand tech, but they will understand numbers. Talk in the language of the business and communicate frequently.

"They implement security tooling and policy, respond to incidents, and harden servers, among other things."

Twitter: @shehackspurple • **Website:** wehackpurple.com

Tanya Janca

Tanya Janca, also known as SheHacksPurple, is the founder of We Hack Purple, a tech startup specializing in online and virtual security training for IT professionals. They also provide coaching services, helping companies launch and improve their AppSec programs. Tanya has been coding since she was a teen. She has worked in IT for more than 20 years, won numerous awards, started her own company several times, been a public servant, and worked for tech giants such as Microsoft, Adobe, and Nokia. She has been a pentester, CISO, CEO, AppSec engineer, but mostly a software developer. She is an award-winning public speaker, active blogger, and streamer and has delivered hundreds of talks and trainings on six continents. She values diversity, inclusion, and kindness, which shines through in her countless projects and achievements.

18

Tanya is also the founder of We Hack Purple, Women of Security (WoSEC), OWASP DevSlop, OWASP Victoria, and #CyberMentoringMonday.

How do you define a blue team?

Blue team are our defenders; they are the ones who ensure we have proper defenses in place and are protected adequately. They implement security tooling and policy, respond to incidents, and harden servers, among other things.

What are two core capabilities that a blue team should have?

Technical capability to get the work done and communication skills to understand what work needs to be done and why.

What are some of the key strengths of an incident response program?

A strong incident response program is mostly about preparation: a well-established incident protocol, training for responders and investigators, tools and access ready and in place, etc.

A strong incident response program is mostly about preparation: a well-established incident protocol, training for responders and investigators, tools and access ready and in place, etc. Other key strengths include always performing a blameless postmortem exercise, keeping metrics and aiming to eliminate or prevent incidents whenever possible, and showing strong, professional leadership during response.

How can blue teamers learn, practice, and grow?

- **Tooling:** Create proof of concepts before purchase to evaluate and to learn. Follow threads and streams online with the tools in use, and/or take technical training if possible. Create your own lab and go to town. A safe space to test and defend means you can't cause harm; use this as a chance to learn the limits of your tools. If at all possible, pair with a friendly red teamer or penetration tester to see whether you can learn from them where you are weak. Consider participating in capture-the-flag (CTF) contests online or in person.

- **Incident response:** Following an incident manager or the investigators as an observer is the best way to learn; however, that is not an option available to everyone. There are many options online for reading, training, or watching videos, and a card game called Backdoors and Breaches helps teach incident response that is quite handy.
- **Theory (the part that is not hands-on that lets you know how to set direction and decide which technical things to do):** There are several other good books from Wiley, and other publishers on this topic, as well as training. The best way to learn, however, is to pair study with either mentoring, job shadowing, or other hands-on training.

How do you reward good blue teaming work?

The same way you reward all good work. Telling your team directly they've done a good job, recognizing them in front of upper management, and giving awards, rewards, bonuses, and high fives.

What are some core metrics that a blue team can use to build, measure, and maintain a successful information security program?

Metrics are likely my favorite topic! When first starting somewhere and/or building a program, you want to see what your overall security posture is. For software (my specialty), this means looking at all the types of vulnerabilities you are finding and related incidents you've had. How many security activities are happening during the SDLC (such as code review or testing)? Do you feel what you are currently doing is enough and/or meeting industry best practices? When starting somewhere new, I usually target the top three issues they are seeing the most often, while I create a plan for modernizing and improving their AppSec program as a whole. Stop the bleeding and then work on long-term healing.

> Stop the bleeding and then work on long-term healing.

For software, have all the test results uploaded to the same place and look for the following:

- Find out whether you are seeing the same mistakes over and over. If so, target those types of issues with education and/or tools and retesting. Has it improved? Keep trying different things until you see improvements.
- Are you finding new types of issues? If not, start looking at new ways to see the things you are currently missing, and measure as you do.
- Are you meeting your SLAs? Are the bugs being fixed within their SLA? If not, why not? How can you get there?
- Are you compliant with all applicable policies and standards? If not, how can you get there? How can ensure you stay there?

Questions for incident response include the following:

- Have you completed an incident report and postmortem activity + report for every incident?
- Are you repeating the same types of incidents, or are you having new types?
- Were any of the incidents avoidable?
- Is there a way for you to prevent some of these incidents in the future?
- Does your team have time to catch their breath after each incident or are they one-after-another (this could lead to burnout)?
- How fast are other teams turning over incidents to your team?
- How long does triage take?
- Could you shorten your recovery time?

Where would you start if you were the only information security staff member at a small to medium-sized business with a primitive security infrastructure?
If I were the first security staff member, I would roll out a companywide password manager and teach them all about

multifactor authentication, password management, and basic security hygiene. I would also instruct all of them to report anything to me they think might be a problem.

Up next: web filtering, email filtering, and firewalls. Not sexy, but absolutely necessary.

What is the most bang-for-your-buck security control?

I would say that multifactor authentication is the best bang for your buck, if you can get your staff to actually use it.

Has your organization implemented any deception technologies?

I have not worked anywhere that has implemented deception technology.

Where should an organization use cryptography?

Data in transit and at rest should be encrypted, always, as well as all hard discs (this includes online cloud storage). Lastly, all websites that are public-facing should be accessible only via HTTPS.

How do you approach data governance and other methods of reducing your data footprint?

My company is currently five months old, so we don't have data governance or reducing our data footprint very well thought out just yet. However, we do off-site weekly backups, duplication of data, and cloud storage for less sensitive information and most content. None of our data is currently classified, although we publish a fair amount of it. Basically it's "published," "draft," or "do no publish" (generally emails, financials, or client information).

What is your opinion on compliance?

I do not find compliance to be an exciting activity, but I do believe that we need to know, for sure, whether we are following our policies. This is the purpose of compliance. That said, whenever possible, I prefer to automate as much as possible, both for convenience and for accuracy.

How do you engage all the different units of an organization to maximize defense?

I try to use a mixture of advocacy/education, policy, and inviting myself to meetings. I feel it's important that first you try to get what you want with honey, teaching people, showing them, and luring them into seeing the value of security. After that, I work on creating policies or standards to get what I think we need. Throughout the whole thing I try to interact with people one on one or in person if possible to ensure I understand how they feel and what they are thinking. With emails it's so easy to misunderstand; engagement requires understanding.

What strategies do you use to communicate the threats you encounter to nontechnical decision-makers?

When communicating to nontechnical people, I tend to use analogies or examples of potential risk that could happen to our business. If I can explain it in terms that they understand (such as describing a specific situation), then usually they can see my point of view and are ready to work together to make change.

What recommendations do you have for managing nontechnical executives' expectations during a significant ongoing incident?

When managing an incident, always make it clear that executives are to talk to you, not to your team (they just slow down the work). Tell them that you will update them whenever you have something significant, as well as every hour. Then I *actually update them*, hourly, as promised. Keeping your promises will ensure confidence, even if the update is that you still don't know. Ensure what you have is fact, not a hunch, before you present anything as fact. Whenever possible, give time estimates, but constantly reassure them you are working your hardest and your team understands the urgency. Reassuring people during an emergency really helps. Always answer the phone if they call. They are counting on you.

> Keeping your promises will ensure confidence, even if the update is that you still don't know.

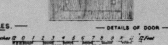

> "The whole concept of blue teaming is to ensure that as businesses digitize, an elite group of resources in the business proactively strategizes against cyberattacks (through policies and procedures), develops secure systems, and detects and prevents cyber events from materializing."

Website: www.linkedin.com/in/ruth-juma-9144b138

Ruth Juma

Ruth is a seasoned cybersecurity engineer with more than five years' experience in various industries. She has versatile skills including web security, penetration testing, and network security monitoring, with a current primary focus on red team operations. Other interests lately include reverse engineering mobile applications.

19

How do you define a blue team?
We have had so many cyberattack cases and cyber breaches across various lines of business. In reality, any business that has data is a target. Compounding this is the fact that digitization is here to stay; therefore, more and more businesses will have more data and offer their services through digital channels.

The whole concept of blue teaming is to ensure that as businesses digitize, an elite group of resources in the business proactively strategizes against cyberattacks (through policies and procedures), develops secure systems, and detects and prevents cyber events from materializing. This is the blue team.

What are two core capabilities that a blue team should have?

Blue teamers should have an in-depth understanding of how cyberattackers operate, including their drive, targets, goals, their resoluteness, etc. As Sun Tzu puts it, "To know your enemy, you must become your enemy."

A blue teamer should have tangible experience around network communications and how data moves through the seven layers of the OSI. Fundamentals in DevOps is also key. Having understood your adversary, you can quickly figure out how they will utilize technology to achieve their goal.

Finally, it is imperative for the blue teamer to possess the ability to quickly analyze situations and determine possible route causes for cyber events, as well as clearly and comfortably communicate to other stakeholders (including nontech) on incidents, events, and the response process.

What are some of the key strengths of an incident response program?

An incident response program should be holistic, from the application development phase to correlation of multiple and diverse events for quick establishment of potential root causes of cyber events. This means the program should support input from multiple disciplines/specialties and optimize response time for every query related to an incident.

How can blue teamers learn, practice, and grow?

For beginners, volunteering in response teams of any nature is a good starting point. Another approach would be using simulators from

> For beginners, volunteering in response teams of any nature is a good starting point.

various online labs that offer this kind of scenario. For practitioners in the field, nothing beats being part of a team that solves cyber incidents, from detection to controls enhancements. Taking part in red versus blue team activities also gives perspective and understanding and at the same time identifies what blind spots in your skillset need enhancing. It's about time these activities were introduced in curriculum for junior high and colleges.

How do you reward good blue teaming work?

At the end of the day, it is the people aspect in the PPT triad that is most critical in handling data and the systems hosting this data. Like any other prized possession, we must take care of our employees. This can be done through improved remunerations, well-defined career paths, and promotions for outstanding performers. More responsibilities, exposure, and opportunities to learn from other experts through conferences and other security events encourage blue team staff to invest more in the discipline.

What are some core metrics that a blue team can use to build, measure, and maintain a successful information security program?

For BAU, performance metrics can revolve around how incidents are managed, e.g., number of incidents over a period, recurring incidents over a period of time, speed of detection and resolution of incidents, and period of time taken to detect an incident. From a strategic perspective, it is practical to customize frameworks for blue team ops maturity via known best practices and global standards.

> From a strategic perspective, it is practical to customize frameworks for blue team ops maturity via known best practices and global standards.

How do you engage all the different units of an organization to maximize defense?

Formerly, the glaring gap that existed was the fact that no one understood the role of cybersecurity in dealing with cyber incidents other than the blue team. Awareness activities to demystify cybersecurity and the blue team to the business has led to a better appreciation to the point of including the business and other departments (legal, risk and compliance, HR) in the CIRT process. Bottom line, if the business appreciates the team input, they are willing to support its efforts.

What strategies do you use to communicate the threats you encounter to nontechnical decision-makers?

The business tends to understand one language: money. Where the communication alphabet uses monetary value, the executives, nontechnical managers, and even HR will quickly understand any threat blue teams communicate. For example, communicating that unwarranted local

> The business tends to understand one language: money.

administrator rights issued to stuff could lead to ransomware affecting all computers in the organization resulting in 14 days of revenue loss to the company, *all* will get the point.

What recommendations do you have for managing nontechnical executives' expectations during a significant ongoing incident?

Prior awareness sessions with management, where a potential event is discussed from a semitechnical and business perspective, help define expectations. During these sessions, blue teams should give a raw picture of what is practical and what is not. They should then recommend realistic actions in light of these discussions with

> Who knows, management may opt to invest more into the blue team activities.

management. Who knows, management may opt to invest more into the blue team activities.

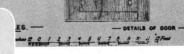

> "Technical security reviews, creating security tools, and managing vulnerabilities are all functions of a blue team."

Twitter: @BrendonKelleyBK • **Website:** www.linkedin.com/in/brendonkelley

Brendon Kelley

20

Brendon Kelley is a resident of Austin, Texas, where he was raised, and is currently a security engineer at a healthcare payment software company where he leads security operations and initiatives. He is a security advisor to a government consulting company focused on military and defense and a former security engineer at Bazaarvoice. He is a graduate of Baylor University in computer science and was cocaptain of the Baylor University Cybersecurity team that won the Southwest Collegiate Cyber Defense Competition (SWCCDC) in 2018 and finished fourth in the National Collegiate Cyber Defense Competition at NCCDC in 2018.

How do you define a blue team?

I'd define blue team as more than incident response. A core responsibility of a blue team is responding to incidents, but that's really a subset of its functions. Technical security reviews, creating security tools, and managing vulnerabilities are all functions of a blue team. They're always continuously working to reduce application and network security threats and mature their organization's security posture.

What are two core capabilities that a blue team should have?

Depending on your function on a blue team, some capabilities might be more valuable than others; just defining two is difficult. I'd say one would be the ability to understand and be cognizant of attack patterns and current threats. I'm always thinking from a red team's mindset. I try to learn some of their techniques by replication or staying on top of new threats and exploits by reading about them. When doing security architecture reviews, knowing about the attack landscape really helps.

> Another important capability for a blue teamer is always learning about other blue teams' tools used and their success stories.

Another important capability for a blue teamer is always learning about other blue teams' tools used and their success stories. Similarly, stay on top of the attack landscape so you can understand and incorporate defense tools or strategies that can be applied or used in your infrastructure.

What are some of the key strengths of an incident response program?

I think that a really strong incident response program consists of security automation, documentation, runbooks, and being prepared for anything. A more mature program has automated processes and procedures in place for incident response. Some incident response programs have the same producers or processes in place, but they're more manual.

For example, when an intrusion detection on a system occurs, an advantaged IR program could automatically isolate resources and aggregate findings for an investigation. An IR program that has to manually collect resources and isolate the system would be very time-consuming. Security automation for incident response separates those programs into being strong. Blue team is always getting security alerts, so having security automation built into the incident response program can make incident response much more manageable. Another key strength would be being prepared by having runbooks, documentation, and policies in place for incidents. Taking the time to evaluate the entire process can keep you focused when everything else is chaos.

How can blue teamers learn, practice, and grow?

Similar to software engineers having to learn about new frameworks or applications, blue teams also have to stay on top of those same developments to know how to defend them. Personally, I believe the security community on Twitter is very close. I learn a lot just by following many of the other Tribe of Hackers. A great way to meet some of them is to attend one of the many security conferences. I learned the most early on from attending local security events around Austin.

Another way to learn and practice is checking out some security Git repos. There are some that offer a collection of tools as well as learning materials about every topic in cybersecurity.

Growing on a blue team involves how to be the most productive asset to your organization in communicating security. That could mean working with software teams to fix vulnerabilities or helping them integrate security into their build process. A blue team is always growing technically, but the next step in career growth on a blue team is the soft skills.

What are some core metrics that a blue team can use to build, measure, and maintain a successful information security program?

Some core metrics blue teams can use in their security program are known vulnerabilities in our applications over time. Are we more secure than we were three months ago? Are we creating more vulnerabilities, or are we helping reduce them? We should be tracking not only incidents but also the resources it takes to fix them over time.

Beyond looking at vulnerabilities, record other metrics such as network and attack traffic and those trends. Visibility into internal traffic communication as well as external, and making sure there's not anything unusual, could prevent

I'm worried about the metrics I don't know. Anything I feel like our security team doesn't have visibility into keeps me up at night.

data exfiltration. I'm worried about the metrics I don't know. Anything I feel like our security team doesn't have visibility into keeps me up at night.

Where would you start if you were the only information security staff member at a small to medium-sized business with a primitive security infrastructure?
Well, I'd start with having really great security automation. Building something from the ground up, you're going to have to be able to scale well. So, having as many tools as possible to incorporate into a SIEM is great. The first thing I might build would be around access controls. One foundational element in building a secure network is having really great ingress and egress rules. This limits the attack vector. Hackers may be able to get in one way, but if you can prevent persistence access and are monitoring ingress and egress traffic, that is super critical.

When building a program from the ground up, the blue team first needs the ability to even detect a security incident. That requires adding visibility everywhere, such as adding intrusion detection systems on hosts, adding network intrusion detection, logging user activity, and adding vulnerability scanning to applications and hosts. After adding visibility into your organization, the next step is making it actionable by aggregating all of those alerts or information into a way a blue team can manage it, usually a SIEM. Presenting those findings to teams and others in the organization will help eventually mitigate the risk and improve security.

What is the most bang-for-your-buck security control?
Well, there are tons of great enterprise security tools on the open source side that have lots of capabilities. One is Wazuh. It has tons of great features and can support tons of different systems. It's an intrusion detection system that can monitor for incident response and help with compliance. It can do Windows operating systems, Linux, Mac, and containers. Wazuh analyzes file systems (even file systems of an application), and it can do configuration assessments, log data analysis, and vulnerability detection. And it's all open source, so Wazuh has to be on the list of best bang-for-your-buck security tools.

However, real-time threat intelligence is something that's missing with open source tools in general. Threat intelligence is something I'd prefer to have an enterprise-level tool for and incorporate those findings into other security tools.

Has your organization implemented any deception technologies?

My organization or any other organization I've been at has never implemented deception technologies. I've played around with them personally but not actually in an organization. However, there are some deception techniques that have been used. For example, when you get blocked by a WAF or just a firewall, you might get a "406 Blocked" response. That can give information to the attackers that they're getting blocked; instead, we can block the request and change the HTTP response code to be a "404 Not Found" response.

Similarly, another technique we've done is change the server information to be the opposite of what it actually is, like IIS instead of Apache, or vice versa.

How do you approach data governance and other methods of reducing your data footprint?

This has had such a profound impact on really everyone. We're always trying to limit the places of data replication, especially with personally identifiable information. It's much easier to prevent a data breach when there's a single data store that every service interacts with. It's so critical to isolate your production environment and have a testing environment with mock data. Data governance also applies to access management and even beyond, such as to a data store with S3 and log files.

What is your opinion on compliance?

My opinion on compliance is that there's a belief that being in compliance means you're secure, and that is absolutely false.

How do you engage all the different units of an organization to maximize defense?

- Education and training
- Making everyone feel a part of the security team
- Getting them to be cognizant and security conscious about phishing emails, leaving their computer unlocked, or even letting people into the office they don't know and who don't have a badge

> We can have all of the security controls in the world, but it's up to everyone in the company to be security conscious.

We can have all of the security controls in the world, but it's up to everyone in the company to be security conscious. It's part of the blue team to engage in the process by sharing examples, engaging in discussions about personal security, and participating in training.

What strategies do you use to communicate the threats you encounter to nontechnical decision-makers?

A strategy I think that works well when communicating threats to nontechnical decision-makers is having all of the risks organized and including recommendations and estimated cost/work to mitigate the risk, as well as stating the impact if exploited. A great way to organize risk is having meetings with technical individuals in the company along with other security stakeholders to evaluate the risks. Then assign priority and come up with recommendations that you can communicate to the nontechnical decision-makers. This whole process is common of a risk assessment. Internal risk assessments are a great way to stay on top of an organization's security threats.

What recommendations do you have for managing nontechnical executives' expectations during a significant ongoing incident?

I recommend being honest with what you know and don't know. Try to come up with set times to sync back up about the status of an ongoing incident. That could be every four hours or every eight hours. Constant communication that manages nontechnical executives is important, but also remember to give the blue team space to operate in times of chaos.

> Constant communication that manages nontechnical executives is important, but also remember to give the blue team space to operate in times of chaos.

"A blue team's goal is to automate the cybersecurity ecosystem of applications to actively and passively protect themselves from threats around the world."

Twitter: @ShawnKirklandCS • **Website:** www.linkedin.com/in/shawn-kirkland-240a6539 and cyberpulse.tech

Shawn Kirkland

Shawn Kirkland began his career in the U.S. Navy as an operations specialist bringing the military's global networks together. He then went to college at Auburn University of Montgomery to study computer programing and while in college began his career outside of the military contracting for the Air Force. Over the next eight years, Shawn became fluent in securing most systems and applications available in the industry today. Shawn leverages this knowledge to educate companies today on how to properly start and maintain an information security program.

21

How do you define a blue team?

Every person within a company is part of the blue team. From the executive assistants to the CISO, all parties hold a certain amount of responsibility to defend their company's network. At a more specific level, a blue team's goal is to automate the cybersecurity ecosystem of applications to actively and passively protect themselves from threats around the world. To be successful at this, it is imperative that a blue team have a modern vulnerability management program and set of processes to ensure best practices are implemented.

What are two core capabilities that a blue team should have?

A blue team should have five core capabilities, and they are listed as follows:

Discover: Map, categorize, and identify every asset on the network.

Assess:

> **Pre-active:** Establish automated pipelines for securing and hardening asset images before they are released into the network.

> **Re-active:** For assets that live on the network for long periods of time, ensure each asset continues receiving vulnerability assessments and updated hardening controls.

Analyze: Report on KPIs and metrics to understand if the blue team is being successful or failing.

Fix: Distribute vulnerability and control findings to the appropriate personnel for remediation.

Measure: Rinse and repeat. Continuously ensure the processes established in the first four capabilities are working and measured against the metrics defined.

What are some of the key strengths of an incident response program?

- **Identify:** To be aware of an incident in the first place, it is necessary to have a robust asset management or discovery program in place to constantly record and track all assets and traffic throughout the network.
- **Monitor:** There are three primary types of data to monitor to have a complete picture of the network from a holistic perspective.
  - **Software:** Software should be scanned by vulnerability scanning software to identify vulnerabilities or compliance controls that can be remediated by patching or hardening mechanisms.

- **Traffic:** Analyze traffic to determine the flow of data throughout the network and discover malicious activities that could be occurring.
- **Logs:** Capturing and analyzing logs is useful in determining the history and possibly predicting the future of a cyberattack. It can also be useful in implementing protection to avoid an incident.
- **Contain:** Once an incident occurs, containing the threat will reduce the probability that it spreads further. Utilizing threat containment software will keep files or traffic isolated to prevent further damage.

How can blue teamers learn, practice, and grow?

A successful blue team is aware and has the "know-how" to operate and understand any form of technology. They also have a good understanding of how this technology and network infrastructure operate within the overall technology ecosystem within their company.

> A successful blue team is aware and has the "know-how" to operate and understand any form of technology.

Here are few steps to stay ahead of the ever-evolving realm of cybersecurity:

- **Communicate:** To stay relevant with the constantly changing network, it is imperative that you establish relationships with all teams or units within the company.

  For example, an information security program is extremely dependent on the network team to be successful. By setting up weekly or biweekly meetings with the network team, you can constantly have discussions about changes in the network or existing infrastructure that will assist you in ensuring those networks have the proper coverage. Without a relationship with the network team, an information security program will be blind with regard to cybersecurity.

Here are a few teams to have relationships with to be successful:
Network team
Server team
Red team
DevOps team
Cloud team

- **Learn:** Great news, you've already taken the first step by reading this book! Technology is constantly changing and evolving, and cybersecurity professionals have to stay knowledgeable on the latest features, software, and best practices to successfully protect the network. Watching videos, going to a SANS class, and reading articles will keep your knowledge up-to-date with the latest happenings in the industry.
- **Practice:** Learning helps with understanding cybersecurity best practices at a high level, but how do we apply that knowledge in the real world? Having a home or work lab to test best practices will send you light years ahead in being able to successfully apply these mechanisms in your production network.

What are some core metrics that a blue team can use to build, measure, and maintain a successful information security program?
By identifying what it means to be successful as a blue team, you can define metrics to measure that success criteria. For example, metrics can be associated with each of these five core capabilities:

- **Discover:** Am I discovering and categorizing 100 percent of my assets?
- **Assess:** Am I scanning for vulnerabilities and controls against all assets discovered?
- **Analyze:** Am I reporting against defined SLAs and success criteria for my blue team?
- **Fix:** Are my asset owners fixing findings according the SLAs?
- **Measure:** If I am not adhering to one or more metrics, how do I change or improve the process to meet the KPIs and metrics in the first four core objectives?

Where would you start if you were the only information security staff member at a small to medium-sized business with a primitive security infrastructure?

Learn the network. The most common issue my customers have today is the lack of understanding of how their network is architected.

> The most common issue my customers have today is the lack of understanding of how their network is architected.

This is usually due to not having a strong relationship with the network team. The network is by far the most pivotal fundamental item to understand to be successful at securing it. Set up weekly or biweekly meetings with the network team to grasp how it is architected today and what improvements or changes will be implemented in the future.

What is the most bang-for-your-buck security control?

Vulnerability scanning technology is quite a useful piece of software due to the vast amounts of information it can gather. Here are some of the tasks a "good" vulnerability scanning solution can do for you:

- **Discovery:** Knowing which assets exist on the network is crucial to many programs throughout your network such as asset management to identify gaps in security, where threats reside, and who should fix them.
- **Vulnerabilities:** Scanning for out-of-date software, misconfigured code, or malicious software will help in securing your network.
- **Compliance:** When taking the next step in your information security program and implementing compliance controls, having a suite of software that can run configuration checks against all systems will help in identifying where the compliance gaps are.
- **Traffic analytics:** Deploying passive scanning technology at TAPs/SPANs will ensure you are analyzing all traffic coming in and leaving the network to identify malicious activity in the network. This scanning method can also be useful for identifying rogue assets as it listens 24/7/365 versus an active scanner, which is a point-in-time scan.

- **Patch management:** The patch management teams will have the responsibility of deploying patches to all systems throughout the network regardless if they are a security patch. Active scanners have the capability to log into an asset and find which patches are required regardless of the vendor. This data can be sent to the patch management teams to ensure their applications are set up correctly and packages created for all software patch automation.
- **Image security:** It is imperative that we continuously scan pre-existing assets throughout the network, but by scanning images before they hit production, you will increase the security posture even more to ensure that nonsecure images/software are not being deployed throughout the network. Integrating a scanning solution into this pipeline will alleviate these issues.
- **Logging:** Some vulnerability scanning technologies will also have logging solutions within their suite of products. Utilize these features or integrate your vulnerability scanning solution with your pre-existing SIEM to correlate logs with active and passive vulnerabilities.

Where should an organization use cryptography?

- **Personally identifiable information (PII):** At a high level, any network segment that has PII information traversing that segment should be encrypted. Even if the segment is not externally available, attackers could exploit the externally available assets and jump to a segment that has PII traversing it.
- **Disaster and recovery:** Backups contain vast amounts of information that, if compromised, can be catastrophic to a company. Ensure your backups are encrypted and keep the data path encrypted for off-site storage.
- **External-facing assets:** Externally available assets such as web servers are typically a hacker's first choice when attempting to compromise a network. If these external web servers are compromised, the attacker could possibly jump to other assets that are not externally available such as database servers. Ensure the connection between your externally available assets is secure and encrypted between the assets they are connecting to inside the network.

How do you approach data governance and other methods of reducing your data footprint?

By answering the question "What does it mean to be successful?" for your cybersecurity program, you can identify which data is most important to you to store, analyze, and report. For example, logs are a great way to monitor activities going on throughout the network, but it can be costly to store them and buy software to analyze them.

After identifying your success metrics, you can define which logs to capture and which logs are not important for you to capture. This not only helps you from a data footprint perspective, but you can take the "useful" logs and report/monitor events based on that data.

What is your opinion on compliance?

Compliance can be a complex world; however, it is absolutely necessary in order to be considered a "good" information security program. To my customers, I call compliance "end game security." I suggest not beginning compliance enforcement until you have a robust vulnerability management program. If you do not already have a "definition of success" for your program and you begin implementing compliance, you will likely fail before you even begin.

Some compliance controls will require months to implement, and some will require an acceptance of risk due to the risk not being applicable to your network or breaking a critical aspect of the network. Here are a few items I would have in place before beginning to implement a compliance program:

- **Risk acceptance workflow:** An approval process defined for controls that will require being accepted if they cannot be remediated in your given SLAs.
- **SLAs defined:** How long should you give your asset owners to remediate each control? This will allow you to measure success for your compliance remediation efforts.
- **Automated remediation tools in place:** Many controls in compliance should be deployed throughout the network and enforced by software such as Group Policy (for Windows), Puppet, Chef, Ansible, scripting, etc.
- **Asset owners identified:** Once scanning and analysis begins for compliance, having the asset owner identified beforehand will allow for a much smoother process in getting the control remediated.

- **Communication channels with all teams throughout the company including non-IT teams:** It is always imperative to have good communication channels established with other teams for all aspects of technology. With compliance, it is even more imperative. Many controls have the capability to bring your network to its knees if implemented. Understanding how each control affects your team's technology will alleviate some of these pains.

Is there a framework that aligns the activities or functions performed by the blue team with regulatory compliance requirements?

Typically, there are two frameworks I always recommend to every customer, depending on whether they are government or commercial, regardless of what types of assets or data they have in their network:

- **NIST:** Government customers are required to implement NIST controls to all assets throughout their network. You can find the hardening standards here: csrc.nist.gov/glossary/term/Hardening.
- **CIS:** Commercial customers should implement CIS controls throughout their network. You can find the CIS benchmarks here: www.cisecurity.org/cis-benchmarks.

You may be required to implement other frameworks such as NERC-CIP, PCI, ISO, etc., depending on your regulatory requirements, data traversing your network, or functions within your company. If so, reach out to the appropriate vendor website for more information.

How do you engage all the different units of an organization to maximize defense?

When beginning down the path of communicating to each business unit (BU) in an organization, using a "How can you help me, how can I help you?" strategy will get you in the door and establish a good relationship with the appropriate BU. Here are a few examples:

Network team:

- *How can you help me?* Giving me a view of what the network looks like today and providing the data necessary for me to analyze the network from a vulnerability and compliance standpoint.

- *How can I help you?* Providing data on what the network "actually" looks like according to active and passive scanning technologies to update your systems. Providing vulnerability and compliance information to better secure your systems.

Patch management teams:
- *How can you help me?* Patching systems in an automated manner using appropriate patch management tools to close vulnerabilities.
- *How can I help you?* Providing the necessary information on which patches a system requires and a more holistic view of assets that may fall under your team's umbrella with regard to patch management.

Development:
- *How can you help me?* Securing software before it is released to production networks.
- *How can I help you?* Integrating vulnerability scanning solutions with your development pipeline to ensure your software is secure before it is released to production.

What strategies do you use to communicate the threats you encounter to nontechnical decision-makers?

At a high level, there are usually two mechanisms of reporting threat data in the company.

- **Asset owners:** These are the people who are actually going to remediate the threat or finding in the network. They want to know as much information about the threat as possible, such as the following:
  - What is the threat?
  - How do I remediate it?
  - Is there other information available on this threat to help me determine my best appropriate action?
  - How long do I have to remediate this vulnerability?

    Distributing this data to the asset owners can be done in PDF, spreadsheet, or even ticketing format to help them understand the variables they need to know to remediate the finding.

- **Executives:** The "higher-ups," managers, or executives typically just want to know one simple thing: "Are we good or not good?" They do not need to know the ins and outs of how to fix a finding but will likely want to know some of the following:
  - How many vulnerabilities do we have on our critical assets last month? How many do we have this month?
  - On a trending chart, are we making progress quarter over quarter on our remediation efforts?
  - Do we have all of the necessary technology in place to monitor/enforce our defined metrics of success?
  - Do we have the staffing in place to monitor/enforce our defined metrics of success?
  - Can we utilize integration points to automate manual labor that may be hindering our workflow?

    Answer these questions and more in a weekly PDF or slideshow presentation to showcase, at a high level, where you stand with your information security program.

What recommendations do you have for managing nontechnical executives' expectations during a significant ongoing incident?

When an ongoing incident is occurring, it can be stressful because executives and upper management want answers as fast as possible to some of the following questions:

- Which systems are compromised, and what data was affected?
- Is the threat still active, or is it contained?
- Was customer data or PII affected?
- When will the threat be contained or eliminated?

Ensure you stay calm and have your teams work as quickly as possible to identify the threat, which assets or areas of the network are affected, and how to contain the threat. Avoid giving unrealistic time frames to the executive staff, and do not let pressure from the "higher-ups" allow you to make a hasty decision that could set you back even further.

"The blue team plays against the red team, like in military exercises."

Twitter: @samilaiho • **Website:** 4sysops.com/members/sami-laiho and samilaiho.com

Sami Laiho

Sami Laiho is one of the world's leading professionals for the Windows OS and security. Sami has been working with and teaching OS troubleshooting, management, and security since 1996. In 2019 Sami was chosen by *TiVi* magazine as one of the top 100 influencers in IT in Finland. He is the 11th most followed person on Twitter in his field in Finland.

22

At Microsoft Ignite 2018, Sami's "Behind the Scenes: How to Build a Conference-Winning Session" and "Sami Laiho: 45 Life Hacks of Windows OS in 45 Minutes" sessions were ranked as #1 and #2 out of 1,708 sessions. This was the first time in the history of the conference that anyone has been able to do this.

How do you define a blue team?
The blue team's focus is to defend the organization from digital/cyberattacks. Basically it includes anything that defends the

company from an enemy, but this usually refers to cybersecurity. The blue team plays against the red team, like in military exercises.

What are two core capabilities that a blue team should have?

- Good knowledge/inventory of hardware and software assets so that they know what to secure
- Trained skills on what to do when an incident happens

What are some of the key strengths of an incident response program?

The goal is to handle the situation in a way that limits damage and reduces recovery time and costs.

A good incident response program has five major steps.

1. Preparation
2. Detection and reporting
3. Triage and analysis
4. Containment and neutralization
5. Post-incident activity

Practice, practice, practice.

How can blue teamers learn, practice, and grow?

Use on-demand learning and follow other experts on Twitter.

How do you reward good blue teaming work?

A successful blue team should be rewarded each year if they keep the environment secure. The management should be educated on the proactive measures taken by the blue team even if they are never actively blocking incidents. The worst example I have is a CISO and a friend of mine who was kicked out of a company because there were no incidents, so the management thought there was no need for his services.

What are some core metrics that a blue team can use to build, measure, and maintain a successful information security program?

Security can't hinder usability. Otherwise, you will never get buy-in from management or end users. So, the measurement should not only be about prevented incidents or fixed breach situations but also the overall satisfaction of the users of the protected systems.

Security can't hinder usability. Otherwise, you will never get buy-in from management or end users.

Where would you start if you were the only information security staff member at a small to medium-sized business with a primitive security infrastructure?

I would implement the principle of least privilege. Most of the traditional malware can be mitigated by removing admin rights. The results are insanely good compared to reactive measures, especially when looking at Office apps and browsers! In 2019, removing admin rights mitigated 80 percent of all vulnerabilities in Windows and 100 percent of vulnerabilities in Office and IE/Edge.

You should remember that removing admin rights is not just about security. Removing admin rights will also allow your computers to run faster, better, and longer, with fewer reinstallations. My bigger customers have also measured 75 percent reduction in the number of help-desk tickets after removing admin rights. This means you can be more secure and more productive for extended periods of time.

What is the most bang-for-your-buck security control?

Whitelisting. A correctly configured whitelist adds no overhead, and you only need an average of one new rule per month. The traditional blacklisting of threats needs to add 1 million new lines per day because of new malware.

A correctly configured whitelist adds no overhead, and you only need an average of one new rule per month.

Where should an organization use cryptography?

Every endpoint needs full-volume encryption. The most important task for the full-volume encryption is to keep the device intact. So, the most important feature is integrity, not data encryption like many think.

An endpoint with no data still needs to be encrypted to keep anyone from tampering with it. A good example is AppLocker whitelisting on Windows. If you put in a good policy, anyone with physical access can just take the system offline and clean the C:\Windows\System32\Applocker folder, which disables the whole whitelisting. When your computer's disk is encrypted, this cannot be done.

How do you engage all the different units of an organization to maximize defense?

In my company, the security department is now included in every project from the beginning and not just auditing/commenting afterward. This has been a big change, and it has really paid off!

What strategies do you use to communicate the threats you encounter to nontechnical decision-makers?

The CISO presents monthly to our board. "Luckily" the news nowadays lists so many attacks and breaches against companies and even cities that it's now easier to get an audience from management.

What recommendations do you have for managing nontechnical executives' expectations during a significant ongoing incident?

Be extremely honest and precise on what functionality the ongoing situation affects and how long you predict the situation to last. Break the expected process into milestones, if possible, as it's always easier for a human to see some light at the end of the tunnel when the tunnel is not infinite.

Don't try to solve everything yourself if outside help will get operations up faster. Budget will rarely be an issue in a serious situation that is not expected to be ongoing for a long time. The person who communicates to executives should have good knowledge on how the company's business processes work normally.

"The primary capabilities of a blue team should be keeping systems secure but also educating other areas of the business."

Twitter: @ctrlshifti • **Website:** codemopolitan.com

Kat Maddox

Kat Maddox is a security architect who frequently calls herself a "one-girl security team." She focuses on helping small companies get a head start on their security posture and works in fields including vulnerability management, application security, compliance, and risk analysis. Having previously worked as a pentester before moving to a blue team, Kat is an advocate for closing the gaps between offensive and defensive security and building a culture of knowledge sharing and collaboration. When not putting out fires, Kat writes tech jokes on Twitter.

23

What are two core capabilities that a blue team should have?

This answer is a little unorthodox, but here goes: The primary capabilities of a blue team should be keeping systems secure but also educating other areas of the business. Blue teams are usually much smaller than we need to be, so it's crucial to get help from other departments. This includes things such as teaching employees what phishing scams look like, empowering people to champion security in their own department, and maintaining good DevSec relationships. The developers have saved me more times than I can count.

One of the coolest things I did in my current role was hold a lock-picking workshop for the rest of the business. You can bet people were way more interested in engaging with my security program and reporting phishing scams after that. People were so interested in learning about security afterward that I had to set office hours!

How do you reward good blue teaming work?

I find that, compared to other areas of the business, blue teamers are critically starved of recognition. We work hard to keep the organization safe, but normally won't get the same shoutouts that someone from sales or product will. I think it's a good security leader's job to make sure their team is given the recognition they deserve within the business.

Where would you start if you were the only information security staff member at a small to medium-sized business with a primitive security infrastructure?

Something that's often over-looked in InfoSec, and tech in general, is the importance of understanding the organization's business goals.

Something that's often overlooked in InfoSec, and tech in general, is the importance of understanding the organization's business goals. A fintech offering a SaaS that's accessible only to approved clients is going to have a way more limited threat surface than an online store that's available to anyone. The company's roadmap might even include expanding into an area that's covered by different security regulations than it currently complies with. If you don't understand the business needs before designing security infrastructure, you're going to waste time, resources, and, worst of all, offend your stakeholders. That takes a lot of hard work and coffee bribes to recover from.

Before designing any security solution, here are the questions I ask myself:

- If this is a product-based company, then who uses the product?

- Who are my key stakeholders? What can I learn from them before starting?
- What regulations or certifications does the company need to acquire/comply with to achieve their business objectives, preferably without the CEO getting fined or jailed?
- What's the one-year business roadmap? Two years? Five years?
- What security measures already exist, if any?
- What's the architecture of the current network and systems?
- What's the budget, and who do I have to sweet talk if I need to get an increase?

Once I have the answers for these questions, it's normally pretty obvious where I need to start. Even the best security professionals sometimes fall into the trap of operating in their own bubble, and it's easy to create disconnect between the security team and the rest of the business. In my experience, the key to running a drama-free, well-funded security program is to get your stakeholders to see it not as a security program but as another business program that we all need to work together to achieve.

> In my experience, the key to running a drama-free, well-funded security program is to get your stakeholders to see it not as a security program but as another business program that we all need to work together to achieve.

What is the most bang-for-your-buck security control?

This depends so much on the business (see my earlier rant!), but I've had the best success with identity and access management. Audit who has access to what, and revoke any access that's not necessary or used. Apply the principle of least privilege wherever you can. This will already ease a large portion of your people risk and make phishing scams way less dangerous (more effectively than phishing simulations ever could—but that's a debate for later). An added bonus of this is while auditing access controls, you'll usually discover numerous rabbit holes of terrible practices that you wouldn't have otherwise known about, just by talking to people about what access they have and need.

Where should an organization use cryptography?

There's no one-size-fits-all solution for each business. The organization I currently work for encrypts data pretty much *everywhere*, because our existing network infrastructure makes this cheap and easy, and we store sensitive financial data. A place that I worked for previously encrypted basically *nowhere*, because they didn't collect or transmit any sensitive data, and implementing sophisticated encryption strategies would have cost the business much more than it'd potentially save. I'd start with understanding *what* the data is, what its sensitivity levels are, and what the data lifecycle is before you decide what stages it needs to be encrypted at.

What is your opinion on compliance?

I *love* compliance. So does the CEO, when we get him not imprisoned. Compliance is a crucial part of the business objectives, and I think it's important for security teams to collaborate closely with the GRC team to understand what regulations affect your business.

The main issue I've seen with compliance is when organizations see it as a checkbox activity without actually investing in security or user safety. I've been in access audits where stakeholders gave some people's access the all-clear because just checking the box would be easier than dealing with the drama of revoking their access. When stuff like this happens, it's a clear sign that people aren't engaged with your security program. Sometimes it's a sign that your security program just needs some marketing, or it could hint at much deeper issues in the business.

What strategies do you use to communicate the threats you encounter to nontechnical decision-makers?

You have to put it into terms they'll understand. If you're talking to risk professionals, you can describe the threats in terms of how it'll affect the organization's risk rating. If you're talking to someone who works in operations, try explaining how the threat will affect the organization's operational abilities. This is why it's important to understand your stakeholders and the worlds they operate in.

At the same time, I think it's important to not underestimate them. Just because someone is nontechnical doesn't mean they're stupid. The more context you can give them, the more opportunity they'll have to offer solutions from perspectives you wouldn't have considered.

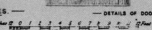

> "What I have come to understand over the past few years is that the blue team is more or less the defenders of the network operations of an organization."

Twitter: @MrJeffMan • **Website:** www.linkedin.com/in/jeffreyeman

Jeffrey Man

24

Jeffrey Man is a respected information security advocate, advisor, evangelist, international speaker, keynoter, host of *Security & Compliance Weekly*, and co-host on *Paul's Security Weekly*. He has nearly 40 years of experience working in all aspects of computer, network, and information security, including cryptography, risk management, vulnerability analysis, compliance assessment, forensic analysis, and penetration testing. He is a Certified Cryptanalyst by the National Security Agency and was part of the first penetration testing "red team" at the NSA. For the past 25 years he has been a pentester, security architect, consultant, QSA, and PCI SME, providing consulting and advisory services to many of the nation's best-known companies.

How do you define a blue team?
This first question is a great starting point but also implies that at least part of the definition of *blue team* involves incident response. To be completely honest, it is not really a term that

comes up in consulting/advisory duties, primarily in the area of credit/debit card security (you know, PCI). I've heard the term numerous times at hacker/security conferences, but it is not a term that comes up often in my day job.

What I have come to understand over the past few years is that the blue team is more or less the defenders of the network operations of an organization. Whether this is a defined role or not doesn't matter to me as much as understanding what activities/tasks/disciplines would fit this loosely defined category of "defense."

I've been asking folks I meet at various conferences and events over the past several years to define the terms they use to describe what we do as an industry, first asking "What is a vulnerability?" or "What is a threat?" and ultimately asking "What is security?" I am continually amazed at the lack of consistency in responses, and that last one quite frankly has stumped many people, even several who are considered to be leaders or influencers in our field.

There seem to be two broad views of security that have emerged despite the lack of concise answers. First is the notion that organizations need to "be secure," meaning they are to achieve a state where they are immune to attack or otherwise not capable of being compromised. Security in this sense is a state or level that is to be achieved (and maintained). The second idea that has emerged, and is the one that I more often suggest, is that security is something you do; it is a set of activities performed on a continuous basis to detect malicious activity, identify/contain the attack or otherwise minimize the damage or loss, analyze the source and/or cause of the exploitation so that the attack can be prevented from being successful moving forward, and assure that either whatever changes/mitigations/countermeasures are identified to stop future attacks are implemented or steps/processes are created to detect if such attacks are attempted again.

These activities start to sound a lot like the activities that one would expect to see in an incident response program, so effectively the blue team is responsible for security of the organization's network. Security = defense.

What are two core capabilities that a blue team should have?

The capabilities that I have seen most consistently over the years within organizations for which I have consulted are a deep knowledge of the systems for which the teams are responsible, a good idea of what is "normal" in terms of its operation, and an appropriately paranoid but tenacious attitude that whatever system they are responsible for will not fall to an adversary. Someone told me once, "Not on my watch and not on my box." Maybe these are more like qualities rather than capabilities, but these are certainly attributes I have most often seen in organizations that I would describe as doing security well.

Unfortunately, as technology has advanced in terms of how it works, the increasing speed, and the complexity of data, applications, systems, operations, and so forth, I am seeing these qualities less and less. I still see folks who know how the technology works, but less and less do I see folks who know what the technology *can* do beyond its intended functionality. There is also necessarily more reliance on automation to collect and sort through all the network traffic, logs, and audit trails that are generated by all the technology, and folks are increasingly becoming experts on the tools they use to perform these activities, often at the expense of understanding what they are actually doing.

What are some of the key strengths of an incident response program?

A good place to start is by having a formal program. Formal means the goals, tasks, steps, and activities are all *written down*. The incident response program needs to involve every employee in the organization, but that seems to be missing too often.

I see too often general users/employees assuming that somebody or something that is somewhere else in the organization is responsible for doing the monitoring detection, prevention, and response. All employees need to be trained to "see something, say something" in terms of any unusual behavior or activity of any of the applications and systems they use in their jobs. They are responsible for more than simply being able to identify phishing attempts and watch a 20-minute security awareness video once a year. Good incident response programs train employees to report if they see something unusual or weird, and they give them the names/numbers/emails of the people they should inform. Beyond that, the key strengths include having knowledgeable analysts who are familiar with business operations and either have the right skills or have good relationships with developers, administrators, and operations folks so they can tap the right resources during investigations.

C-level and management support is essential as well, as the incident response team must be able to tap into whatever resources are required during its investigations and response.

What is the most bang-for-your-buck security control?
Knowledge.

Where should an organization use cryptography?
There are several possible applications for cryptography in an organization. From a data security perspective, you can use cryptography to promote the three classic aspects of data security: confidentiality, integrity, and availability. Cryptographic functions are also commonly applied to authentication mechanisms such as the protection of passwords and the use of digital signatures both for authorization and for nonrepudiation (the protection against someone denying that they agreed to, consented, and signed off on an agreement or contract).

I think the question is asking mostly about data security, so first and foremost the organization should create a data classification standard or guide that can then be used to determine what types of data the organization deals with that require the type of protection afforded by the use of cryptographic solutions. The organization should also perform a business process/data flow analysis to determine such things as how the data is created or introduced into the organization, where it flows, who or what consumes the data or needs access to it, if it is required to be retained, where and how it is retained and for how long it is needed, whether it leaves the organization, and when and how it is destroyed when no longer needed.

Cryptography then becomes appropriate to protect sensitive data when it is being transmitted into/within/and out of the organization's network and also to protect the data when it is being stored or retained.

What is your opinion on compliance?
I believe that most organizations in America (and probably worldwide) have limited exposure to or interest in or appetite/budget for security and are interested in security only to the extent that regulatory/compliance standards make them do anything.

I have been almost exclusively involved with the Payment Card Industry Data Security Standard (PCI DSS) since its introduction in 2004 and was a qualified security assessor for nearly 10 of those years. In those 10 years I worked with more than 100 organizations, many of which were Fortune 500 (including at least two that were ranked Fortune 1 at the time). Several of my customers were victims of some of the largest data breaches of the time. Those companies were certainly interested in security after their breaches, but none of them was prepared at the time for what transpired.

But these types of companies were the exception. Most of my other customers had little apparent interest in setting up a security program, wanted to do the bare minimum to be found compliant, and would spend an inordinate amount of time trying to "reduce scope" and avoid having to do what most would consider to be best practices.

I spent a lot of my time during assessments explaining what the PCI DSS requirements meant, why they mattered, and why my customer should not only do all the things within their cardholder data environment (CDE) but everywhere in their organization. I would often receive feedback such as, "That was the toughest thing we've been through; thank you for helping us understand." I also heard things like, "What are our competitors doing, because we want to do no more nor less?" and "Why do we have to worry about security; we just sell clothing?" and my favorite, after spending a good bit of time explaining how encryption worked and what the PCI DSS requires, "Yeah, but we don't need DoD-level security."

So, my opinion about compliance is very well defined at this point, and this is explicitly in reference to the PCI DSS.

- All the pentesters and red teamers who are around today largely have their jobs because PCI requires an annual penetration test.
- I talk to a lot of PCI haters and naysayers in the hacker/ security community, and their beliefs are always based on a misconception or misunderstanding about how PCI actually works and/or what the PCI DSS requires.
- I most often hear that PCI is the "bare minimum" in terms of actual security practices/requirements, and yet I have worked with so many companies that find out it is extremely hard to actually follow the requirements put

forth in the PCI DSS and do it consistently and do it well. When I hear these statements, I try to ask the person what is missing or what else should they do from a security perspective that is not in PCI. I rarely get any response.

- I also hear "You can be compliant and not be secure" to which I respond in one of two ways: "Yes, you can, if I assessed you" and "You can be secure and not be secure."

Bottom line: If you treat the PCI DSS as a framework and not just a security standard for a specific type of sensitive data and follow the principle or spirit of the major goals/requirements, you will have set up a pretty decent security program, including incident response and whatever you call a blue team (if at all).

Is there a framework that aligns the activities or functions performed by the blue team with regulatory compliance requirements?

The concern that people have about "only doing what regulatory compliance requires" is that this is less than what security requires and therefore leaves you open to compromise, or worse that the compromise goes undetected. The reality is that most companies are only going to do what regulatory compliance requires, so you better know how to work within those constraints to be effective as an incident responder/defender/blue teamer.

That's where I had my greatest successes with my PCI customers. I define success by feeling like I at least helped them make more informed decisions about how they would/wouldn't really follow the PCI DSS requirements and ideally helped them to understand the necessity of each requirement, the interdependencies of all that is required, and all those in the organization who make it all work.

So, yes, there is a framework; it's PCI DSS. It's not a question of whether it's wise to do this; it's a question of so many organizations have to do it anyway, so the challenge becomes using PCI as a means to an end. The wise organization will embrace whatever framework they apply; understand that it points you in a certain direction and that it does not embrace all of the specifics of what you need to do, but ideally you recognize that it covers all of the aspects of a mature security program.

How do you engage all the different units of an organization to maximize defense?

When I was a qualified security assessor (QSA), I had the opportunity to engage all the different players in an organization, including the business units, HR, legal, internal audit, developers, admins, and even the security teams. This was made easy because of the nature of PCI DSS, which requires the involvement of all the different units if they wanted to be found compliant (and that was always a strong motivator).

I often came away from a PCI compliance assessment with a better overall picture of the business operations/security posture of my customer than any one group with which I engaged. I would use that to my advantage to help with the discussions of what they needed to do new and differently in order to be compliant (secure) by helping to educate the various groups as to how they fit into the big picture of the business and ideally instill in them the desire/motivation to do their part for the greater good of the organization.

What strategies do you use to communicate the threats you encounter to nontechnical decision-makers?

Generally speaking, I follow the lessons I have learned from my 25+ years of consulting, which I put forth in a training course entitled "The Art of the Jedi Mind Trick" (www.cybrary.it/skill-certification-course/art-of-the-jedi-mind-trick-certification-training-course).

Basically my strategy involves things like "knowing my audience," in which I try to learn something about them, so if I need to use examples or analogies, I can try to draw on something they already understand. I also attempt to learn their language—whether it is the language of business, executives, HR, legal, techies, or whatever. I am not trying to get them to learn my technical jargon; it is on me to explain it to them in the way they will understand.

A key strategy is also listening, which helps not only with learning their backgrounds or interests or the language they speak, but also gauging whether they are understanding or tracking what I am saying. Telling stories, making analogies, finding common ground or a basis of understanding, being patient, trying more than one method, and asking "What did you hear me say?" are all different techniques that help the nontechnical decision-maker to get to the point of making the right, or at least an informed, decision. (This is called *persuasive speech*.)

"My dedicated cybersecurity team is entirely focused on defense, but that defense stretches to incident response, risk management, business continuity planning, and disaster recovery."

Twitter: @aprilmardock • **Website:** www.linkedin.com/in/aprilmjwork

April Mardock

25 April Mardock has supported cybersecurity and InfoTech in 132 different companies. She is well-versed in complex, multilayered environments and is currently the functional CISO for more than 60,000 users at Seattle Public Schools. She holds a master's in IT and a CISSP security certification, as well as several other industry-specific certs. April's current responsibilities include site-based technology audits, InfoSec policy management, disaster recovery and business continuity consulting, firewall management, penetration testing, email spam and web filtering, and on-site network forensics.

How do you define a blue team?
For me, the blue team is everyone involved in the defense of the business cyber assets. Some are involved in it full-time, some part-time, and some only occasionally, but in reality, we're *all* on the blue team, as each of us has responsibility to practice defensive cyber safety in our daily work. See something, say something.

My dedicated cybersecurity team is entirely focused on defense, but that defense stretches to incident response, risk management, business continuity planning, and disaster recovery. We are also doing board policy work to change business operations to better manage confidential data. We are working to change the organization from the inside out, using every lever at our disposal. My blue team even extends to my external partners like the SOC that watches my organization nights and weekends while the employees sleep.

What are two core capabilities that a blue team should have?

Blue teams need two things to be successful: empathy for the end user and persistence to push through the necessary changes. Most exploits aren't stopped by threat hunting; exploits are stopped by following best practices by patching regularly, following up on alerts, removing admin rights, and blocking lateral movements.

What are some of the key strengths of an incident response program?

A good incident response program understands the threat at both a tactical level and a strategic level.

- Tactical, in that as many steps as possible are detailed so that the least skilled players can still be successful
- Strategic in that it reaches across the organization to include executives, public relations, legal, risk management, and other teams and actively involves them as part of the response effort

Once established, the incident response plan needs to be tested regularly and revised, at all levels of the organization.

How can blue teamers learn, practice, and grow?

The InfoSec blue team in an organization our size has a chance to learn, practice, and grow every day. That's one advantage of having 60,000 managed computers; there's never a lack of threats. The key is protecting the team's time so they don't get tapped out by other organization demands like forensic requests and investigations.

How do you reward good blue teaming work?

Reward often depends on each member of the team. For the introverts, a small gift card may be appreciated. For the extroverts, it might be calling out thanks in a public meeting. Blue teams are often motivated by a recognition of service, especially when they perform above and beyond the call of duty. I once had the superintendent give my senior security engineer a "fly to the ball" signed football because he was so good at anticipating and intercepting threats.

What are some core metrics that a blue team can use to build, measure, and maintain a successful information security program?

Blue team metrics depend on the role. It might be as simple as "%systems with up-to-date patches within the past 30 days." But it should be metrics against those things that are considered high risk for the organization.

Where would you start if you were the only information security staff member at a small to medium-sized business with a primitive security infrastructure?

Take a good long look at the NIST CSF. Then create an inventory of your systems. What do you have? What does it do? Then prioritize your current vulnerabilities and weaknesses, ranking them by calculating your Worry Index = (%impact on biz) × (%probability of event). Focus your limited resources on your top five concerns. For us that would include phishing and ransomware.

What is the most bang-for-your-buck security control?

There is no one answer. As far as low-cost/no-cost options, stop giving users admin rights and simultaneously turn on LAPS (blocking lateral movement). It will slow down any potential attacker. Then force MFA for use from the outside. Create an exception group if you must, but MFA is a massive game-changer.

Has your organization implemented any deception technologies?

Yes, we've leveraged a few simple deception technologies. We've turned on internal email relays and set up a simple BLAT alarm when someone tries to use it. We've used more elegant tools like Kushtaka to set up a network of "fake" FTP services to capture bad actors looking for unprotected data. We've even used honey tokens to mark data extracts so we can fingerprint them if the data shows up elsewhere. All of these give us early visibility of probing activities by both curious students and bad actors.

Where should an organization use cryptography?

We all need to be in the habit of encrypting data at rest, and that's perhaps the most critical use of cryptography in my book. But cryptography should also be used to globally authenticate each host and help the organization clearly delineate trusted from untrusted hosts and users. As a side note, we also need to be a lot more intentional about protecting our cryptographic private pairs and API keys.

How do you approach data governance and other methods of reducing your data footprint?

Partner with your legal teams; find out what they're using for e-discovery and leverage the same system to identify risky data like SSN and credit card data across your network. Then isolate and consolidate the risky content, putting additional controls around it to audit and control use. You can also sometimes leverage the same systems to identify stale data: Work with the organization to delete what you don't need! If it's gone, it can't be stolen. Examples include automating removal of home drives of departed staff, including cloud data.

What is your opinion on compliance?

Leverage the compliance checklist as an opportunity to catch missed opportunities, but *never* assume a compliance checklist means you're secure against an attack. Every organization's risk fingerprint is different, and all mitigation plans should differ as a result.

> Every organization's risk fingerprint is different, and all mitigation plans should differ as a result.

Is there a framework that aligns the activities or functions performed by the blue team with regulatory compliance requirements?

There is no perfect framework. There are some that will try to sell you alignment strategies and solutions that sound good, but it's up to you to hold the line for your team. Your focus should be on your inventory and your customized risk profile. Most of your work should be aligned with both business priorities and assessed risk. The compliance exercise is a necessary evil, but you will need to work to avoid a false sense of security. "Checking all the boxes" will never prevent you from getting pwned.

How do you engage all the different units of an organization to maximize defense?

For me, everyone is involved in cybersecurity. I call it the human firewall. Every single one of us is on the hook for defense. For blue team work to be successful, you must be embedded at every level of the organization. For my end users, it's about educating them on how their passwords are like tooth-brushes—not to be shared and to be changed often. For my developers, it's reaching deep into the SDLC process and helping them evaluate risks before they become liabilities. For my operation teams, it's helping them prioritize the patching so that the highest risks are addressed first. And for my cybersecurity and response teams, it's learning and improving after every incident, in a tight loop of continuous feedback.

What strategies do you use to communicate the threats you encounter to nontechnical decision-makers?

My most successful strategy with the executives is proving their most competent peers are doing it. If other agencies like mine are taking the same precaution, executives are often more willing to consider the request. The same goes for warnings that come from official channels at the state or federal level—if they feel there is some level of external "credence" to the request, they're more likely to allow an interruption in service or provide additional funding.

The other thing that helps nontechnical decision-makers are viable analogies. Explain things in such a way that they can represent it to someone further up the line. Keep it simple, keep it relevant, and keep it memorable, like the password analogy of not sharing the toothbrush.

What recommendations do you have for managing nontechnical executives' expectations during a significant ongoing incident?

It helps if you've already communicated an incident response plan and done tabletop exercises before. It's best to go into an emergency having already built the trust of the executives. They need to have seen you and have trust in both your data and your team's decision-making abilities.

"The blue team identifies intrusions, performs incident response, analyzes malware analysis, and addresses strategies to avert future potential attacks."

Twitter: @BRIGHTZEED • **Website:** www.linkedin.com/in/dr-bright-gameli-mawudor-phd-4324b238 and www.brightzeed.com

Bright Gameli Mawudor

Dr. Bright Gameli Mawudor is the head of Managed Security Services at Internet Solutions and Dimension Data (MEA) and has more than 13 years of professional experience. He is also the founder of the Cyber Security collective Africahackon, which has been running for seven years.

Dr. Mawudor acquired a PhD in IT convergence and application engineering with a concentration in information security from Pukyong National University, South Korea, and has presented at more than 120 cybersecurity conferences as well as lectured at various universities.

Dr. Mawudor has performed various evaluations and selections of cybersecurity tools and successfully implemented IT security systems to protect the confidentiality, availability, and integrity of critical business environment to curb and mitigate risks.

26

How do you define a blue team?

A blue team is a defensive security team that focuses on improving an organization's security posture. The blue team identifies intrusions, performs incident response, analyzes malware analysis, and addresses strategies to avert future potential attacks.

What are two core capabilities that a blue team should have?

Intrusion identification and incident response.

What are some of the key strengths of an incident response program?

- **A plan:** A good incidence response plan helps the team deal with threats, outlines how to isolate events, assigns a severity scores, and stops the attack.
- **People:** A blue team requires complementary and good communication skills, which when used together increase the odds of stopping adversaries.
- **The right tools:** Using the wrong tools in a blue team can greatly increase the mean time to respond (MTTR) on incidents.

How can blue teamers learn, practice, and grow?

- Keeping current with present and previous threats according to frequency, methodology, and severity
- Understanding what input data (logs, SNMP, NetFlow, etc.) they gather from their environment and how to interpret it to detect and correlate incidents
- Proper communication and information sharing to reduce MTTR
- Conducting purple team exercises in controlled environments to learn adversary behavior

How do you reward good blue teaming work?

Monetary rewards are usually considered great for team members, but an agreement was made at our organization to recognize the team's work during company meetings and team dinners and, most importantly, to let the organization sponsor certification courses for their career development, which are usually expensive.

What are some core metrics that a blue team can use to build, measure, and maintain a successful information security program?

Measure MTTR for incidents on a regular basis for unique events.

Where would you start if you were the only information security staff member at a small to medium-sized business with a primitive security infrastructure?

Identify a framework that fits the business and automate tasks to have visibility at all times using open source technology as it does not involve a lot of capital expenditure. This will be supported by conducting frequently scheduled security awareness training to the staff and testing some of the lessons, such as phishing campaigns.

What is the most bang-for-your-buck security control?

Have visibility at all times, and have strategies in place to respond to incidents to determine root cause within the shortest possible time. Mostly have a disaster recovery site ready with an up-to-date backup to allow for easy failover when necessary.

Has your organization implemented any deception technologies?

On the upside, the blue team gets to learn adversary evasive techniques and gain insights on how to stop them. The downside is surges in false positives if the deception technologies aren't demarcated from the production environment. This allows the tweaking of honeypots planted in the environment, and a really good example is RedCanary tokens, which can be placed in networks, systems, applications, and web servers.

Where should an organization use cryptography?

Cryptography assures an organization of its data confidentiality and integrity. Such data could include passwords and intellectual property. Data in transit and memory should employ cryptography to avoid compromise from intruders who may get access to it in the event of a successful attack.

> Cryptography assures an organization of its data confidentiality and integrity.

How do you approach data governance and other methods of reducing your data footprint?

Organizations need to adopt frameworks that will be used to govern data. There has to be an enforcement of rules and policies such as assigning liability to staff who takes care of the data asset. Reducing data footprint requires classification of data and adequate archiving, compression, and backup. Old data that is not required anymore can be archived with attention on de-duplication and planned backup.

What is your opinion on compliance?

Compliance is still a difficult concept to be adopted by organizations that do not understand the consequences it can bring in relation to the legal entities. Protection of personal data and privacy needs a lot of awareness of not only what it takes to execute, but also the penalty and costs to an organization should they fail to embrace it. Such awareness starts with one understanding if they are a data controller, a data processor, or a joint controller.

Is there a framework that aligns the activities or functions performed by the blue team with regulatory compliance requirements?

Frameworks to apply to blue teams will differ from company to company. Some might have to be governed by ISO and others by PCI DSS if there is card data involved. PCI DSS focuses on the following domains:

- Build and maintain a secure network
- Protect cardholder data
- Maintain a vulnerability management program
- Implement strong access control measures
- Regularly monitor and test networks
- Maintain an information security policy

It is wise and paramount to have such frameworks as it binds the blue team and their activities to follow standards of best practice.

It is wise and paramount to have such frameworks as it binds the blue team and their activities to follow standards of best practice.

How do you engage all the different units of an organization to maximize defense?

The business gets to understand the conversation is about the risks exposed and identified by the blue team as well as the potential extent of damage that could have been caused if had not been dealt with. Further discussions go on about potential areas of exposure and remediations plans to be put in place as strategy for implementation.

What strategies do you use to communicate the threats you encounter to nontechnical decision-makers?

I like to use live demonstrations to mimic some of the threats seen on the day-to-day basis. An example is ransomware attacks via phishing email embedded in an Excel sheet as a macro. I explain by replicating a similar scenario and use sample similar domains to send the attachment as a compressed file to a nontechnical user. Upon opening, I use simple frameworks such as Metasploit to show the level of control that one can have on a target just by them opening a simple document laced with a macro embedded or DDE.

Should there be a need to purchase software or hardware for the organization, I make sure I have done sufficient comparison of the best on the market and have proof of concepts ready to show the value of how they can stop such attacks. An example in this case can be an endpoint detection and response tool.

What recommendations do you have for managing nontechnical executives' expectations during a significant ongoing incident?

Swift decision-making is needed during an incident, and I make nontechnical executives know they are stakeholders involved in the well-being of the organization. This ranges from communication to acquisition of a tool needed immediately,

> Swift decision-making is needed during an incident, and I make nontechnical executives know they are stakeholders involved in the well-being of the organization.

enactment of the incidence response or disaster recovery plan that has been drafted for failovers, etc. Business impact analysis and getting the buy-in of executives is always important for the future state of the organization.

Twitter: @InfoSecwar • **Website:** mcalynn.com

Duncan McAlynn

"Blue teamers are a special breed."

27 Duncan McAlynn is the founder of Operandis and the host of the podcast series Cyber Speaks LIVE. He is an InfoSec professional with more than 25 years of industry experience, and now, semi-retired, he develops technical content for the cybersecurity industry and is mentoring the next generation of cyber champions. Throughout his career he has consulted with numerous Fortune 500 companies, government agencies, and educational organizations on enterprise management and security strategies.

Duncan is active in his local community, supporting security BSides events, attending local hacker association meetups, and going to ISACA and ISSA meetings, and he is a member of the FBI InfraGard.

How do you define a blue team?

Blue teamers are a special breed. They tend to be the empathetic type who sees someone in need and does something to help. Those same heartfelt principles apply when these frontline defenders of the world take on the role of blue teamer. They become the protectors and defenders of the nation's corporations, government agencies, nonprofits, and learning institutions. They stand up to the challenges and face their attackers head on. I applaud their efforts daily.

What are two core capabilities that a blue team should have?

While it may seem obvious, I can't emphasize enough how important it is for a blue teamer to be a team player. To be an effective blue team member, you must work not only with your core team but also with those of network engineering, desktop support, the server team, and not to mention the CISO and CIO. This means that teamwork and communication (both verbal and written) are essential. You can't be a blue teamer and a lone wolf at the same time.

Second, blue teamers should have a passion for learning new things, whether that be by reading a book, watching YouTube videos, attending a conference, or asking a colleague for assistance. Blue teamers should possess enough humility to know what they don't know and demonstrate a willingness to learn.

What are some of the key strengths of an incident response program?

Something I learned from being a first responder to cyber incidents is that proper, preplanned communication can be the difference between a successful incident response and absolute failure leading to loss of trust, as well as the potential for legal and financial repercussions. An incident response plan should include a well-thought-out communication plan, involving key stakeholders, and should clearly state who says what and when to ensure that the statements made (both internal and external) are not causing more harm than good.

You never know what you're going to require when you have a cybersecurity incident. So, be sure to have a jump bag ready to go. This jump bag is literally a backpack that is filled with a fully patched laptop, pens, pencils, paper, mini printer, digital camera, cellular phone, memory cards, USB sticks, flashlight, etc. This backpack should be rotated monthly among the CIRT members and duplicated—one on-site, one off-site always.

How can blue teamers learn, practice, and grow?

There are so many ways for people to learn stuff today that at first it can seem overwhelming to know where to begin. Most adults, however, will know which type of learner they have become: audible, visual, or kinetic. Thankfully, there are tons of resources available for each today. We have largely the internet to thank for this massive advancement in learning. So, I say take advantage of whichever works for you!

If you're an audible learner, sign up for Amazon's Audible service or listen to some of the great podcast series that are available.

If you're more of a visual learner, search out some of the cybersecurity topics on YouTube and Vimeo or stream some of the content available on Cybrary.it and Pluralsight.

For you kinetic learners, there's no better way than building out your own lab environment to tinker with, blow up, and then have to start all over again. Some of the best hackers I know have had to do it dozens, if not hundreds, of times. It doesn't have to be terribly expensive either, thanks to cloud computing and virtualization.

How do you reward good blue teaming work?

I'm not suggesting that *attaboys* will pay the bills or anything, but in reality, public praise of a team member's contributions does go a long way. Blue teaming can be a thankless job much of the time because when things are going well, nobody notices, and when an incident does occur, you have only one chance to get it right. So, when the little accomplishments happen along the way, it's nice to have them recognized. The higher up the chain to do so, the better.

What are some core metrics that a blue team can use to build, measure, and maintain a successful information security program?

I have found that the key performance indicators (KPIs) that one organization uses can greatly vary from the next. But the most successful that I see are short-term, measurable, and repeatable. Perhaps it's lowering the MTTD or improving the response times for applying software updates, or even participating in and the results of implementing a new bug bounty program. Whatever the case may be, its success is dependent upon the team members, and they should be recognized for their accomplishments.

Where would you start if you were the only information security staff member at a small to medium-sized business with a primitive security infrastructure?

This is where I would lean on the Center for Internet Security (CIS) Top 20 Security Controls, focusing on the Implementation Group 1 (IG1).

- Inventory and Control of Hardware Assets
- Inventory and Control of Software Assets
- Continuous Vulnerability Management
- Controlled Use of Administrative Privileges
- Secure Configuration for Hardware and Software on Mobile Devices, Laptops, Workstations and Servers
- Maintenance, Monitoring and Analysis of Audit Logs

This framework is based on the input from industry experts from around the world and provides a simple way to help organizations of different sizes to focus their security efforts in the just the right places, at the right time, while still leveraging the value of the CIS Controls program. More information can be found at www.cisecurity.org.

What is the most bang-for-your-buck security control?

Patching. Patching. Patching.

Has your organization implemented any deception technologies? If so, what effect has that had on the blue team's detection capabilities?

High-fidelity sensors, like that of the open source Kushtaka (maintained by fellow Tribe of Hackers contributor Jared Folkins), have their place in the enterprise as part of a defense-in-depth approach. The key is "high fidelity." When implemented and used properly, these solutions can help prevent an infrastructure breach from becoming a data breach by decreasing the mean time to detection (MTTD). These sensors allow the blue team to be immediately notified once a malicious actor trips on one of the cleverly placed assets. They can then act on the alert, such as blocking the IP address of the attacker or using SOAR playbooks to automate the process.

Where should an organization use cryptography?

Rather than address the where, I'd like to address the why. With growing regulations regarding the safe handling of consumer data, it's becoming increasingly challenging for organizations today to conduct business as usual.

> With growing regulations regarding the safe handling of consumer data, it's becoming increasingly challenging for organizations today to conduct business as usual.

While this is good news for data privacy and protection advocates, it does mean that companies must be quite cautious when handling any personally identifiable information (PII), as more and more new laws are being written to the books at a rapid pace.

If this type of sensitive data (e.g., dates of birth, health records, Social Security or credit card numbers) are being collected, then state, federal, or industry regulations may require that this data be encrypted while at rest, in transit, or in use.

If your organization is unsure what requirements are applicable to them, a good place to start is with your local Secretary of State department for U.S.-based companies, or in Europe check with your National Data Protection Authority: edpb.europa.eu/about-edpb/board/members_en.

What is your opinion on compliance?

Compliance ≠ Secure. Far too often organizations will focus so intensely on obtaining a specific compliance level that they can't see the forest for the trees. In their quest to obtain some industry or federal compliance badge, they overlook some of the most basic security controls that mitigate risk and reduce vulnerabilities.

> When you design, build, and develop security into your stack, compliance comes much more easily.

Is there a framework that aligns the activities or functions performed by the blue team with regulatory compliance requirements?

Yes. The National Institute of Standards and Technology (NIST) Framework for Improving Critical Infrastructure Cybersecurity has quickly become the industry darling for addressing an organization's cybersecurity risks as part of its overall strategy. The framework is flexible enough to be implemented by organizations of all sizes and industries based on their unique types of threats, vulnerabilities, and risk tolerances.

How do you engage all the different units of an organization to maximize defense?

Early and often. The last thing that another overworked group wants is for us to dump more upon them unexpectedly and at the last minute. The more we can communicate and collaborate with other groups, the better. I've also learned that breakfast tacos are the key to success with multiteam-smelting.

What strategies do you use to communicate the threats you encounter to nontechnical decision-makers?

Risk is the language of the board room. When speaking with executives, I have learned to talk about subject matters that resonate most with them.

In terms of what we're doing out there, that means speaking to the risks to which they're vulnerable.

> When speaking with executives, I have learned to talk about subject matters that resonate most with them.

What recommendations do you have for managing nontechnical executives' expectations during a significant ongoing incident?

Establishing trust early on is a critical factor for setting expectations during a cybersecurity-related incident. This holds true whether you're speaking with those in the trenches or helicoptering up to the board room. Trust comes with confidence, and confidence comes with experience. That is the trifecta.

"Guess what? You are part of this blue team. There are no walls. We are all in this together with one goal in mind."

Twitter: @FrankMcG • **Website:** www.frankmcg.com

Frank McGovern

28

Frank McGovern is a founder of Blue Team Con, an information security conference focused on community for blue teamers. He is also a senior information security engineer in Chicago, Illinois. Frank has a unique aspect of being in a large organization with a small cybersecurity team. Due to this, he aids in cybersecurity architecture, implementation, and operationalization. He also currently oversees writing the organization's cybersecurity policy and implementing its cybersecurity GRC program. He comes from a Marine Corps intelligence foundation, which has helped him throughout his cybersecurity career.

How do you define a blue team?
Blue team is the culmination of people who are working toward defending an organization's assets. This means that your title doesn't matter; it's the work you're doing. Are you an IT person at a high school who manages antivirus? You are blue team. Are you GRC, such as an auditor? You are blue team. Are you coding securely? You are blue team. Are you even an offensive security

red teamer? Guess what? You are part of this blue team. There are no walls. We are all in this together with one goal in mind.

What are some of the key strengths of an incident response program?

A strength is the ability to maintain a lessons-learned document and reflect on those lessons via subsequent meetings. Adapting the environment through a continual maturation method is key to successfully guarding against any future risks.

How can blue teamers learn, practice, and grow?

Learning is not one set path for every individual. Some learn by reading; some learn by doing. The best way you can learn, practice, and grow is to find what works for you and don't gauge yourself by others. You are following your own path, and you know what works for you better than anyone else. Focus on that, and you will find yourself meeting milestones.

Where would you start if you were the only information security staff member at a small to medium-sized business with a primitive security infrastructure?

Removal of admin rights with the installation of host protections will return the largest amount of ROI. From there, you need a complete understanding of what is in your environment through inventory management. Once you've taken care of these basic ideas, start working down the CIS Top 20 controls and solving those questions.

What is the most bang-for-your-buck security control?

Removal of admin rights. This is closely seconded by multifactor authentication in as wide a breadth as you can do. Too many people focus on implementing a solution to 100 percent. Even removing local admin rights from 75 percent of machines is still a win. Implementing MFA to 50 percent is still a win. Start the journey, and you will eventually reach the endpoint.

What is your opinion on compliance?

Compliance is a great checklist to view yourself at a defined baseline. From there, you should discover gaps and what else in your business is of concern and implement more controls. There are always problems to solve that compliance doesn't highlight, and it's your role as a blue team member to shine the light on those risks.

> "A blue team must have a core membership that is intellectually curious, thoughtful, and passionate about their field of work."

Twitter: @dsmcf • **Website:** www.linkedin.com/in/dmcfarlane

Donald McFarlane

29

Donald McFarlane provides management/board consulting and "vCISO" services, mostly in the enterprise sector. He is a passionate information security architect and risk management evangelist who helps run DEF CON's Skytalks and donates his time to several other industry conferences.

His experience implementing, operating, and protecting IT systems started early on, running his own BBS in prep school and dumpster-diving line printer output from the local university. His first paid InfoSec job was to secure Unix systems for the UK's version of DARPA. Since then, he has secured online trading systems, global data centers, and branch networks in more than 100 countries and advised on several billion-dollar acquisitions, mergers, and divestitures.

When he's not thinking about how things might go awry, he cooks, plays golf, and runs a small ISP. He lives with his wife, son, and dog in a log cabin that he built himself on the side of a mountain in New Hampshire.

How do you define a blue team?

The concept of a blue team/red team is that of simulating engagement with a threat to try to improve the enterprise's defenses and to learn better defensive strategies and recovery strategies. It is the responsibility of the security team at large to adopt these lessons by understanding the hazards involved and fostering appropriate reductions in the risks. After-action reports should involve both red and blue teams, security leadership, and other IT and BU leadership as applicable, and they should be transparent and honest regardless of politics.

Most organizations will want to rotate key security talent in and out of the blue team based on the mission of the exercises at hand. This—and indeed the whole blue team/red team approach—works only if you have deep and broad strength in your core security team. You should also be prepared to identify talent from outside the security team, which may benefit the mission.

With that said, you should recognize that many in the industry have not adopted this understanding of a blue team and instead use the term to apply broadly to all of the organization's defenders, or at least all of them with "security" in their job title. This is not a helpful definition. Everyone in the firm, let alone the security team, has a role to play when it comes to security. That work doesn't start or stop at any single discipline, and blue teamers should take their experiences back to their primary role, upping everyone's game in the process.

What are two core capabilities that a blue team should have?

To engineer something well, one must understand the use cases and the normal failure modes; to secure something well, add to this an appreciation for the potential avenues of abuse and unexpected failure modes and to some extent the threat models and actors who might participate in that abuse. All of this demands a capacity and desire to understand and explore all layers of the stack.

First, then, a blue team must have a core membership that is intellectually curious, thoughtful, and passionate about their field of work. A broad knowledge of the technology stack and lifecycle as well as of the risks and processes embodied in those technologies must be nourished within the team.

Second, no matter how clever individual team members or groups may be, a blue team can work best only when its members spend time engaged closely with counterparts in the other teams across the IT and business landscape, collectively understanding the specific environments, activities, challenges, and frustrations. They must appreciate the business risks and processes, recognizing the priorities of what makes the business run and what's worth defending.

Like the blue team, the whole IT security team should understand that their mission is to enable the business (or other entity) to survive and to thrive, rather than to defend it beyond any possibility of doing so. Encouraging a long-term view that looks beyond next quarter's earnings or the next annual report—or even beyond the appointment of a successor CEO or CIO—is likely not a bad thing at all, but failure to appreciate the broader context of "security" decisions is. Dogmatic team members who cannot recognize nuance and conceptualize the interplay between different risks are likely to promote bad decisions or to perpetuate a dysfunctional "department of no" model, which ill befits a security team. Security teams should be called in on incidents because they are considered helpful, not viewed as a necessary evil. Nevertheless, to advocate properly, the team must, at its core, be articulate and versed in reason, argument, and historical context.

How can blue teamers learn, practice, and grow?
Spend time talking and collaborating with people. Go to conferences (to learn from and interact with others, not just listen to talks). Try your hand at a local CTF and learn some red team techniques. Read broadly, not just InfoSec books. If your management is not supporting cross-training, ask them to and explain why. If you don't feel challenged at your company, ask yourself why; and if you don't like the answer, refresh your résumé and be willing to try your hand at a different role. Even if you're a security guy or gal at heart, consider stepping outside of InfoSec for a few years to gain some other perspectives.

As a company, practice the art of failure. If this sounds odd, take a look at what Netflix has been doing for the last decade with chaos engineering, and consider whether your own DR, BCP, and incident management testing programs are achieving the right ends. Play "what if" scenarios. Talk to people who've had breaches. Oh, and you do have a red team, right?

How do you reward good blue teaming work?

I try to be sensitive to the needs and interests of that individual. Sometimes the traditional employer's performance incentives and positive reinforcement techniques will work best, but be willing to adjust your approach to the case at hand. It might be giving praise and recognition outside the usual corporate forums (a tweet even), adding training/tools, giving some time to work on personal projects that keep it interesting and raise skill levels, providing flexibility in work hours and location, or allowing publication of (suitably redacted/sanitized) tools/techniques/experiences to the hacker community. There's almost always an approach that will satisfy and provide mutual benefit to both parties.

There should be a competitive ethos between blue and red teams, and you should remember that the opportunity for practice afforded by the work is often as valuable as the specific outcomes and lessons learned.

What are some core metrics that a blue team can use to build, measure, and maintain a successful information security program?

The most important thing is always to remember that, one way or another, metrics are incentives. They create behaviors. By measuring the same problem in different ways, people can and do end up driving dramatically varying—or even oppo-site—effects.

A lot of the time, organizational metrics are only given lip service by hard-core blue (and red) teamers, who are more interested in the meat of their work than in the corporate politics or compliance/audit aspects of the job. Even to the extent they do care about the metrics, these folks often look at the numbers and actually read them carefully, seeking to interpret how they are derived and what they really mean to contextualize them properly. If this is you, know that this is not how the majority of the audience will read them.

So, the first question is, what changes are you trying to drive, and with what relative priorities? To answer this, understand the maturity you're at and where it is reasonable to get to the next level. Brainstorm with a few of your smarter and more naturally devious colleagues, who understand the human condition, to understand the ways in which your first attempt at creating the right metrics will actually drive negative behaviors. And iterate. Then, and only then, publish. Be prepared to adapt the metrics as the maturity advances, but know that in doing so you are losing (or creating disjoint) trend data, so as much as possible design for each metric to last throughout the lifecycle of the change it is intended to spur.

As a general rule, quantitative metrics should be risk-based, not compliance-based. Your goal should be to reduce risk effectively, which will naturally yield a compliant posture. You can then assess compliance qualitatively and close any small gaps that remain. If your priority in measurement is compliance, then do not be surprised when the solution turns out not to have delivered the level of risk reduction you expected.

Oh, and the red team versus blue team metrics? Sure, you can measure the simple success or failure of specific mission objectives. But if the intent is to encourage and reward good work, then that's better arrived at by a subjective assessment by peers and by leadership of the work that has been done. If you really want to turn this into a metric, then add a mean opinion scoring round into your next after-action report.

Where would you start if you were the only information security staff member at a small to medium-sized business with a primitive security infrastructure?

Know yourself. Sure, as you tour the battlements, you will want to kick off a few parallel threads to address some of the most obvious and gaping holes as you go along. But spend several weeks getting to know your assets—the systems, the networks, the software, the data, the business model and key processes, the people, the risk tolerance, the history, the failures, the root causes, the available budget. Do a SWOT analysis. Pick some topics and go ask people the five whys. Know where the keys to the kingdom are, both at a business level and at the IT level. Know what keeps your board of directors (or partners or owner) and your senior leadership up at night. Know your customers. Then drink a nice cup of tea, read over the SANS top 20 list or your other favorite cheat sheet for the umpteenth time in your career, and think carefully about your next step.

If this is too daunting, start with the network diagram, firewall rules, and software/application list.

What is the most bang-for-your-buck security control?

DNS logging. Trap and manage all DNS requests (on all transports), log them, and establish monitoring and alerts. You can use blacklist/whitelist approaches to reduce the noise, you can baseline and look at volumetric anomalies to detect C2 channels, or you can even look at other contextual detail such as when the domain was registered.

Has your organization implemented any deception technologies?

I've been using simple honeypots and other false and misleading targets since the 1990s. Even if there are now a bunch of vendors looking to invade this space and separate some companies from their spare revenue as those companies pursue a "no security tool left behind" approach, the truth is it's not hard or expensive to do. If you have basic logging and alerting in place, or for that matter a DevOps team that is halfway competent with scripts, then you should already be using some of these techniques (along with some basic configuration monitoring) up and down the stack to separate the wheat from the chaff and to help you identify when there's a malicious actor at work inside your environments. Security by obscurity is a much-maligned term: Good operational security is a valid and extremely useful tool in your arsenal.

Yes, OpSec is key here. These should be small things, spread across your environment—files, user accounts, API calls, credentials, client settings, networks, etc. Understand the attacker's TTPs, especially for lateral movement and persistence. I would love to give more concrete examples, but then people would know what to look for. And the same holds true in your organization: Information sharing is important for most things, but this is one of the times where few people should have the whole view up and down the stack. It's okay for some operational SMEs who need to know about these "tells" to be aware of their piece of the pie, but they don't need the whole view, and risk/compliance/audits don't need a granular view either. As with fraud controls (e.g., forgery detection), one should always keep a few tricks up one's sleeve.

Where should an organization use cryptography?

First and foremost, don't let crypto give you a false sense of security. Use it judiciously, when the use case demands it. Doing it right is hard and needs lots of careful review. Maintaining it is expensive.

These days, encryption is ubiquitous, and everyone wants to see inside to monetize the plaintext, whether lawfully or unlawfully. In the consumer space, cryptographic techniques are being used at least as much to gain or keep competitive advantage as to actually protect the consumer's information. As an enterprise, it's not hyperbole to say that there are difficult balances to strike between protecting competing interests of the customers, workers, investors, governments, and mankind.

So, know where your key controls require cryptography. Understand why you are using it:

- What is the purpose of the control?
- Who or what is the threat?
- How are the keys stored, derived, exchanged, and otherwise managed?
- What trust models exist, and how are certificates validated?
- What roots of trust have been installed?

Last but not least, remember that many of today's solutions are architected so as to concentrate risk in fewer places. You have enterprise root certificates, MITM TLS inspection proxies, escrowed keys, and the list goes on. While these centralized solutions can be as convenient for the enterprise as they are for the cloud vendor or the nation-state, you should at least recognize that these keys to the kingdom exist within your environment—and defend them accordingly. Or, perhaps, tackle the slightly harder problem of decentralizing risk and segmenting and protecting critical assets and processes in a differentiated fashion.

What is your opinion on compliance?

That's a pretty broad question. Done right, compliance teams can be a boon to business teams and IT teams, fielding requests on their behalf from hundreds of different regulatory agencies and thousands of customer entities, mapping those requests to the organization's control assessments and other relevant records, and dealing with all the responses and evidentiary detail. Whatever your opinion of regulators, the simple reality is that most of them do not have adequate tools and resources at their disposal to allow them to be less prescriptive if they are to do their jobs in a consistent and equitable fashion.

However, one definitely runs a risk with compliance in that there is a temptation to structure the controls framework and even the controls themselves, not so much to address the inherent risks but rather to address the perceived regulatory requirements. This is reasonable for some specific controls (e.g., trade monitoring) but for IT general controls is typically a mistake.

Then, too, does regulatory capture exist? To what extent do we have these regulations for good purposes versus as barriers to new market entrants? Whatever the answers, there is no denying that even for a large enterprise, the compliance burden is often substantial. The tail should not wag the dog.

How do you engage all the different units of an organization to maximize defense?

Do more than by-the-numbers security awareness training—awareness should be a frequent and open dialogue. People need reminders and practice to create good habits, and most will learn better when they understand and believe in the why-should-I-do-it, not just the what-to-do. Host education sessions where you brief different business units and leadership teams on security-related topics of particular interest to them. Engage the audience and draw out their fears and interests and other questions. Talk to them about security outside of the workplace and in their personal and family lives.

The IT security team should be partnering with operations and development and non-IT personnel and making sure that security is understood as a shared responsibility in which many teams have a role to play and in which everyone knows how to and feels empowered to do their bit. Run tabletop drills, involve the security team in business continuity and disaster recovery exercises, run attack simulations to practice incident handling, and involve the leadership teams in your incident management scenarios.

"In my opinion, the term *blue team* shouldn't be so squishy that it is unclear who is included in that group."

Twitter: @nathanmcnulty

Nathan McNulty

30

Nathan McNulty is the security architect for a large school district with more than 40,000 students. With a BS in computer science, his career started on an IT help desk and then transitioned to desktop engineering for a civil engineering firm. He later took a role as the client architect for the school district where he has managed everything Microsoft. For the past four years, he has been doing security-focused work utilizing Graylog, Nessus, Panorama, Microsoft 365 E5 Security, and Kali for internal pentesting. Nathan also serves on the board of OpsecEdu.com, a community for empowering and building up InfoSec people in education.

How do you define a blue team?

I personally define blue team as those responsible for actively and directly protecting the organization, whether through implementing security controls to prevent incidents or by responding to incidents. I prefer more defined roles, so while a network admin may perform blue team activities such as making security changes to the firewall, I wouldn't consider them blue team as that is not their primary responsibility. In my opinion, the term *blue team* shouldn't be so squishy that it is unclear who is included in that group.

What are two core capabilities that a blue team should have?

Good interpersonal skills and an attention to detail.

In my experience, the technical side of things is rarely the blocking issue. Implementing positive changes usually hinges on the ability to accurately explain the risk and impact to the organization at multiple levels, and you need to be able to change language between the C-suite, security team, operations team, help desk, and end users.

As you focus on communicating with others inside or outside of your team, you gain empathy, which usually results in better-designed solutions that minimize impact on your users and help gain their trust for future projects. Long term, this is more important than any singular security control you are trying to implement.

Attention to detail gets tossed around lightly on every job description I've seen, but with the increasing complexity of our systems and skill level of attackers, those nuanced details can be the difference between catching or missing an attacker or accidentally breaking a business critical system.

What are some of the key strengths of an incident response program?

Preparation and attitude are everything. Because IR is stressful for most people, our brains simply don't filter and process our responses in the same way we normally would. Training, table-top exercises, and reviewing previous cases are important and can equip us to remain level-headed during the real thing. A major part of this training should be to focus on staying positive, encouraging one another, and avoiding calling out failure or passing blame at all costs. Think of how you respond when co-workers get severely sick. You don't blame them and get upset they aren't working; you look for ways to help them.

During a crisis, it's easy to get tunnel vision and focus only on your stuff. Keep an open ear for those who are struggling or stuck, especially in areas that you may have expertise. Good relationships built ahead of time can be huge here. When opportunities to help do come up, be sure to ask questions or ask permission to provide feedback. This makes them feel less threatened, leaves them in control, and makes it easier to respect their decisions.

How can blue teamers learn, practice, and grow?

I truly believe that the best learning and growth happens in the context of community. There are so many experiences that we each have that others will never have, and we gain better understanding and empathy through sharing those experiences. This may also look like signing up for a project outside of your comfort zone or temporarily filling a gap in another team.

For personal learning, there are tons of free resources available online: YouTube, podcasts, social media, course catalogs like Cybrary or Lynda, and content from groups such as SANS or CIS. The most important part is to make it a priority. Determine how you learn best and who you learn from best, and make it happen.

For practicing, nothing beats hands-on learning like a home lab, Raspberry Pi, or cloud developer accounts. I regularly try new products, test the efficacy of controls, or walk through guides that I wouldn't normally be able to at work. While many would consider this bringing work home, I would challenge everyone to think of it as investing in yourself. It will pay off.

How do you reward good blue teaming work?

It's a good idea to know what "reward" means to each person on your team. Some people are motivated by words of affirmation, some by gifts, and others by public recognition. This could be a simple text saying you appreciate someone, recognition for their contribution at a staff meeting, extra PTO, or a gift card or bonus. The reward itself is less important than how you make people feel. Make your team feel valued, not just through your words but through your actions.

What are some core metrics that a blue team can use to build, measure, and maintain a successful information security program?

For a simple model, mapping to a framework or even the CIS Top 20 can be an easy way to set goals and track progress. Metrics can be achieved by mapping values to each of these controls whether you are implementing or improving them, and then you can prioritize them based on your organization's threat profile. Vulnerability management can map into this as well.

My process is to create a document for each data domain based on my teams (for example, email security, endpoint hardening, SIEM, identity, etc.). In each document, I create categories based on frameworks or whatever makes sense. Now, as I learn new techniques, ideas for improvements, or things to look out for, they are put into the appropriate categories as a to-do, created as an issue for change management, and then removed when completed.

Now I can look back at my commit history on each of these and track the progress of what has been completed. I tend to get frustrated when I focus on all of the things that I haven't finished yet, so it's incredibly helpful to have this progress to look back on and recognize just how much good work has been done.

Where would you start if you were the only information security staff member at a small to medium-sized business with a primitive security infrastructure?

My biggest return on investment has been educating and delegating to my operations team. You will never be able to keep up with the number of changes your operations team makes, so instead, you need to focus on getting them to understand "secure by default," making security part of the culture and part of their normal thought processes. Additionally, there is no way around this; you will need to rely on them for asset inventory.

Especially when first starting, I think it's crucial to focus most of your energy on what you know best, do it well, and work on learning your next strongest knowledge area, working your way down the list. For me, email, endpoints, and identity are my strongest areas, and because those have been done well, it has built trust with my team, making tackling weaker subject matters an easier task.

If I'm building a network from the ground up, it's going to be all about NAC controlling what is allowed to connect and what network segment it gets dropped on. This makes monitoring much more manageable because I can now better define what I'm looking for on each segment and really reduce the size of the haystack of data I'm working with.

What is the most bang-for-your-buck security control?

Privileged identity management. This means removing admin rights from end users and not sharing admin rights across endpoints. Separate the regular and administrative credentials for your system, network, and security teams, and only allow those administrative credentials to be used on hardened systems where no other accounts are allowed to log on. Enable multifactor authentication for these administrative accounts on absolutely everything that you can. Finally, when possible, use a privileged access management solution to kick off an approval workflow that escalates those administrative accounts into administrative roles only for the period of time required to do the work.

Has your organization implemented any deception technologies?

I have had several honeytoken accounts in place for a few years now, and these are spread across several different permission levels throughout most of our services including AD, Office 365, and G Suite. For honeypots, I originally started with OpenCanary, and I am now using a prerelease version of Kushtaka.io.

My sensors go off fairly frequently, but to be fair, I have probably a couple hundred students out of a little more than 40,000 who actually know how to poke around and look for things. They are curious and trying to learn, and this gives me an opportunity to redirect that energy to appropriate learning sources before they get themselves in too much trouble. I really appreciate the peace of mind the sensors give me, and my response time would suffer without them. I like to view it as an insurance policy while I continue to build and enhance my detection capabilities in other areas.

Where should an organization use cryptography?

Wherever possible. More and more, we are recognizing the need for encryption at rest, in memory, and in transit. If I were to create a short list of examples, it would include full-disk encryption, TLS 1.2+ for all browsing, VPN, network access (EAP-TLS, 802.1x), and digitally signing scripts and other code.

How do you approach data governance and other methods of reducing your data footprint?

Since we have state policy to comply with, we must base our retention policies on what the state requires of us. Being aware of your legal requirements is crucial, so the most important thing here is to get guidance from your legal counsel. In my experience, they usually do not want to keep data any longer than we are legally required to, and this external pressure from legal can really help move the conversation forward with your operations and security teams.

What is your opinion on compliance?

This really depends on what we are complying with and the maturity of the security program. In general, I agree with the sentiment that compliance is a point-in-time checkbox exercise, and sometimes this can even require less secure settings to be "in compliance."

Having said that, there are many organizations that are not under any compliance requirements and have neglected security for a long time. In these cases, compliance could be helpful because it could force them to make noticeable improvements.

Is there a framework that aligns the activities or functions performed by the blue team with regulatory compliance requirements?

There are plenty of frameworks that do this, but you still need someone who is able to interpret those generic controls into the specific technical implementation. One of the neat things about some of the current frameworks is that they are starting to map to one another. My favorite example is in the NIST Cybersecurity Framework; you'll notice ISO27001, NIST 800-53/171, PCI DSS, etc., being mapped into each category and control. This can be very helpful in the early stages of a security program or when training those new to the field.

I don't think it is wise to only follow a framework and expect to be secure as a result. Frameworks are guidelines, not an exact playbook, and there are certainly going to be misconfigurations and issues that don't map directly into a chosen framework. Frameworks can still be helpful to explain the goal or desired outcome, but you need to know their limitations.

How do you engage all the different units of an organization to maximize defense?

To reach all of my users and scale myself, I use systems such as email security, DLP, content filter, etc., to perform just-in-time training. Most of these systems allow for custom block messages, so when a user attempts to send an SSN, they get a block message explaining that email is not a secure method of communication and more details.

In general, I'd say it is important to know your target audience and change the language and narrative depending on who you are talking to. For end users, relating security controls to their personal lives is far more effective: Use stories. For your technical teams, you need to be able to teach, and that means you need to understand it well enough to be able to break it down and explain it well. For management, you need to know their limits and what kind of details they are looking for to make informed decisions.

What strategies do you use to communicate the threats you encounter to nontechnical decision-makers?

I get excited nerding out on details and jump right into teaching mode and then watch their eyes glaze over. To avoid this, it's helpful for me to ask them questions to better determine what they understand and how to best relate it to something they are familiar with. I tend to use a lot of analogies, and I've seen a lot of security folks effectively relate threats to common examples ranging from military to business or even to agriculture that everyone is familiar with.

What recommendations do you have for managing nontechnical executives' expectations during a significant ongoing incident?

When we are under significant stress, it's hard to remember that they are incredibly stressed as well. It is difficult to balance time with them and time spent on the incident, but it's extremely helpful that they know they are being heard. That line of communication needs to be healthy.

As far as content, keep it clear and concise, and focus on the impact and outcome. At some point, you will be tempted to blame a system, person, or team for a failure, and you will gain nothing and lose everything if you go down that path.

It never looks good, and it always creates conflict that will outlast the incident.

"The blue team is responsible for the detection, assessment, investigation, correlation, and recommendations to the system owner to remediate an incident."

Twitter: @SATCOM_Jim

James Medlock

James Medlock is a 25-year Army veteran with multiple job skills, a cyber operations specialist, a satellite network engineer, and an SME. He also has worked on designing and supporting communications systems for the military as a senior satellite engineer and staff engineer for General Dynamics, has written his name on a Milstar communications satellite before it was launched into space, has a bachelor's degree and a master's degree in management of information systems, has eight years working with IT and OT in the oil and gas industry, has a bunch of certificates in a box in his closet, serves as a high school cyber patriot mentor, was the technical editor for three books, has written multiple technical manuals for Army communication equipment, is a board member for a couple of conferences, is a DEF CON walker of 15,000 steps a day, was an illuminati party-goer, and is a friend to many, father of five, and spouse to one.

31

How do you define a blue team?
The blue team is responsible for the detection, assessment, investigation, correlation, and recommendations to the system

owner to remediate an incident. They should also be involved in post-remediation validation. This does not mean they are the only ones who have input or perform these activities within a business. In several cases, initial event detection might initiate from a user, or the system owner might have identified the initial events.

What are two core capabilities that a blue team should have?

- An active personal interest in staying updated in the security field
- The desire/personality/mentality to actively hunt and research different opportunities/avenues for adversaries to ingress or egress the network

What are some of the key strengths of an incident response program?

- Being active even when nothing is known to be going on.
- Having leadership flexibility for individuals to research and try new detection techniques or tools. However, never 100 percent trust your tools; they will lie. Define ways to verify accuracy; otherwise, you may unknowingly be blind.

How can blue teamers learn, practice, and grow?

- Find some projects for your team to research and tests.
- Stay up on current technology and try to keep your finger on the pulse of security.
- Attend or watch conference topics of interest and workshops; tons are available on YouTube.
- Join and participate in local security groups in your area; examples are OWASP, ISSA, AHA, BSides, DEF CON, 2600, IEEE, ISACA, and ISC2. If there are no local ones, several groups have larger chapters that stream their events.

How do you reward good blue teaming work?
Everything from "crisp high-fives," stickers, time off, to financial compensation.

What are some core metrics that a blue team can use to build, measure, and maintain a successful information security program?

- Measure time from notification/discovery through escalation and investigation to approved recommended actions.

- I treat blocking and remediation separate from the previous measurements as many BT do not have access or authorization to block activity as they are not the system owners.
- Use individual and team training simulators that have realistic scenarios. I recommend being tool-agnostic, though some shops might want to focus on their team's speed and familiarity with the tools in their environment.
- Run your individuals/teams against similar scenarios and assess their speed and accuracy on solving the problem; repeat a similar scenario routinely during internal BT training.

To that point, have routine BT training sessions on the calendar. In a previous role I had, the SOC team would come in an hour early on Fridays and spend the first two to four hours doing internal BT-specific training or conducting an internal BT exercise/challenge. This was also an excuse to do team building and leave work a little early every Friday.

Where would you start if you were the only information security staff member at a small to medium-sized business with a primitive security infrastructure?

It's hard to pick one; it would depend on what hat you are wearing.

- **Programmatic:** Establish business policies.
- **Technical:** Understand your perimeter and apply common best practices.

What is the most bang-for-your-buck security control?

Managing controlled traffic types with intention; examples include DNS, NTP, FTP, and certificate authorities (CAs) to name a few. Manage the traffic flow and direction via rules and architecture. Let's use DNS in the following examples. A business should not honor unexpected external to internal DNS traffic. Internal to external can only go via known and designated internal DNS server/relay; all other attempts are tagged and blocked. These essential services and protocols are ripe for attack and exfiltration.

Has your organization implemented any deception technologies?

In a previous organization of mine, there were some deception technologies in place. They ranged from honeypots to actively separating origin-based traffic through different unrelated domains to splitting the traffic source and return from the expected corporate traffic domains.

In most cases, a business or entity will use these deception techniques as learning and alerting opportunities. When an unauthorized person starts toying with areas they should not be in, they cause an alert to system admins who have the choice to black-hole them or monitor their activities to learn their tools and techniques. It makes it much easier if an invader is nice enough to accidentally announce themselves; it saves time hunting them.

Where should an organization use cryptography?

At minimum, where they are required by regulation or govern-ance. For business that do not fall under a compliance umbrella, establish a risk management program and assess what your business's highest risks of data exposure are.

For most, the first steps would be following best practices for external to internal access to your company (think remote user VPNs) and for data at rest (laptop-disk encryption), data in motion (online transaction, HTTPS/TLS/SSL, email-PKI), or data in use (the hardest).

How do you approach data governance and other methods of reducing your data footprint?

This world is driving to a big data collection mentality, so we are collecting a lot more data than we were in the past, with multi-ple tools on the market to enrich your current data consump-tion needs.

Either don't collect data you do not need or, if you do, have a known period that it gets erased. A technique might be to put it in a folder to be deleted after 15/30/60/90 (whatever you decide) days.

Reduce the collection of unnecessary data. I was brought into a company once and found that they were hashing, encrypting, and backing up their workstations and servers; however, they did not groom their servers/workstations, so they were backing up and storing the active Windows partitions as well as the Windows installation files that were being left on all of the devices. The most common way to address this is to establish a Data drive for important documents and store only that data.

What is your opinion on compliance?

It is a necessary frustration for the greater good, but the regula-tions can easily get out of control and therefore should be implemented with great care and concern. Previously, several business regulations were self-assessment or self-reporting; companies like Enron that ran without external (third-party) verification crushed employees' and investors' financials.

Is there a framework that aligns the activities or functions performed by the blue team with regulatory compliance requirements?

NIST, PCI-DSS, etc. They provide a framework to align the masses to speaking the same vernacular and clearly categorizing systems and services into an auditable activities format. I think standardization in many areas allows us to remove some of the FUD and communicate in a risk-based language to the business owners/leadership.

How do you engage all the different units of an organization to maximize defense?

One word: buy-in. Establish a common scope relevant to the customer or business unit, baseline common understanding, and provide clarity of intent focused on the mission/vision/risk to that organization.

What strategies do you use to communicate the threats you encounter to nontechnical decision-makers?

Nontechnical business leaders are mostly focused on risk and financials, so the quick and off-the-cuff answer is, "Risk, risk, money, risk, money, without the fear, uncertainty, and doubt."

In other words, elaborate on the threats using quantifiable measures for the following:

- Risk to brand
- Risk to current revenue
- Money lost in remediation efforts
- Risk to future revenue streams
- Money (minimal cost of mitigating measure to reduce risk of exposure)
- Without the fear, uncertainty, and doubt (minimize the old "Sky is falling" tactics that security managers use to leverage to get more funding for security)

What recommendations do you have for managing nontechnical executives' expectations during a significant ongoing incident?

Keep them informed, keep reassuring that your team is on top of it, provide executive summaries, remind them not to make any promises, limit the amount of FUD, and provide nontechnical talking points.

"I define a blue team as the group that defends an organization from both real attackers and red teams by employing adversarial empathy."

Twitter: @danielmiessler • **Website:** danielmiessler.com and www.linkedin.com/in/danielmiessler

Daniel Miessler

32

Daniel Miessler is an experienced security practitioner and virtual CISO with more than 20 years in information security. His areas of interest and focus are web application security, IoT security, OSINT/recon, and security program design.

How do you define a blue team?
I define a blue team as the group that defends an organization from both real attackers and red teams by employing adversarial empathy. Adversarial empathy is the ability to not just use similar TTPs to the enemy but to successfully think like they do.

What are two core capabilities that a blue team should have?
Deep visibility into the environments being attacked through widely deployed, detailed, and centralized logging/alerting, and a deep understanding of normal that can help the blue team when something is amiss.

What are some of the key strengths of an incident response program?

- Adoption of an attacker mindset as a culture
- The use of metrics to objectively understand current-state and future-team performance goals
- The capture of every step of the response process so that continuous improvements can be made
- Formalized improvement based on lessons learned from regular reviews of previous incidents

Similar to fixed versus growth mindset in individual learning, strong IR teams focus not just on how good their metrics are but on how much they are improving and at what scale.

How can blue teamers learn, practice, and grow?

The best way for most blue teamers to grow is by learning to think more like their adversary. That should not only mean taking technical training and becoming proficient in various tools but should also include education in the motivations and capabilities of various real-world adversaries they're likely to face. Learning what their metrics are, how their rewarded, and the history of previous attacks will help blue teamers anticipate their actions as much as knowing specific techniques.

How do you reward good blue teaming work?

The first way is by not immediately moving them to the red team. Blue teams should not be treated as the red team reject pool or the red team proving ground. There are people with red team–level skills who are simply aligned around defense, and those types should be rewarded with additional mentorship, training, and speaking opportunities (according to preference), and they should be encouraged to stay and teach the next generation.

What are some core metrics that a blue team can use to build, measure, and maintain a successful information security program?

Specific timings on all aspects of the incident lifecycle, such as how long from the event to it being logged, how long from there before it was analyzed by a system or human for maliciousness, how long it took to get to a blue teamer, how long it took to triage, how long it took to contain and eradicate, and how long it took (if at all) to make an improvement to the existing process based on a lesson learned.

Where would you start if you were the only information security staff member at a small to medium-sized business with a primitive security infrastructure?

Extensive, centralized logging at all layers of the stack.

What is the most bang-for-your-buck security control?

Logging. You can't respond to what you can't see.

Has your organization implemented any deception technologies?

I've seen many organizations experiment with deception technologies, but all but a few ended up realizing sometime later (months or years) that the time would have been better spent on the fundamentals. More logging. More automated analysis of logs. Better triage methodologies. Better IR process, etc.

Where should an organization use cryptography?

Anywhere they're looking to keep information safe from unauthorized viewers.

How do you approach data governance and other methods of reducing your data footprint?

The best method is to capture the main use cases for data usage over time from key stakeholders and then ask yourself what you can delete and how often. The key principle should be not storing anything that's not explicitly needed for some reason.

What is your opinion on compliance?

Compliance has its place in security just like high school has its place in education. It's meant to be a formal requirement that gets people thinking

> Compliance has its place in security just like high school has its place in education.

about the right things. It should be respected as a catalyst for positive action in cases where it works as such and should be deprioritized where certain managers fetishize it to the point of spending too little time on real security.

Is there a framework that aligns the activities or functions performed by the blue team with regulatory compliance requirements?

Not that I know of or would recommend, no.

How do you engage all the different units of an organization to maximize defense?

A great method is by posting your response metrics, your lessons learned, and the number of successful interactions you've had with other teams that lead to better security for the organization.

What strategies do you use to communicate the threats you encounter to nontechnical decision-makers?

The use of narrative examples combined with quantitative metrics (e.g., this person did this, because they were motivated by this, which we see in news stories like this, which could result in this type of damage to our business, and we've seen 47 of those attacks in just the last 10 days, which is why we are recommending that we do this).

What recommendations do you have for managing nontechnical executives' expectations during a significant ongoing incident?

Do these two things simultaneously:

- Provide them with crisp, high-level updates that convey the status of the incident.
- Remind them that the details are transparent if desired but that the situation is being handled.

This reminds them that everyone in the organization is an SME in their own area and that this is a moment for trust, not for continued probing or micromanaging.

"Within an organization, the blue team is often a team of people with various disciplines ranging from security operations to incident response and forensics."

Twitter: @AlyssaM_InfoSec • **Website:** www.linkedin.com/in/alyssam-infosec and www.alyssasec.com

Alyssa Miller

33

Alyssa Miller has been a hacker and programmer since her pre-teens when she bought her first computer. While IT was not her original career plan, she ended up working as a developer and later a penetration tester in the financial services industry. As she moved into consulting, her focus on defending corporate systems grew to the point where she was advising Fortune 100 companies on how to build comprehensive security programs. She's a security advocate, public speaker, and author with a passion for sharing her ideas and knowledge to help improve the ways we defend our digital world.

How do you define a blue team?
To me, blue team refers to anyone who is responsible for designing, deploying, maintaining, supporting, or operating security controls and defenses. Within an organization, the blue team is often a team of people with various disciplines ranging from security operations to incident response and forensics.

What are two core capabilities that a blue team should have?

Every blue team starts with the security operations capability. These are the frontline people who are responsible for monitoring and responding to security systems and events. Actively watching for signs of attack and being able to initiate responses as needed is crucial for any blue team organization.

Additionally, every blue team should have a security architecture capability. This is the group of experts who design and deploy the necessary security controls infrastructure that actually defends the systems and enables monitoring and response. The architecture capability is the foundational element needed to ensure a comprehensive program of security defenses.

What are some of the key strengths of an incident response program?

Incident response programs are most successful when they establish a clear shared responsibility across all areas of the organization. It is important to recognize that incident response is more than just leveraging technological means to combat an attack and gather forensic data after an attack. The best incident response programs understand the need for documented communications strategies, notification requirements (both internally and externally to the organization), impact assessment methodologies, and even rules for engaging third-party response services. Additionally, a good program should be ready for all forms of incident, from data breaches to ransomware/malware outbreaks, disinformation campaigns, and even attacks against personnel.

> Incident response programs are most successful when they establish a clear shared responsibility across all areas of the organization.

How can blue teamers learn, practice, and grow?

There are a couple activities that can be helpful for blue teamers to refine their craft. Tabletop exercises in which different scenarios are played out and discussed allow blue teamers to really consider the implications of their actions. Labs and workshops focused on optimizing security technologies in use or being considered for use are also effective at developing skills for blue teamers. Additionally, purple team exercises, where the blue team works collaboratively with a red team, can provide not only a powerful view into the current capabilities of the blue team today but also a strategy to refine and improve those capabilities going forward.

How do you reward good blue teaming work?

The difficulty with rewarding good blue teaming work isn't so much how do you reward it; it's how you measure it in the first place. Clearly, the goal of every blue team is fundamentally to prevent all breaches of the defensive systems. However, this is idealistic but not realistic. So, developing key metrics around vulnerability management and remediation, speed/accuracy of security event response, and successful deployment of strategic security initiatives is imperative. Setting realistic goals and measure improvement can then lead to rewards.

Rewarding good work is of course crucial. Smaller successes can be rewarded with simple recognition tactics. However, for more significant successes, monetary compensation becomes a great reward system. But there are other options as well. Extra days off is one possible option. Given the high-stress environments security practitioners work in, a day off can be extremely valuable for ongoing mental health.

> Given the high-stress environments security practitioners work in, a day off can be extremely valuable for ongoing mental health.

However, the organization has to make sure that the person actually takes this time off. It's ineffective to give someone another vacation day but then let their workload prevent them from using it.

Another common tactic that can work well is company-sponsored attendance at a conference or training of the employee's choice. The crucial part here is ensuring that it's something the employee chooses and is not dictated by the organization. Direct job-related training and employee development should not be withheld as rewards. These are investments the company should be making in every individual. It's important to set clear differentiation between job training and rewards systems.

Finally, travel rewards can be a great way to reward an employee. For employees who travel a lot, it could be allowing them to purchase a first-class fare for their next business trip or buying them a membership for their favorite airline's club. For all employees, particularly high-profile successes could be rewarded with a company-sponsored trip for the employee and their family.

What are some core metrics that a blue team can use to build, measure, and maintain a successful information security program?

Metrics for measuring the success of a security program need to focus on measurable elements. Since we're talking ultimately about something that cannot be easily measured, that being how many attacks were prevented by our efforts, it's important to focus on measures that show our processes and procedures are continuing to improve. For instance, instead of measuring the number of vulnerabilities fixed, which is ultimately a direct result of vulnerabilities created in the environment, organizations should instead track the time to resolution of vulnerabilities. Adding additional characteristics such as severity, risk profile of the affected system, etc., can provide additional clarity. Similar metrics can also be used for measuring security event response.

Within architecture teams, metrics should focus on measuring automation, response time to emerging threats, and new capability deployment. To do this, a clear roadmap and strategy needs to be defined for the security program.

Where would you start if you were the only information security staff member at a small to medium-sized business with a primitive security infrastructure?

Assuming there was nothing, the best place to begin would be with a comprehensive patch management strategy. Many of the breaches that occur exploit vulnerabilities of out-of-date systems. When I say comprehensive, this includes a full asset inventory across hardware and software. It's challenging but required. If you don't know what you have and can't keep them up-to-date, you've already opened major attack vectors into your enterprise.

What is the most bang-for-your-buck security control?

The human element has become the single biggest source of breaches. Whether it's exposed S3 buckets due to insecure configurations, poor coding practices that result in vulnerabilities in applications, or malware/ransomware infestations because a user clicked a bad link, it's humans who are creating the issues. So for me, the most bang-for-your-buck security control is culture. Organizations need to develop a culture that truly embraces security as a shared responsibility of everyone. DevSecOps has taken us closer to this goal, but we need to extend beyond just specific technical functions. Everyone from the legal team to marketing to development to customer service needs to understand that they are responsible for the security of the company, and they need to be enabled with tools and processes that make it easy for them to complete their day-to-day tasks in a secure way (and this is the crucial element that is often missed).

Has your organization implemented any deception technologies?

I'm not sure about my current organization, but I have worked with a number of companies in the past that did have honeypots and honeynets in place. The problem I find with these is that it's really difficult to measure whether they're successful. Sure, you can look at the attacks coming in, you can try to track metrics on the number of attackers landing there, but at the end of the day, there's really no context to say if that helped identify an attack that could have or will hit elsewhere. It's often tough to make that correlation because after getting caught in a deceptive defense system, attackers typically change their approach.

From a blue teamer perspective, they are fun to watch. It sometimes is comical to look at the logs and see how attackers behave as they slowly figure out they've been attacking a decoy. But at the same time, these systems and networks can take a lot of resource time to manage and keep running. Without a good way to correlate decoy attacks to defended attacks against production systems, it's hard to really demonstrate that they're worth the effort.

Where should an organization use cryptography?

Is this a trick question? Literally anywhere and everywhere there is data that they care about protecting, whether it's credentials, personal information, or corporate secrets. The old adage of data at rest and data in transit applies here as well. Cryptography should be used to protect all of it at all times. Now that's a very idealistic view of things; however, it's not realistic.

The reality is cryptography technologies have still failed to address some key issues. For example, data in databases to this day can still be very problematic. How do you encrypt it? At what context? Full DB encryption is great, but when the service accounts that access the database and have the ability to decrypt are the ones being exploited directly or indirectly, that defeats the defense. Should you go higher level and do it at the application level? Well, now you've got issues of performance, key management, etc., that complicate the equation.

So, while it may seem like a cop-out, the answer is there is no one answer. Every organization needs to look at what their business assets are and design a plan of defense that starts from the IT systems that support or enable those assets and builds out. This can include cryptographic controls, or it may leverage other mitigating controls. There is no one-size-fits-all approach to security, and that includes when/where to leverage cryptographic security.

How do you approach data governance and other methods of reducing your data footprint?

I can't stress enough the need for us to stop looking at data as an asset. Data is *not* an asset; it is a liability. Every piece of data that a company holds comes with obligations. From a technical debt perspective, it has to be stored. From a compliance per-spective, it has to be protected, cataloged, and managed. To derive value from it, it has to be analyzed. And that's the key. Data by itself has no inherent value, the way true assets do. I like to use the example of a UPS truck. They own probably millions of those custom-built trucks. Even if no one had any other use for them, the components they're made of, metal, fiberglass, etc., have some inherent value. That's simply not the case with data.

I know this is an unpopular opinion right now. We have massive tech giants building entire business models on data monetization and treating data as an asset. We've built massive data lakes that store all the data we possibly can collect. Unfortunately, we've become hoarders of data. Data gets stored in the hope that one day we can monetize it, rather than stored for a specific purpose. However, if we start to think of data as a liability and really commit to treating it that way, it drives behav-iors in which data must have a purpose before it is collected and stored. Data is cataloged and tagged. Those tags define specific security controls, retention periods, etc. What we need is the Marie Kondo approach to data: If it doesn't bring you revenue or compliance, get rid of it.

> What we need is the Marie Kondo approach to data: If it doesn't bring you revenue or compliance, get rid of it.

What is your opinion on compliance?

Regulatory requirements are something business leaders complain about all the time—and in some respect, rightfully so. Rarely do they drive a true measure of security. Worse, because they tend to be quite onerous, companies approach them with a minimalistic attitude. How do we do the bare minimum needed to check the boxes and move on? Organizations use the term "intent of the requirement" to do exactly the opposite and avoid what the authors had intended. It's all a vicious game with no end.

The reality is most compliance and regulatory requirements are more about shifting liability than actually securing anything. PCI is a terrific example of this. It's no secret that card brands were able to leverage PCI to shift their liabilities onto processors, who then shift to issuing banks, who then shift it to retailers. It's not about protecting cardholder information; it's about who gets blamed and who gets sued when there is a breach.

Now with all that said, we in the business world have no one to blame but ourselves. Had business being doing a good job of being responsible with data, being responsible with fraud prevention technologies, etc., legislators and governing bodies wouldn't have felt the need to create these regulations. But the fact of the matter is, until you threaten the bottom line, businesses aren't motivated to take action. This is where compliance steps in to provide that impact to the bottom line to create artificial risk to the business that in turn should motivate the business to follow the intended practices. So, sadly, compliance has become a necessary evil.

Is there a framework that aligns the activities or functions performed by the blue team with regulatory compliance requirements?

NIST is probably the closest to this at this point. 800.53 was a prescriptive set of controls and unfortunately was too granular.

I tried to establish that one-size-fits-all approach and wasn't terribly effective. However, when you look at the Cyber Security Framework (CSF), it does a much better job of focusing on core concepts and aligning those with activities that blue teams should be performing within an organization. I think something like this is a good model to follow. It gives the organizations the flexibility they need to not only design a security strategy that fits their business but also helps them establish a roadmap for continuous improvement.

From the regulatory and compliance perspective, implementing the NIST CSF "can" bring a company in line with regulatory requirements. However, that's changing in light of recent privacy legislation (GDPR, CCPA, etc.) that goes beyond simply how organizations secure their systems and protect consumer data. Compliance with these new regulations requires organizations to create new processes and implement new technologies not for the purpose of security but rather for giving consumers some level of control and authority over their own data.

How do you engage all the different units of an organization to maximize defense?

Again, while it may seem ethereal, it has to begin with culture. From the CEO down to every individual employee, everyone has to understand their role in securing the organization and be enabled to do so. I've seen companies that have hosted internal security conferences where they give employees valuable information not only on how to secure the company but on how to secure their own personal lives. This is effective in fostering cooperation with the security team.

I've worked with companies who implement a "walk a mile in their shoes" program where resources from security spend time working in other areas of the business, and vice versa. This creates an empathy between teams that is crucial for collaboration. I've even seen organizations that have found unique training ideas for security awareness training such as escape rooms, or fun activities that employees want to do and still teach valuable information.

Finally, I personally really like to leverage threat modeling. This is an activity that when done properly should bring many areas of the business together to collaboratively discuss the threat landscape and security posture of various systems.

What strategies do you use to communicate the threats you encounter to nontechnical decision-makers?

Let me start with what I don't do. I don't go down that old, tired path of using fear, uncertainty, and doubt (FUD) to try to convey my message. I make sure that I come to the table with a solution defined. I then focus on connecting that solution to how it will improve the business. It could be a cost savings, it could be that it enables additional business revenue, or the best-case scenario is that it can actually be leveraged to create a new business differentiator.

Simply telling a nontechnical business leader that "You must do this or this really bad thing will happen" is actually counterproductive. It doesn't motivate them to action; it motivates them to ignore you, to freeze and do nothing, and, in the long run, to avoid you all together. You have to show benefit in terms of business goals and objectives. Provide a tangible result from implementing that security control that will address the threat you're concerned about. It's not easy; FUD is easy, but this is the process that works and wins support.

What recommendations do you have for managing nontechnical executives' expectations during a significant ongoing incident?

The single most important thing you can do is set up regular communications of updates. Executives understand that there won't always be a simple answer to what comes off as a simple question, like how long with this take or how much will this cost us? However, they start to get nervous when they feel like they're in the dark. So, be honest and share information regularly and in a detailed fashion. Focus on objective information, not guesses, not estimates, but tell them what you have in hand.

They may ask for guesses or estimates. When they do, be ready to provide a confident answer that's grounded in objective information. Quite often we get caught unprepared; we're asked for an estimate, so we throw out a swag on the spot. If you can't justify your answer with facts, it's a garbage answer. Make them feel confident that you're on top of things by anticipating and being prepared for their questions. Give them a reason to trust you and communicate with them regularly, and they will give you the space to get the job done.

"Blue teams are traditionally the teams actively and directly engaged in assessing the operating environment to ensure security and thwart attacks by opposing forces."

Twitter: @magg_py

Maggie Morganti

Maggie Morganti is a technical staff member for the Power and Energy Systems team at Oak Ridge National Laboratory focusing on electric grid cybersecurity and resilience research. Prior to joining Oak Ridge National Laboratory, Maggie was a graduate intern at FireEye and worked as a threat intelligence analyst on their iSight cyber-physical team. She holds an MS in intelligence studies with a focus on cybersecurity from Mercyhurst University. As a graduate student, she worked as an intelligence analyst for the university's Center for Information Research Analysis and Training (CIRAT) program and served as an active member of the university's cyber-threat research analysis, data science, and nuclear nonproliferation clubs. She is an IEEE member and active in local chapter events.

34

How do you define a blue team?
The lines of blue team roles have definitely become more encompassing and blurred with the addition of so many folks doing tangential system security tasks.

I find the easiest way to think about "What defines a blue team?" is by going back to the military origins of red team/blue team. Blue teams are traditionally the teams actively and directly engaged in assessing the operating environment to ensure security and thwart attacks by opposing forces. There are countless roles that support these teams in military operations such as communications, transport, and logistics personnel. All of these roles are necessary to facilitate an exercise or operation, but when attacks begin to hit the perimeter (kinetic or network), blue teams are the ones that are actively participating in the response. I think by and large this same premise can be carried over into the cybersecurity space to help us more easily think about blue team definitions.

What are two core capabilities that a blue team should have?

I think two core capabilities a blue team has to have are the following:

- In-depth understanding of the network they are trying to defend
- Tight communication loop with management about organizational risk and the "crown jewel"

In essence, we need to know what we need to prioritize defending and the digital terrain in which it exists.

What are some of the key strengths of an incident response program?

Two key strengths of an incident response plan that I think are particularly important are adaptability and clarity. Certain pieces such as roles, key steps, and reporting must be clear easily identifiable. However, the plan must also not be so bogged down in excruciating details that it cannot be adapted on the fly to meet the demands of an incident.

How can blue teamers learn, practice, and grow?

Rotate your blue team to spend time with the red team, threat intel team, business development teams, etc.

The easy answer here is training, but I think that this needs to be more than simply checking the continuing education box.

Rotate your blue team to spend time with the red team, threat intel team, business development teams, etc. This exposure will give them better tools, perspectives, and partnerships.

How do you reward good blue teaming work?

Full-disclosure: I outsourced this question, because I felt uncomfortable speaking for everyone. The overwhelming answers I got from my co-workers and peers when I asked how they wanted to be rewarded were advancement and training. This is such a hopeful metric that we as defenders want to be rewarded with tools to help us be better at our mission.

What are some core metrics that a blue team can use to build, measure, and maintain a successful information security program?

I think there are some really easy "gimme" core metrics we can often look to for successful security programs: training scores, time between incidents, types of incidents, patch cycles, etc.

In operational technology (OT) environments, I think these metrics are often similar with several caveats.

Given the prevalence of legacy equipment and/or equipment not easily patchable due to interoperability, metrics focusing on accurate asset inventories, network segmentation, and whitelisting should be employed in networks where common security metrics may run into complications.

Where would you start if you were the only information security staff member at a small to medium-sized business with a primitive security infrastructure?

I think the starting point and fundamental element of starting from zero generally has to be figuring out what the highest value assets for that business are, assessing risks associated with those assets, and prioritizing security manpower and investments around those assets.

What is the most bang-for-your-buck security control?

People. Hear me out. I came into this space with a manufacturing engineer for a husband and an oil and gas executive for a

I think all too often companies want to "buy a solution" to cybersecurity, so they go purchase the newest blinky box that then, due to lack of dedicated staff to manage, sits on the shelf with unknown ANY/ANY rules and unmonitored alerts.

parent. Both organizations operated with an IT staff that doubled as both their enterprise security staff and their ICS security staff (if and when they were thinking about ICS security at all). We have some amazing technology currently on the market, but no vendor solution can magically give small, over-tasked, IT shops time in the day to also be a robust blue team. Only people dedicated to those tasks can lighten that load. I think all too often companies want to "buy a solution" to cybersecurity, so they go purchase the newest blinky box that then, due to lack of dedicated staff to manage, sits on the shelf with unknown ANY/ANY rules and unmonitored alerts.

Where should an organization use cryptography?
Organizations should use cryptography where it is most needed and operationally can be supported. Especially in ICS environments, factors such as latency must be taken into consideration.

How do you approach data governance and other methods of reducing your data footprint?
Data governance is so vital to organizations such as research and government institutions like ours. Government-owned research labs must simultaneously manage data pertaining to high-value intellectual property as well as classified intelligence material. Simple steps such as not uploading sensitive documents to sites like VirusTotal and Google hacking for sensitive data relating to your organization can go a long way in reducing digital footprints and unnecessary data exposure.

What is your opinion on compliance?
I think compliance is a great place to start with giving organizations a benchmark. However, it is crucial we not allow stakeholders to fall into the trap of thinking "compliant" equals "secure."

Additionally, we should not reach a place where asset owners are more afraid of compliance audits than actual breaches to the organization.

Additionally, we should not reach a place where asset owners are more afraid of compliance audits than actual breaches to the organization.

Is there a framework that aligns the activities or functions performed by the blue team with regulatory compliance requirements?
In the critical infrastructure and power system space, I think NERC-CIP is a great example of this. In addition to outlining measures to be taken to secure key assets and systems, NERC also conducts an annual GridEx exercise in which these controls are tested under simulated cyberattack conditions. This is highly valuable as it allows blue teams to fall back on coordinated established training in the case of a real-world event.

How do you engage all the different units of an organization to maximize defense?
Communication and buy-in between teams. This sounds painfully obvious, but sadly it still needs repeated. Still far too often, the SOC does not communicate with the IT staff, who in turn doesn't communicate with the engineers or operators. Fluid communication between those administering, securing, programming, and operating critical assets is crucial to maximizing defense of these networks. Tabletop security exercises should include folks from all of these teams. Especially in ICS environments, partnership with asset engineers and operators is needed to understand and properly defend the networks.

Fluid communication between those administering, securing, programming, and operating critical assets is crucial to maximizing defense of these networks.

What strategies do you use to communicate the threats you encounter to nontechnical decision-makers?

The most important strategies for me when trying to communicate threats to nontechnical decision-makers are as follows:

- **Humility:** We shoot ourselves in the foot when we swagger into a situation with the attitude that we know a company or environment better than the decision-maker. The person we are sitting across from must consider the entire picture, not just "the cyberz." In a manufacturing shop, we may walk around and scoff at the legacy and unpatched equipment. We can rub our temples and pontificate about how it all needs "fixing yesterday." However, in doing so we fail to appreciate that an impromptu patching overhaul or "rip and replace" solution would likely cause as much if not more disruption to operations than the actual attacks we are attempting to defend against.
- **Dollars and sense:** Decision-makers likely do not care about the latest novel attack details. They care about their people and their bottom line. Therefore, that is what we should also care about when talking to them about threats: Days of downtime. Dollars lost. Reputation degraded. These are the metrics that mean something to decision-makers without bogging them down with the nitty-gritty technical details when it is not necessary.

What recommendations do you have for managing nontechnical executives' expectations during a significant ongoing incident?

I don't think executives need technical chops to oversee and work through an ongoing significant incident. Like any other communications with decision-makers, we should strive to be clear in communicating the information they need to inform the decision-making process without bogging them down with unnecessary details. We should also strive to anticipate misinformation or misconceptions they are bringing to the incident with based on knowledge of previous incidents affecting other organizations. Managing expectations of impact, scope, and time to recovery is crucial as they largely rely on us to distill the chaos into these digestible metrics for them.

> "Through organized log management, hardening techniques, and cybersecurity analysis coupled with threat intelligence, blue teams bolster the SecOps department's ability to improve security maturity while maintaining the integrity of business continuity."

Twitter: @masofmoss • **Website:** www.linkedin.com/in/justin-moss-090206132

Justin Moss

Justin Moss is a cybersecurity enthusiast who currently works as a sales engineer for the endpoint security company CrowdStrike. With a CompTIA Security+ certification as well as CrowdStrike's Proactive Hunting, Incidence Response, and Administration certifications, he's passionate about informing the industry on how to be proactive with their security tools. Justin stays proactive in his workplace by creating and delivering workshops that bridge the gaps between security vendor solutions and practitioner needs.

35

How do you define a blue team?
Blue teaming represents proactive practices put in place to expedite the identification and response processes needed to address malicious events that target greater IT business assets with speed. Through organized log management, hardening techniques, and cybersecurity analysis coupled with threat intelligence, blue teams bolster the SecOps department's ability

to improve security maturity while maintaining the integrity of business continuity.

Leveraging existing toolsets, blue teaming enables cross-departmental communications. This helps security teams identify, asses, prioritize, and mitigate IT business threats.

In other words, links of a chain, in isolation, offer limited protection. Together, their strength improves the ability to secure. Though blue teaming introduces specific practices and skillsets, the ideology is the same. Regardless of the work done outside of incident response, blue teaming enables inter-department communication that maintains overall business operations.

What are two core capabilities that a blue team should have?

Two core capabilities blue teams should have access to are tools that enable security augmentation through automation and cloud-based management platforms.

The cyber-threat landscape has modernized, meaning our defensive strategies must follow suit. According to the 2020 Global Threat Report released by endpoint security company CrowdStrike, the year 2019 experienced an 11 percent drop in attacks leveraging malware from a consistent 60 percent from 2017 to 2018. This means attackers are using malware-free and script-based attacks more often to compromise systems and access sensitive data.

Technology that automatically identifies and alerts defenders of the misuse around trusted/built-in applications, alongside cloud-enabled log management platforms, assists the availability/integrity around incident response and forensic investigation workflows.

What are some of the key strengths of an incident response program?

The three key strengths of an incident response program are as follows:

- Pre-incident process
- Incident process
- Post-incident process

Objectives around the pre-incident process are simply to confirm if an incident is present and initiate the incident response process. Baselining what to look for in an incident and who to call when one is present can reduce the risk of falling susceptible to the 45 to 150 average security breach dwell time, documented by the Verizon 2019 Data Breach Investigations Report (DBIR).

During an incident, there are a plethora of tools one could use to assist the analysis of disk, file, memory logs, and more. Regardless of the technology used, the process of who manages the incident, internal/external communications, and incident goals should remain the same.

The post-incident process should be used to reflect on wins and areas of improvement. Most importantly, this is a time for key business and IT stakeholders to get together and evaluate the effectiveness of their internal/external incident response (IR) resources against its cost in comparison to the duration of the incident and its monetary effects.

How can blue teamers learn, practice, and grow?

Blue teamers can learn, practice, and grow their overall security competency using staple guides and frameworks like these:

- The Lockheed Martin Cyber Kill Chain
- Mitre ATT&CK Framework
- National Institute of Standards and Technology (NIST) Cybersecurity Framework (CSF)

Blue teaming is often seen as a process synonymous with reactive security. It's common for practitioners to believe blue teaming means reacting to the latest malware and/or ransomware family type. Though important, blue teamers should focus on applying security controls that combat core tactics and procedures of modern and old threats alike to protect their people, processes, and products.

> It's common for practitioners to believe blue teaming means reacting to the latest malware and/or ransomware family type.

How do you reward good blue teaming work?

In Daniel Pink's book *Drive*, he constructively breaks down human motivation into two components: intrinsic motivation, which describes individuals who respond to workspaces where project autonomy is present and see themselves as purpose maximizers, and external motivation, which describes individuals who react to workspaces where projects are closely metered and performance is tied to a preset reward. Based on the research presented in this book, externally motivated individuals often saw themselves as profit maximizers for their respective organizations.

There are plenty of examples in the book to draw from that could provide assistance on an approach that best fits your organization. One example that stood out to me was the difference between the "If-Then" and "Now That" reward system. If you're a supporter of the intrinsically motivated workforce, it's offering surprise rewards after completed projects (e.g., "Now that you've finished X and it turned out well, let's celebrate with Y"). This approach versus the If-Then reward system has the potential to show your appreciation and can boost team morale. On the other hand, according to the research provided in the book, If-Then entitlements have the potential to crater effective performance.

Ultimately, blue teaming is a thankless job that may or may not have rewardable projects because of limited security event activities/resources. One sure way to highlight the value of your worker's performance is to tie it back to the business operation's KPIs. The book *Traction* by Gino Wickman lays out a practical guide on how to stand up and practice this method flawlessly.

What are some core metrics that a blue team can use to build, measure, and maintain a successful information security program?

Once the blue team has baselined the level of uncertainty surrounding risk, they can begin to measure the improvements around the following:

- User education (e.g., phishing email attempts, emails sent, emails opened, etc.)
- Detection/prevention automation (i.e., measure speed of toolsets in place to identify, notify, and prevent malicious activities)

- False positive rates (i.e., measure effectiveness of toolsets in place to reduce signal-to-noise ratios)
- Time taken for analysis and triage alerts

Measure effectiveness of risk assessment methods (e.g., is success metered by compliance acceptance or security risk management improvements?).

Where would you start if you were the only information security staff member at a small to medium-sized business with a primitive security infrastructure?

To architect a building that has the potential to withstand unknown weather conditions and unexpected damages, you'd start with a blueprint. Blueprints allow practitioners to see what success looks like as an end result as they begin to lay the foundation. When building a security program, there's no need to re-create the wheel. Standards like NIST CSF are modular. Practitioners can build with confidence toward a mature security posture, while simultaneously assessing and prioritizing overall security risk.

What is the most bang-for-your-buck security control?

The security control that will give you the most bang-for-your-buck is preventative control. The less time security teams can spend analyzing and dispositioning security events, the more time practitioners can devote to proactive threat hunting. Proactive threat hunting should be one of the only manual processes, alongside IR, that practitioners use to maintain business operations and combat modern live-off-the-land type of attacks.

> Proactive threat hunting should be one of the only manual processes, alongside IR, that practitioners use to maintain business operations and combat modern live-off-the-land type of attacks.

Where should an organization use cryptography?

An organization should always use cryptography when possible. Encrypting data that leaves your network is a staple part of maintaining the confidentiality of your intellectual property, personally identifiable information, and sensitive data. Due to the changes in the threat landscape, encrypting internal data channels will provide an additional layer of needed security. Living-off-the-land techniques, such as increasing the attacker's footprint presence, has become an integral part of their schemes to complete nefarious objectives.

Ransomware is often the nosiest and last method an attacker would use to disrupt business operations.

Most businesses are afraid of being hit with ransomware, which is a legitimate concern. Unfortunately, it's only the tip of the iceberg when it comes to things defenders need to protect themselves from. Ransomware is often the nosiest and last method an attacker would use to disrupt business operations. Prior to deploying the ransomware, attackers often do the following:

- Gain initial access to vulnerable host/users
- Establish persistence
- Monitor/exfiltrate data to offshore C2 servers

Utilizing internal/external cryptography practices and limiting system access to data should reduce the scope of your risk exposure to the preceding attacks.

What is your opinion on compliance?
Compliance, if required, should be used as a bridge between security and business operations from defenders to nontechnical executives. An organization that enables security understands the shortcomings of aligning security with compliance alone. For non-security-enabled organizations, defenders can use compliance as the catapult to aligning business and security goals.

Compliance, much like periodic physicals, can be used as a beacon for baselined posture. Just like one would use the diagnostics from their physical to follow a prescribed diet, compliance should be used as a checkpoint on the road of improved security posture.

Is there a framework that aligns the activities or functions performed by the blue team with regulatory compliance requirements?

Yes, there are a few such as NIST CSF and the ISO 27000 series. Most recently the Cybersecurity Maturity Model Certification (CMMC) combines the like of the preceding frameworks alongside parts from the American Institute of Architects (AIA) anti-trust compliance. Like NIST, the CMMC has plans to offer implementation processes around security programs, in addition to guided steps for executing these processes.

What recommendations do you have for managing nontechnical executives' expectations during a significant ongoing incident?

In addition to the techniques addressed in the employee reward question earlier, practitioners could apply similar techniques for nontechnical executives on a quarterly/semi-annual basis. Through key stakeholder tabletop exercises or briefings around business-driven security metrics, defenders can build company-wide confidence around their proposed security programs.

Start by speaking in terms of the executive by showing them what's worth protecting, why they should care, and how blue teaming will achieve the overall business goals. This can ensure that when an incident occurs, they would know the following:

- What to expect during the IR process
- How to forecast the incident's cost based on effects to the business

Keeping the nontechnical executive informed before, during, and after an incident will pay great dividends to your security team and, more importantly, your business.

"When the game is on the line, high performers don't rise to the occasion, they fall to their highest level of preparation."

—John Wooden, *A Game Plan for Life*

"Obviously, security is a shared responsibility for many different groups and individuals, but the key differentiator is responsibility for taking some action, even if that action is simply to identify and escalate."

Twitter: @markaorlando • **Website:** www.linkedin.com/in/marko16 and www.bioniccyber.com

Mark Orlando

36

Mark started his security career in 2001 as a SOC analyst and, since then, has been both fighting for blue team resources and trying to automate them out of a job. He has built, assessed, and managed security teams at the Pentagon, the White House, the Department of Energy, global managed security service providers, and numerous Fortune 500 clients.

Mark's passion is finding new and innovative ways to help defenders scale through the right application of foundational knowledge and assistive technology, as well as helping people in leadership and nontechnical roles navigate the many challenges of information security. In 2012, he designed and launched a managed detection and response (MDR) service offering and helped to invent an automated cyber-threat hunting technology, both of which were later acquired. Today, he is the cofounder and CEO of Bionic, a technology company dedicated to bringing advanced defensive capabilities to organizations everywhere.

Mark has presented on security operations and assessment at DEF CON's Blue Team Village, the Institute for Applied

Network Security (IANS) Forum, BSidesDC, and the RSA Conference and has been quoted in the *New York Times*, the *Washington Post*, *Forbes*, CNBC, *SC Magazine*, and many other publications. He holds a bachelor's degree in advanced information technology from George Mason University and served in the U.S. Marine Corps as an artillery noncommissioned officer. In his spare time, Mark enjoys reading, going to rock shows, and sneaking in the occasional Netflix binge.

How do you define a blue team?
The blue team responds to threats in defense of an enterprise. Obviously, security is a shared responsibility for many different groups and individuals, but the key differentiator is responsibility for taking some action, even if that action is simply to identify and escalate.

What are two core capabilities that a blue team should have?
Every blue team should have network security monitoring and host security monitoring capabilities. In most multistage attacks, there are actions you'll see at the network layer and actions you will see only at the host layer, so both are equally important. A skilled team gets an honorable mention here, since it also takes a skilled analyst to identify events of interest and pivot through host and network data in a deliberate way.

What are some of the key strengths of an incident response program?
A key strength is the ability to improve the organization's security posture as a result of the incident response process. This means capturing lessons learned, identifying controls that might have prevented the incident or enabled better detection, and feeding new requirements into the planning process. If you can't look back on cases you've worked in the last month or the last year and identify ways you've improved your overall security, you're just playing whack-a-mole. Another key strength that's often overlooked is communications. An incident response program must include internal and external communications to ensure that business owners, users, customers, and other stakeholders have timely and accurate information. This latter element can have long-lasting impacts to an organization if handled poorly.

How can blue teamers learn, practice, and grow?

This is a lesson I take from my military service. You won't always be in combat; in fact, you'll hopefully spend relatively little time there. But your success in that situation is directly related to how much and how well you train. For blue teamers, this means continuous training and improvement. If you aren't sharpening individual skills through mentoring and formal training, then you're sharpening team capabilities through structured exercises, purple teaming, and testing new detections. Cross-training is also important. Sometimes it's tough to pick out the things you know that your teammate doesn't, and vice versa. Training in multiple disciplines, including those outside of your area of expertise, helps reduce over-reliance on specific team members.

How do you reward good blue teaming work?

People should be compensated for good work in the form of more pay and advancement opportunities. But rewards and incentives don't always have to be formal or monetary. It's important to understand what drives your people and offer a range of rewards for quality and initiative. These rewards could be time and resources to pursue a passion project, verbal or written recognition of their work, or more responsibility within the team. I like informal recognitions that anyone on the team can "award." You can get very creative with them, and it encourages the team to recognize each other's work.

What are some core metrics that a blue team can use to build, measure, and maintain a successful information security program?

Every blue team needs two types of metrics: one for internal operations and one for impact to the organization. Internal metrics help the team improve technical operations. Mean time to identify incidents, mean time to respond, false positive and true positive rates by detection source, and monitoring coverage are all useful metrics that a team can track to improve its own capabilities. External metrics are more strategic and measure the blue team's value and contribution. Examples might be mean time to recover from incidents and incident discovery by phase (which ideally trends to the left, meaning the team is reducing impact of successful attacks). I'm also a fan of objectives and key results (OKRs), which measure progress toward specific finite goals.

Where would you start if you were the only information security staff member at a small to medium-sized business with a primitive security infrastructure?

Good security starts with situational awareness. I would try to get at least minimal visibility at the host and network layers to better understand what is happening in the environment, investigate the things I find, and work outward from there. Before you can respond to incidents, enforce policy, and address recurring issues, you must be able to monitor the environment. Visibility into core services like DNS, SMTP, and HTTP are a good start at the network layer, and event logs are a must at the host layer.

What is the most bang-for-your-buck security control?

A complete and up-to-date asset inventory. The first two controls in the CIS Top 20 are hardware and software inventory, and with good reason. So much in detection and defensible network architecture is based on understanding what you have in your environment. If you have a solid grasp of that, you can make a huge impact without deploying a single security product.

Has your organization implemented any deception technologies?

I've used honey tokens to trigger detections for heavy recon or post-exploitation activities. I love the technology because it's unsophisticated and inexpensive but highly effective. For blue teams, honey tokens sprinkled throughout the environment offer high-fidelity detections that flag some of the most damaging phases of an attack.

Where should an organization use cryptography?

Assuming it's applied correctly, cryptography can be a boon for the blue team. It underpins the trust frameworks we use to cut down on spam and validate web resources we want to access, among many other things. Blue teams should embrace the use of cryptography for these controls but understand how cryptography impacts security monitoring and other defensive measures. The recent adoption of encryption in DNS over TLS and

DNS over HTTPS is a good example of a move that improves privacy but presents challenges for network security monitoring.

How do you approach data governance and other methods of reducing your data footprint?

When I first started in security operations, our approach was to collect all the data we could get, even if we weren't sure how we'd use it for detection. We didn't need much of a data collection strategy beyond that (or didn't think we did). Today, the privacy and regulatory landscape is much different, not to mention there is a lot more data to gather. I'm a big advocate for collecting only the data you need to support detections and investigations. There might be some cases where capturing sensitive data is unavoidable, but it's easier and safer to mask the data if you can or avoid collecting and storing it altogether. A data collection strategy that accounts for the cost of retention as well as regulatory implications for what you're collecting is no longer optional.

What is your opinion on compliance?

I think compliance has had some positive impacts in terms of awareness and, in theory, enforcing minimum security standards in certain industries and infrastructures. Where compliance breaks down for blue teamers is when we confuse compliance and security or think that because we are compliant, we don't need to take additional steps to be secure. In my experience, it's a *great* forcing function to get certain controls deployed or policies published that I can build upon as a defender.

Is there a framework that aligns the activities or functions performed by the blue team with regulatory compliance requirements?

I think the NIST Risk Management Framework is a solid concept in terms of bridging compliance—in this case, categorizing systems and cataloging security controls—and blue team activities like security monitoring. The downside of this framework and others is that it is still up to the individual organizations for how they implement this guidance and what constitutes success. The advice I give to my clients is to follow both the letter and the spirit of the guidelines wherever possible. For example, if you're collecting data to meet a "monitoring" requirement but no one is making any use of that data, you may be compliant, but you still aren't practicing good security.

How do you engage all the different units of an organization to maximize defense?

You must get out of the SOC. There is an internal marketing element to blue teams where you must constantly "sell" security to your users and stakeholders, not beat them over the head with it. It's an ongoing effort including training and awareness, briefings, and inclusion in blue team exercises. Users can be powerful allies in security, but you have to engage with them regularly and constructively.

What strategies do you use to communicate the threats you encounter to nontechnical decision-makers?

The first step is realizing that organizations do not exist to be secure, so you can't expect all decision-makers to care about everything the blue team takes seriously. I like using the "'five whys" method of taking an issue and asking iterative questions until you find the root cause.

Using it in reverse ("Why do I care?") is a great way to abstract a technical vulnerability or other issue to a larger business impact. The further away your decision-makers are from being technical, the more "Why do I care?" questions you need to answer before you can communicate with them effectively.

What recommendations do you have for managing nontechnical executives' expectations during a significant ongoing incident?

Taking control of the effort or at least presenting a clear plan and rules of engagement up front can help you avoid frustration on all sides. There is an art to analysis and investigations, but that is of no interest to the nontechnical executive during an incident. Response efforts must begin with a clear plan of action, specific goals, and a communication plan that has been agreed upon by all parties. In a vacuum, the executive will step in and create these things for you, and you'll find yourself sitting on conference bridges giving constant updates and going down rabbit holes.

"The blue team uses all the information they can gather and combines it to inform and create strategies and tactics to assess and address threats."

Twitter: @mitchparkerciso • **Website:** www.linkedin.com/in/mitchparkerciso

Mitch Parker

37

Mitch Parker is the CISO at IU Health, the largest health system in Indiana. He started his information security career as a contractor information assurance analyst for a defense agency. Through the years, he has picked up significant experience in defense through running the information security organizations as both a consultant and CISO. Mitch has written for *Ars Technica, Healthcare IT News, CSO Online, Healthcare IT Today,* and numerous other publications. He has also spoken and guest lectured at conferences and universities.

How do you define a blue team?

I define the blue team as the part of the organization responsible for defending against cyber-based threats to the enterprise. They take the information from those parts of the organization that are building secure systems and platforms and combine that with their own knowledge and sources of intelligence. The blue team uses all the information they can gather and combines it to inform and create strategies and tactics to assess and address threats.

What are two core capabilities that a blue team should have?

The two capabilities that a blue team needs are to be able to have are a strong understanding of the environment they are operating in, including team members who can help find out who owns or is responsible for what, and the ability to quickly learn and decode new methods and processes for both legitimate and attack traffic.

What are some of the key strengths of an incident response program?

I believe that the key strengths of a program can be summarized in several key areas.

- **Understanding:** Knowing your base operating environment and who maintains the key systems
- **Detection:** Being able to detect changes to the base environment and trace them back to the people or third party that made them
- **Communication:** Effectively communicating what you have discovered to the right people
- **Education:** Constantly educating yourself and your team on techniques and tactics and the latest technologies being used

How can blue teamers learn, practice, and grow?

The best thing they can do is to take advantage of containerization and virtualization to build their own environments. Like red teamers, you need to have that understanding of how everything works and what normal and abnormal behavior looks like. There's a lot of behavior that applications and systems have that you have to understand. Systems get very

> Systems get very chatty. The best way to learn is to build the systems yourself or get images of them to observe how they work and how they send and receive data.

chatty. The best way to learn is to build the systems yourself or get images of them to observe how they work and how they send and receive data.

I also recommend learning the same way the red teams do. Get virtual machines. Learn how to reverse-engineer code. Keep up with what is presented at the conferences and on Twitter. There is a lot of material out there. You just need to apply and understand it.

You also have to keep continually learning. There is a lot of material out there. Take advantage of what the best members of our community put out there for free, like Ian Coldwater, Gabrielle Hempel, Marcus Carey, and Mudge. Ask questions. Do not be afraid to approach the big names and ask them.

How do you reward good blue teaming work?

You need to always recognize great effort. Use whatever mechanisms you have available to make sure you can engage and retain your team members. Don't base your rewards on one engagement. Keep your team happy, well-compensated, and well-educated. Make sure your goals reflect the work they are doing. Help them build a career, not just expect them to read logs all day. Build plans for them to follow and succeed.

What are some core metrics that a blue team can use to build, measure, and maintain a successful information security program?

The most convincing one I have found has been with the number of targeted attacks stopped. This demonstrates how well intelligence works to find spear phishing attacks. The others are with the number of logs and sources analyzed, the number of devices monitored, and the number of vulnerabilities discovered. You'll want to also report on the average remediation time.

Where would you start if you were the only information security staff member at a small to medium-sized business with a primitive security infrastructure?

You need to have a good log analysis platform in place to analyze the data from all of your devices. No human being can accurately eyeball them anymore. Start by putting up a small ELK Stack server to collect logs and monitor the network. Start querying it and analyzing your data to see where the pain points are. Start scanning for vulnerabilities using open source tools. Address what you discover to meet immediate needs while you plan for better long-term controls. Start assessing and addressing as soon as you can.

> You need to have a good log analysis platform in place to analyze the data from all of your devices. No human being can accurately eyeball them anymore.

What is the most bang-for-your-buck security control?

Log analysis in depth from multiple systems. I learned this when I had several cases earlier in my career where attackers or insider threats would be able to disguise their presence on servers by bypassing logging or deleting logs. However, they can't disguise their path through the network, and I was able to detect a zero-day attack by piecing together information from several sources. I also had an insider threat at a customer attempt to use a service account to bypass several controls. We were able to correlate multiple levels of logging to compensate for their ability to delete logs from their own workstations and provide sufficient evidence that this person was acting to bypass controls.

Has your organization implemented any deception technologies?

We have not implemented these technologies yet because we believe the market is still maturing and that the use of these technologies needs to be very thought out. This technology has significant promise and will eventually be used.

Where should an organization use cryptography?

Where they can effectively manage it. Badly managed cryptography is worse than none at all because it gives the false sense of assurance that confidentiality and integrity exist where they do not. When you put this in place, think of how you're going to manage private and public keys, passphrases, and server certificates. Don't use the defaults, and always generate your own certificates. Make sure you keep your operating systems and cryptographic libraries up-to-date.

The act of putting in self-signed certificates or expired ones and telling your sys admins to click to bypass them means that they're going to do it when someone sends a phishing message. We don't manage crypto well, and this can lead to bigger compromises.

Use cryptography for data in motion and at rest and for any kind of remote access or system administration in combination with two-factor authentication.

How do you approach data governance and other methods of reducing your data footprint?

Data governance is an avenue to use to reduce your data and application footprints. It's actually most effective because it can identify the systems of truth used to generate the most important data the organization uses. This allows you to focus defenses on the most critical systems. In a way, data governance allows you to perform an indirect risk assessment. This is because the processes are built to identify critical data elements and the systems that generate them.

What is your opinion on compliance?

Compliance is something that many think they know how to do well and don't. In healthcare, we speak of HIPAA compliance as the gold standard. However, the intent of it is not to meet all the requirements at once. It's to assess and address risks and build plans to follow up. You don't, and should not, try to get it all done right the first time. If you do, it's like running system hardening utilities on a standard corporate desktop. You end up fixing everything you broke. Take the assess/address/plan approach and work toward measurable and smart goals, rather than breaking yourself trying to comply with a framework 100 percent.

One of the best lessons I learned when I first started was from an old Marine who got into information assurance, Ron Lauzon. Ron told me that organizations that focus 100 percent on compliance go out of business. You've got to focus on what's important and what's highest risk. When you do that, you address a number of others.

Spending your time arguing over packages you don't use in a Linux install that showed up on a vulnerability scan distracts you from the bigger picture.

Is there a framework that aligns the activities or functions performed by the blue team with regulatory compliance requirements?

I recommend the NIST Cybersecurity Framework as it is extensible enough to map to these activities and already has mapping to major regulatory compliance frameworks such as HIPAA. You will need to demonstrate that you are mapping to a framework if you are in a regulated industry. NIST is the standard many organizations use, and there are multiple crosswalks to regulatory frameworks.

How do you engage all the different units of an organization to maximize defense?

Engagement is consistent and necessary. You have to know the organization to know how to protect it. Technical assets and applications will always change. Culture and team members change less frequently than they do. We often overlook this aspect of organizations. We also overlook the connectors that make large companies function despite the silos and fiefdoms created by upper management. We need to understand who the connectors are, who understands the culture and history of the organization, and who we need to talk to. We need to know what we are defending, speak to it in their terms, and have the defense to help them meet their objectives. You don't do that without doing a lot of legwork, speaking with people, and participating in the business. The days of being aloof are over. You are expected to contribute, and you will get much in return when you do. No one is going to trust you to help defend them unless you understand what you are protecting.

What strategies do you use to communicate the threats you encounter to nontechnical decision-makers?

You can't communicate the threats unless you understand what their effects are. We think superficially of vulnerabilities, servers, applications, and devices. We don't normally think of the business, customer impact, or loss of trust. We need to be able to comprehend what the business is, how it will be impacted, what the impact will be, how much it can potentially cost, and what we can do to mitigate this.

Too often people in information security rely upon numbers, mainly from vendors, that give worst-case scenarios of multimillion-dollar fines that are attributed to data breaches. These organizations receive penalties for one of three factors, which are no risk assessment, no risk management plan, and/or not following up on addressing security risks. We have gone as far as telling our senior leaders every time the Department of Health and Human Services' Office for Civil Rights, better known as the OCR, notches another multimillion-dollar settlement. We discuss why the target organization received the penalties. It has been at least one of these three factors since we started doing this in 2016 with every organization we have analyzed. We trust these vendor numbers and claims as much as the falsified claims that there will be millions of unfilled cybersecurity positions within five years.

We set the expectation with our senior leadership team that we will develop risk assessments and risk management plans with an eye on using the assessment to learn more about the business and stakeholders. We follow up with the customers. We let our customers know, in their terms, that we understand the trust others place in them and that we want to support it. We do it in their language and with their support.

What recommendations do you have for managing nontechnical executives' expectations during a significant ongoing incident?

The best recommendation is transparency. An incident command system (ICS) relies upon giving a report each operational period. You want to keep your key stakeholders continually updated. You also want to use an ICS because cyber incidents now have serious business impact. You only need to take a look at how a ransomware attack can shut down a business to see how important the use of an ICS is in an organization.

Be transparent, understand the business and its impact, involve the customers, and use a management framework (ICS preferred) to manage the incident. Lean on people in your company with similar experience to help you out. Most of all, keep everything in writing, explain it, and be transparent about the needs of your customers and yourself. Don't try to be the hero. Be the connector your organization needs to help get them back to 100 percent.

> "The ultimate objective of a blue team is to detect, contain, and eradicate threats."

Twitter: @cybersecstu • **Website:** www.linkedin.com/in/itsecurity

Stuart Peck

Stuart Peck is the director of cybersecurity strategy for ZeroDayLab and runs the situational threat awareness program for executives and general employees and has personally delivered threat briefings to many FTSE 100 and FTSE 250 board-level executives and directors throughout the United Kingdom and Europe. He is also the incident manager and has responded to many major international breaches including global ransomware attacks and data breaches.

Stuart has more than 13 years' experience in the information security industry, including delivering threat intelligence, social engineering, application threat modeling, GRC, and incident response projects. Stuart also founded The Many Hats Club, an online community and podcast. He is a well-known public speaker at conferences and events in the United Kingdom and Europe.

38

How do you define a blue team?

Everyone who performs some action to detect, react, and respond to an attacker is part of the blue team, not just the SOC (although arguably this is the standard definition). For example, a well-formed computer security incident response team (CSIRT) should be comprised of SOC analysts, incident manager/responders, specialists from infrastructure security, AppSec, service desk (as these are usually incident handlers and coordinators), and other usual suspects such as the information security lead (CISO/director), etc.

What are two core capabilities that a blue team should have?

Everyone in the blue team should try to develop the investigator's mindset, always asking questions about the information, verifying everything through internal and external sources, and drawing logical, evidence-driven conclusions. I personally have found developing my investigation skills through competing in open source intelligence (OSINT) capture the flags (CTF) has helped greatly.

The blue team also needs to be able to quickly analyze data and define malicious traffic/behavior and contain threats, whether this is through tooling, log analysis, or reverse engineering. The ultimate objective of a blue team is to detect, contain, and eradicate threats.

What are some of the key strengths of an incident response program?

For me the most important thing in incident response is good and clear communication between the incident response team and key stakeholders such as the executives. I personally have seen where key decisions have been delayed or overridden due to miscommunication; it's vital to get this right early, especially when hard choices have to made quickly.

Next is good and relevant documentation such as incident response plans, workflows, and runbooks that are updated post-incident or at least every 12 months. On runbooks, ensure they are relevant and limited to a small number of scenarios. I've seen cases where there have been in excess of 30 runbook scenarios. There is nothing worse than mid-incident, spending ages trying to find the right process!

Finally, regular incident scenario testing either through desktop simulations or through red versus blue live events is great to not only "stress test" the incident response plans but also ensure that incident response teams are prepared for those perfect storms.

How can blue teamers learn, practice, and grow?

Twitter is a highly effective resource for learning about the latest vulnerabilities, attacker techniques, and trends. The blue teamers should follow red teamers to learn about their tactics, and vice versa; we've got to keep each other on our toes!

In terms of intelligence, the National Computer Emergency Response Teams—US-CERT, CERT-UK, etc.—offer good advisories on critical attacks and vulnerabilities. In addition, intelligence groups in the United Kingdom such as the National Cyber Security Centre (NCSC)'s Cyber Information Sharing Program (CiSP) are great to collaborate with other blue teamers across industry as well as keep up-to-date with the latest threats.

There are a number of really good blue team CTFs such as opensoc.io and companies like Immersive Labs lite .immersivelabs.com/objectives that provide free real-world simulations for threat hunting, SOC, and incident response.

On a personal note, I really like Cybrary and YouTube for digging into a subject quickly. We are lucky that there is so much good content available for free—almost too much!

Where would you start if you were the only information security staff member at a small to medium-sized business with a primitive security infrastructure?

I've always worked off the theory you can't defend what you don't know about, and in this scenario, I would start with the core fundamentals by ensuring the asset register is up-to-date. It's one of the questions I ask organizations I work with the most: Do you have an asset register? If not, let's start there. If so, when was it last updated?

An up-to-date and relevant asset register provides visibility into what assets there are, whether they are patched, what controls there are, ultimately where the critical assets reside, and how exposed they are. This helps build a strong foundation to implement the relevant logical controls to defend the critical assets first, by mapping how an attacker could compromise them.

What is the most bang-for-your-buck security control?

Multifactor authentication is easy to deploy and prevents a lot of common attacks such as credentials stuffing, credentials phishing, etc. There are still a lot of companies that don't have company-wide MFA and wonder why they see so many account take-overs; it's a really fundamental control that currently works pretty well.

Where should an organization use cryptography?
Cryptography should be used to protect sensitive and critical information at rest and in transit; the reality is that a lot of companies still don't encrypt data at rest. This is important especially in a data breach situation, as this renders the data useless in most cases to an attacker. We encrypt our laptops because it's become easier to do so, and with cloud providers such as Azure and AWS this is becoming more attainable. However, with on-premises databases we still see encryption as being a lot further down the priority list.

When it comes to passwords, hashing + salting is so important; there have been many recent breaches where passwords were only hashed using a weak algorithm, allowing the attackers to either hash-match or brute-force using tools like Hashcat.

How do you approach data governance and other methods of reducing your data footprint?
Luckily in the United Kingdom we have regulations such as EU GDPR and UK Data Protection Act 2018, which provide a robust framework for helping organizations manage how they process and control personal identifiable information (PII). This includes stipulating that personal data may only be kept in a form that permits identification of the individual for no longer than is necessary for the purposes for which it was processed. Data subjects have more rights on who can process their data and how, which of course creates its own set of challenges.

However, those rights are also valuable in ensuring that individuals have the power to reduce their own digital footprint through "the right to erasure," also known as the "right to be forgotten," which through subject access requests (SARs) allows the data subject to request that their information is deleted from the processor or controller.

Outside of this I have written some articles on how to reduce your digital footprint through following good OpSec and have trained many organizations' employees on these tactics to remain safe online and reduce the risk of exposing too much information online that an attacker could use to craft spear phishing emails, etc.

What is your opinion on compliance?

Attackers don't really care about compliance. Moreover, they are banking on you focusing on it! Compliance is important, but a lot of companies that were compliant to standards and regulation still have had security breaches. There is a balance between compliance and being secure; for example, policies and procedures provide coverage only if they are fully implemented, teams are following them, and everyone understands why the policies exist. Being secure is as much about the culture of security (the organization's attitude toward it) as it is about the process of undertaking an information security program. If your only focus is on being compliant, then you might be focusing on the wrong thing.

How do you engage all the different units of an organization to maximize defense?

Training is one of the most powerful tools for helping provide insight into why information security is important. These sessions are usually face-to-face to help maximize the engagement and include real-world and relevant attacks and breaches, why they happened, and how those companies responded. Most important, helping people understand how basic cyber hygiene techniques can protect them not only at work but at home, this really helps with buy-in and engagement. I find humor works over fear from experience.

What recommendations do you have for managing nontechnical executives' expectations during a significant ongoing incident?

Clear, concise, and honest expectations are the most important thing when dealing with executives during an incident. Emotions and pressure are usually at a breaking point, especially the longer the incident goes on. Use the data you have to make clear recommendations about what critical systems can be recovered first to relieve the pressure, always focusing on what can and cannot be done within time frames. Also, set expectations about curveballs or the "uh-oh" moments when you discover that the incident is worse than originally expected, especially during those early hours into the breach.

It seems obvious, but sometimes during the heat of a significant incident the obvious goes out the window!

"In addition to threat hunting and incident response, the blue team is the team that looks for unsecure configurations, finds security flaws, and monitors for unauthorized behavior in the internal infrastructure, be it internal or external."

Twitter: @Carlos_Perez

Carlos Perez

39

Carlos Perez has been active in the security community since 1999 working for the government of Puerto Rico to secure networks and perform internal pentests. He later joined Compaq/HP where he worked as a senior solution architect for the security and networking consulting practices covering 33 countries in Central America, South America, and the Caribbean. He helped customers to design and implement security solutions to meet their business needs in a secure way.

Carlos also worked as the director of reverse engineering at Tenable, Inc., where he was in charge of all remote code execution checks and finding zero-day vulnerabilities on products tested. He is currently the practice lead for research at TrustedSec, where he researches and develops both offensive and incident response tools for the consulting teams. He is best known for his contributions to open source security tools such as Metasploit, DNSRecon, and others. He has presented and provided training at conferences like Derbycon, DEF CON, Troopers, PSConfEU, HackCon, and BSidesPR.

How do you define a blue team?

In addition to threat hunting and incident response, the blue team is the team that looks for unsecure configurations, finds security flaws, and monitors for unauthorized behavior in the internal infrastructure, be it internal or external. This team will also update and check security metrics to ensure that the internal security measures are providing value and results. A blue team is not an operations team; implementation of best practices, security products, and monitoring infrastructure should not be part of what they do.

What are two core capabilities that a blue team should have?

One is deep knowledge on how the different infrastructure components work individually and with each other, in addition how these relations relate to business processes and their importance to the overall operation.

The second is the ability and conviction to record as much as possible knowledge that the team has and knowledge that has been gained via operation or research to ensure that the weakest link is a strong one. Knowledge is what makes a blue team strong, not so much the specific tools they may use.

> Knowledge is what makes a blue team strong, not so much the specific tools they may use.

What are some of the key strengths of an incident response program?

A part I see missing many times is the collection of lessons learned. A great deal is invested into the hunting and processing of information, in part because the hunt is the most exciting part, but this has led to not develop other areas such as actions to contain, remediate, and ensure that the knowledge gained is recorded and shared.

How can blue teamers learn, practice, and grow?

On the learning side, by adding learning to the metrics used for evaluating teams and individuals, people will behave in an organization by how they are measured. This can be done by requiring that teams have a development plan for their teams by area of focus. The team needs expertise in areas it focuses on to maintain proficiency. This will help reduce human error due to lack of knowledge and skills in day-to-day operations, ensure a flexible and nimble decision-making process because there is no time wasted trying to gain knowledge at the last minute, and also reduce risk based on badly founded decisions.

The practice part is a bit more challenging since management has to make sure to rotate personnel on tasks to ensure that every member of the team has experience in different fields. There will always be subject-matter experts, but the rotation ensures everyone has at least a base level of experience to support their decision-making process. A lab will help, but many organizations do not have the resources or even the capability to allow personnel to practice. A yearly hackathon, capture the flag, or any other type of event is an alternative that can be looked at.

How do you reward good blue teaming work?
The number-one way is recognition. People who do a good job should be told they are doing one, if possible publicly to the whole team. This includes the specifics as to why they are being rewarded so as to highlight the core principles, values, and actions that lead to being recognized. Rewards will vary from organization to organization; some will be in the form of bonuses, and others in terms of prices, but public recognition is one that should be standard no matter the policy or culture.

What are some core metrics that a blue team can use to build, measure, and maintain a successful information security program?
Some are as follows:
- Time of incident to detection
- Time between when new public threats are acknowledged and when a brief with IOCs is produced
- How quickly action items generated from the end-of-exercise are addressed

I try to keep metrics in terms of time and not quantity since the variables for quantity in terms of threats, IOCs, and resources to address volume will vary considerably. Time for addressing identified and estimated tasks is a simpler and more realistic measurement.

Where would you start if you were the only information security staff member at a small to medium-sized business with a primitive security infrastructure?

Gather a clear and up-to-date inventory of systems and their roles. Without knowledge of what battlespace one is in, we cannot start to prep it or even operate in it.

> Without knowledge of what battlespace one is in, we cannot start to prep it or even operate in it.

More specifically, without knowing what makes up the environment one is operating in, we cannot know how the infrastructure supports the different business processes or how they may impact or influence one another. Having a basic inventory allows for prioritization of other tasks and aids during the entire response process of an incident.

What is the most bang-for-your-buck security control?

It's not so much of a control, but in my opinion configuration management is the most important. The ability to configure an environment in an automated way that will ensure that assets are maintained in a known state means that human risk is reduced from day-to-day operations and that new controls can be deployed in a more efficient manner.

Has your organization implemented any deception technologies?

Yes, canaries are set for known common TTPs used by attackers. This allows a higher return of investment since setting canaries for things like fake service accounts that will entice attackers to use Kerberoast on the account tends to provide great value since it is a technique many execute. Like anything based on TTPs, a constant review/update is mandatory since attackers change their behavior as new techniques are developed and adopted.

Where should an organization use cryptography?
An organization should use cryptography in three main places.
- Communication of information between systems where possible
- Data at rest based on a risk assessment as to what should be protected first
- Hashing of credentials to ensure that the cost of leveraging such credentials is as high as possible in the case of a compromise so as to gain time and be able to operate inside the decision loop of the attacker

How do you approach data governance and other methods of reducing your data footprint?
Reduction, in my limited experience as it relates to governance, is the reduction of silos of information so as to make it easier to adhere to governmental regulations. By knowing what information is on hand and having as much of it centralized as possible, it is easier to apply policies that are developed by a committee or internal group that helps define them. The type of data and how it fits in the business operation will determine the policies and how they will be applied.

What is your opinion on compliance?
Compliance to regulation is just a minimum baseline that one should strive to, not only in the controls one must implement to comply but the system one implements to maintain and account for it. This same process is the base for a secure and efficient operation.

Is there a framework that aligns the activities or functions performed by the blue team with regulatory compliance requirements?
A recent one that I believe to be a good foundation is NISTIR 8183 Rev. 1 that was released by NIST covering identify, protect, detect, response, and recover.

How do you engage all the different units of an organization to maximize defense?
One simply plays the game of interdepartment politics and culture. Each environment has their unique structures and power players, but an approach that may apply to many

environments is to focus on what one can do to help them to minimize risk and ensure their success. By projecting one's self and the team as an asset to their goals, relations are easier to build.

What strategies do you use to communicate the threats you encounter to nontechnical decision-makers?

Ensure that they are communicated within the context of how they affect their business process. This is where all the work of having an accurate and up-to-date inventory of assets that is then used to build a clear view on how they relate to the different business processes shows its value. One is able to clearly quantify the risk and impact to the business in terms that decision-makers can relate to because they are measured on the performance of their part of the business.

What recommendations do you have for managing nontechnical executives' expectations during a significant ongoing incident?

Understand the business and operation to better communicate risk and impact. By knowing this, one can better translate the goal into a certain area of concern.

> Executives care about the business and not so much about the technical details.

Executives care about the business and not so much about the technical details.

Focus on what parts of the business were impacted, and if possible, provide time estimates for more information to be provided. Here is where having knowledge outside of the technical realm and understanding laws, business operation, and soft skills come into play. Developing these skills pays in dividends in hard times and allows you to "play the game" of interdepartmental or general business politics better to achieve the goal of securing the environment or addressing a situation better.

"A blue team is a set of individuals who prepare and monitor for, detect, and respond to security incidents."

Twitter: @itsquiessence • **Website:** www.linkedin.com/in/quiessencephillips and www.itsquiessence.com

Quiessence Phillips

40 Quiessence is a cybersecurity professional with 12+ years of experience working within the financial industry and most recently in the public sector, where she joined the City of New York as the deputy CISO. At New York City Cyber Command, she leads the threat management function, which encompasses the City's Security Operations Center, Computer Emergency Response, Cyber Threat Intelligence, and Counter Threat Automation teams.

Quiessence has been recognized as "Best of New York" by City Tech Foundation, published in *Women Know Cyber: 100 Fascinating Females Fighting Cybercrime,* and awarded Security Team of the Year for the public sector by FireEye. Additionally, in an effort to assist women interested in forging their path in the industry, Quiessence created Securing Your Path.

How do you define a blue team?
A blue team is a set of individuals who prepare and monitor for, detect, and respond to security incidents.

What are two core capabilities that a blue team should have?

Two core capabilities that a blue team should have are a strong understanding of their network and the capability to identify, detect, and respond to threats.

What are some of the key strengths of an incident response program?

Some key strengths of an incident response program are as follows:

- Diverse skill sets across the team, including, but not limited to, network and host-based forensics, malware analysis, a strong understanding of operating systems and architecture, and strong documentation skills.
- A continuous cycle of procedure and process development, including an IR plan, a formal incident management process, processes for various incident types, agreed upon taxonomy, etc.
- An integrated program with cyber-threat intelligence, along with all other support groups within the organization and/or business lines, such as risk, governance, audit, and legal.
- A methodical process for modeling threats and risk scenarios.
- Defined metrics based on effectiveness, efficiency, and efficacy that are calculated, reviewed, and shared.

How can blue teamers learn, practice, and grow?

Blue team members can learn, practice, and grow through various means. A few are as follows:

Internal to an Organization

- Post-incident reviews are extremely helpful to look introspectively at our work and assess what went well and what did not, to review gaps that we've identified and how to plug them, to determine how we could have reached certain milestones earlier, with more efficiencies, etc.
- Capture-the-flag events are helpful to continue to hone our skills and also allow for members of the team who tend to focus on a particular activity within incident response, to broaden their scope.
- Targeted threat modeling and development of risk scenarios allow one to delve deep into the business lines of an

organization, to truly understand the risk of certain threats to your organization.

- Coordinated defense exercises allows your blue team and other technology teams (i.e., web application team) to focus on attack scenarios and their response to them.
- Red/blue team exercises allow for a simulated attack and the opportunity for the blue team to test their defenses against particular threats and tactics.
- Demo days are a great way to take a topic in which you've been studying and show your team how this can be helpful to the organization. Topics that directly impact the way we work are found to be more interesting.

External to an Organization

- Training and conferences
- Networking with other security teams

How do you reward good blue teaming work?

An organization and/or team lead can reward good blue team work by implementing a process for recognition. Internal to my organization, we reward this type of work with challenge coins. This can/should be different based on your organization.

What are some core metrics that a blue team can use to build, measure, and maintain a successful information security program?

While metrics and their value may be different based on the organization and type of program, some core metrics are as follows:

- Total # of incidents investigated
  - By incident type
  - By category
  - By severity
  - By detection source
  - By reporting type
- Total # of incidents requiring escalation
- Mean time to detection (MTTD)
- Meant time to response (MTTR)
- Mean time to closure (MTTC)
- Total # of cases with external tickets opened
- Total # of cases created by automation
- Total # of security alerts and alert trend

Where would you start if you were the only information security staff member at a small to medium-sized business with a primitive security infrastructure?

If I were the only information security staff member at a small to medium-sized business, I would assess the current security posture, develop risk scenarios based on the vertical in which that organization fits, determine the most needed area of investment (time, resources, finances), and focus on the implementation of that. Based on the percentage of investment needed in other areas, it may be worth it to bring in external resources.

One of the foundational elements required in building a secure network is visibility. You cannot protect or respond to what you cannot see.

What is the most bang-for-your-buck security control?

Email and identify security controls (i.e., multifactor authentication).

Has your organization implemented any deception technologies?

I will not comment on technologies that my organization has implemented. I personally think that deception tools have a place in the security stack, at the right time in the development of your program.

Where should an organization use cryptography?

I believe that an organization should assess its environment and use cases for cryptography and implement where there is a need. However, general and standard use cases include cryptography applied to data transmission and storage of data.

How do you approach data governance and other methods of reducing your data footprint?

Data governance acts as the oversight of the data management program, such as the establishment and auditing of particular practices around data quality, retention, policies, etc.

What is your opinion on compliance?

Compliance is a necessary aspect of an information security program and allows for a dedicated practice to ensure the laws and policies that are in place to reduce risks are being adhered to. Where compliance becomes counterproductive is when/if the program functions only as a means to pass an audit. A holistic compliance program can be extremely effective when it is used as a proactive method of ensuring compliance to technology and security controls, which have an effect on policies, standards, and the letter and/or intent of the law.

Is there a framework that aligns the activities or functions performed by the blue team with regulatory compliance requirements?

I am not familiar with a single framework that aligns activities performed by the blue team with regulatory compliance requirements, as regulatory compliance varies depending on a variety of factors. There are various checklists and/or guidance documents that assist with ensuring that an organization is meeting the requirements of a particular regulation.

I think frameworks in general are helpful, especially to organizations that lack resources to build the proper strategies for managing topics such as this. I think the framework should encompass the larger information security program, not just the blue team.

How do you engage all the different units of an organization to maximize defense?

Communication with all areas of the organization is paramount. We go about this through a variety of methods, including the following:

- Incident response readiness
- Security posture reports
- Cyber-threat intelligence briefings
- Incident management coordination
- Coordinated defense exercises

What strategies do you use to communicate the threats you encounter to nontechnical decision-makers?

We communicate threats to nontechnical decision-makers using a risk-based approach. One does not have to understand the technical aspects of a threat to understand the risk to the business/organization, if delivered effectively. Data is also a driver for how we represent risk. Depending on the data, it can be gleaned from open source (i.e., OSINT) or our own internal data; gleaned from network telemetry, vulnerabilities, and cases investigated; and so on. We believe our own data to be one of our largest sources of collection.

Communication of threats occurs in various ways, depending on the cause for communication. Comms may be required due to an active incident, a critical vulnerability, post-incident response, and others. Based on your organization, the blue team might be the bearer of the communication, so having processes in place to hand over necessary information to the appropriate group so they can effectively communicate the concerns is paramount.

What recommendations do you have for managing nontechnical executives' expectations during a significant ongoing incident?

The following are a few recommendations whether executives are technical or nontechnical during a significant and ongoing incident:

- Make your executives aware of the stages of the incident and at which stage you are in.
- Set the expectation that during an active incident, facts are likely to develop over time.
- Words matter, so define and document them. For example, to avoid confusion and miscommunication of terminology within incident response, explain particular words (e.g., incident) that are being used at the onset.
- Develop clear protocols and communicate them.
- Set the cadence for updates and meet them.
- Depending on your executive team, develop a dashboard for them to see pertinent information related to the case, which is automatically updated based on the work of the team. This will reduce the number of incoming questions.
- Communicate clear measures in relation to the closure of an incident.

"Make no mistake, everyone's job ultimately boils down to defending our enterprise; we just take different approaches to defense."

Twitter: @jotunvillur

Lauren Proehl

41

Lauren is an experienced incident responder and threat hunter who has helped identify and mitigate cyber adversaries in Fortune 500 networks. She has led investigations ranging from data breaches to targeted attacks and continues to focus on defining some part of the limitless unknowns in cyberspace and making cybersecurity less abstract and more tangible. Lauren sits on the CFP board for BSides Kansas City, heads up SecKC parties, and attends all the cons. She currently holds GCIH and GREM certifications. When she is not behind a screen, you can find Lauren outdoors, trying not to crash her mountain bike.

How do you define a blue team?
To me, a blue team is any group of individuals who actively identify, mitigate, eradicate, or weaken threats and threat actors. A blue team is evolving daily with each new attack. Make no mistake, everyone's job ultimately boils down to defending our enterprise; we just take different approaches to defense.

The key factor of a defined blue team is that they are always on, constantly evolving, and constantly improving themselves and their enterprise. I worked in incident response for years, and you constantly have to be on your toes for the next event. Ransomware doesn't wait to execute until you're done writing your last report, and attackers certainly don't care that you were up until 3 a.m. last night combing through logs (in fact, they probably prefer that). Though incident response is highly reactive, the goal should always be to either prevent future use of that attack vector or decrease dwell time in the next attack. My first boss taught me that "prevention is nice, but detection is a must," and I believe a blue team should always have the ability to see what is happening.

Now I lead a threat-hunting team, which is mostly proactive, but our goal is still the same. We try to use data and intelligence to try to predict the next move of threats and close those gaps. If we can't close those gaps, we make sure the next time some- one talks about what we hunted, it is the IR or SOC team using our detections.

What are two core capabilities that a blue team should have?

> Logs are gold for the blue team, and when you don't have them, especially parsing properly in a central location, you make the blue team's lives so much harder or impossible.

- The ability to detect any type of attack or the ability to create a detection for an attack that was missed with existing detections. Logs are gold for the blue team, and when you don't have them, especially parsing properly in a central location, you make the blue team's lives so much harder or impossible.
- The ability to drive process change, policy change, and tool changes in the business. If a blue team is not empowered to work with finance to get a phone call check added to the process, then all you are doing is making sure your blue team will continue coming in after business email compro- mise (BEC) has occurred and some great monetary sum has been wired to a Western Union halfway around the world. Empower your blue team to make changes that will make the lives of attackers harder.

What are some of the key strengths of an incident response program?

A strong incident response program is reflective of the people on the team. IR is hard; every time that phone rings, you are walking into a fire where you don't have all the details. Strong IR programs have a manager who is not afraid to get in the trenches and take care of their people. They have people who want to boot attackers out of the network and want to make sure they never get in again. They have people who are continuously curious, even if sometimes you have to dive in after them to pull them up for air. They have people who can handle pressure and a manager to protect from toxic politics and being stretched too thin. They have people who are okay with the unknown and a manager who will walk in front of them shining the light. Strong IR programs look for incident responders from all walks of life and are open to hiring help-desk gurus, music education majors, and stay-at-home moms. You can always teach technical skills, and strong IR programs make sure to look beyond that.

Strong IR programs seek to evolve with attackers. They track current trends, TTPs, and intelligence, and they understand potential weak points in their organization. Every day in security is new, so it is critical that teams are empowered to learn and grow with the times.

Additionally, strong IR programs know their baseline. They know what tools cover what portion of their security stack. They know how available logs are and where they need to go to get them, or at the very least, they know who to ask for the logs they need when the time comes. Strong IR programs know their organization's weaknesses and strive to close the gaps whenever possible. Ultimately it boils down to being prepared, and if you don't know what is in your own backyard, you won't be able to tell the holes from the shadows.

How can blue teamers learn, practice, and grow?

Blue teamers should look to attend conferences, read blogs, build labs, and try their hand at some controlled red team work in order to grow. Collaboration with my red team counterparts has leveled up my blue team work tenfold. I would rather get woken up at 2 a.m. by my friend Eric in adversary emulation instead of a real attack. I always make sure to ask Eric for copious notes on what he did and why he did it. This helps me understand the mind of an attacker and uncover gaps we may have never known about before. The best part is, I can give Eric logs so he knows how to be more stealth in the future, and it only matures our defenses as we progress.

How do you reward good blue teaming work?

Time off and competitive pay!

The adage about defenders having to be right 100 percent of the time and attackers only having to be right once is so true, and quite frankly, it is exhausting. You have to take care of your people and watch for burnout, because it can happen fast and hit hard in blue team roles.

Beyond that, a reward is recognition for the work that is put in by the blue team and investment in training and keeping skills sharp. Look, most people coming into the field I talk to want to be a pentester. They want to get paid to pull up the hood of their hoodie and click that magic Hack button, and that's okay. That is reflected in a lot of conference talks I attend and a lot of what is highlighted by enterprise security programs, but when you get MFA deployed for 60,000 users and stop the annoying password spraying from Bangladesh, you have to celebrate as hard as getting shell.

What are some core metrics that a blue team can use to build, measure, and maintain a successful information security program?

Metrics are hard, but they are so important. If you aren't doing metrics for your blue team, change course and start putting those together this year. If you don't have solid metrics, you are literally leaving money, staff, training, and resources on the table because your story isn't being effectively communicated to the board.

There are a few good metrics that blue team should look to highlight. Using industry-accepted frameworks, like Cyber Kill Chain and ATT&CK, are great, but remember, they are not comprehensive and are constantly evolving. Also, do not treat the two as the same. Cyber Kill Chain highlights the timeline of an attack, while ATT&CK highlights the technical elements of an attack. An easy first metric is to map all of your incidents or attacks to the Cyber Kill Chain to show at what point attacks are being stopped or detected. Ideally, you'd like them to never get in, but since we live in reality, detection at delivery should be the goal.

Blue teams should also focus on tracking true positive, false positive, true negative, and false negative rates, especially by tools. Tools are constantly changing, and if you find that tools begin misclassifying items as malicious (and thus creating more work for you) or are missing malicious items, it may be time to reevaluate your tool. I love mean time to detect (MTTD) and mean time to resolve (MTTR) because these can outline the ugly truths of understaffing or incomplete security stacks. Several industry reports use these as well, so you can compare yourself against industry averages.

The number-one thing you should not do is turn your blue team into a ticket shop and track things such as the number of incidents worked or the average time to close a ticket. If you must meet a number of tickets worked to justify staffing, make sure you have a strong story backing it up that does not encourage your IR team to close a ticket versus completing quality work.

Finally, remember, what gets measured gets managed (that isn't always good), and as the wise Wu Tang Clan once said, "Cash rules everything around me," so make sure you are talking to upper management in terms they understand: cash.

Where would you start if you were the only information security staff member at a small to medium-sized business with a primitive security infrastructure?
I would start by collecting all the available logs in a central location with proper configurations. There is a lot of detection and alerting you can do with a good data lake and properly parsed logs. Microsoft has amazing documentation for handling EVTX logs, which can give you insight into so many various activities. Once you get logs parsing right, you can leverage frequency detections to search for anomalies and trend analysis to see where the most detections occur and the least occur. For most purchasing or hiring decisions, you need supporting data to justify the expense, and centralized logging can help you realize those initiatives.

What is the most bang-for-your-buck security control?

I truly believe a good endpoint detection and response (EDR) tool is worth its weight in gold, silver, and any other gems combined. With the expanse of remote work, combined with global organization spread, we are rarely in the same offices or even on the same network as our colleagues on any given day. The endpoint is still heavily leveraged by attackers, whether to get credentials through Mimikatz or install a backdoor for future sneaky activities. Having the ability to detect process changes, registry writes, scheduled task setups, or file exfiltration at a granular level is key to defense work. Make sure to look for EDR solutions that allow for process or hash blocking and remote containment as well in order to control intrusions.

Has your organization implemented any deception technologies?

I *love* deception. I am a self-proclaimed "blue teamer with a vengeful side." One time someone phished my grandma, so I wrote a Python-based credential stuffer to flood attackers' databases full of junk. We have used this on multiple incidents to try to make it a needle-in-the-haystack situation, and it has bought more time before an attacker can use potential legitimate credentials.

Our organization has used honeypot and honey token defenses as early warning systems as well. These do tend to generate noise and potential false positives but can be great for identifying attack patterns and teasing out threats that may have been lying dormant. I encourage all blue teams to use deception techniques. They are a blast to execute and have legitimate payoffs as a defense strategy.

How do you engage all the different units of an organization to maximize defense?

This starts from the top down. My organization has great leadership in our C-suite who has made sure that security is aligned from the C-suite down. We do our best to educate and collaborate so finance, HR, and others understand the role they play in defense and why it really does matter.

I constantly reach out to other leaders in the business to discuss new ways to collaborate and find ways to make sure

I like to ask other business units to participate in blue team work, especially threat hunting.

we are feeding back to benefit them. I like to ask other business units to participate in blue team work, especially threat hunting. So many people see cybersecurity as this highly abstract concept that they are only exposed to on the nightly news. We try to make it accessible and give them a role to play in threat hunts or adversary emulations so they feel valued. This is also a huge benefit to us because we get to see how people think who haven't been doing this day in and day out and find things we never even thought of before.

What strategies do you use to communicate the threats you encounter to nontechnical decision-makers?

Personally I try to write out what the threat and impact are three times in a way that my spouse, my dad, and my grandma could understand if I sent it via email. I heavily rely on analogies to paint the picture as well. One thing a lot of people do understand is money, so I try to quantify a threat's impact in monetary terms. When people hear BEC emails were the biggest threat last year, they tend to tune out versus when people hear BEC emails were the biggest threat *and* resulted in $1.7 billion in loss last year.

What recommendations do you have for managing nontechnical executives' expectations during a significant ongoing incident?

Always stay calm, always be prepared, and don't blame anyone.

Always stay calm, always be prepared, and don't blame anyone.
I have walked into a room full of yelling executives, and the ability to calmly explain the situation with all of the facts available to you at that time can do wonders. They might have questions you don't know the answers to yet; that is okay. Make sure you are giving clear, consistent updates, and continue steering the ship away from the iceberg with a confident stoicism. Remember, incidents are stressful for everyone involved, and no one wants to be the next front-page breach story.

"An individual who foremost thinks about the implications of an action, event, or decision, and the impact that has on a user or an organization, is utilizing the practices of a blue team."

Twitter: @MSAdministrator • **Website:** letsautomate.it, www.linkedin.com/in/josh-rickard, and www.github.com/msadministrator

Josh Rickard

Josh Rickard has a diverse background from system administration, digital forensics, and incident response to managing teams and building security products. As an automation and security expert, Josh focuses on creating tools to help defend and automate everyday processes using PowerShell and Python.

42

How do you define a blue team?

Most believe that a blue team is comprised of security professionals who specialize in different security verticals. This team could be part of a security operations center (SOC), a team of security analysts, or some other combination. You would not be wrong if you believed this; in fact, this is probably what most think of when asked how to define a blue team.

   I believe the definition of a blue team is anyone who supports, drives, trains, implements, or cares about the defense of an organization. You do not have to be a security specialist to be part of a blue team. An individual who foremost thinks about the implications of an action, event, or decision, and the impact that has on a user or an organization, is utilizing the practices of a blue team.

A blue team is not a segmented pool of employees within an organization. Yes, an organization will have a specialist on the security team who focuses on defensive goals. These individuals may have expertise in reverse engineering, memory forensics, operating system hardening, or network forensics, but these are not the only members of the defensive (blue) team. The blue team is comprised of much, much more.

The individuals who define, write, review, and implement policies, procedures, compliance, and legal requirements are also part of the blue team. Examples of this can be seen at many levels: an organization's frontline support (e.g., help desk) that scrutinizes someone during a password reset attempt; the IT analyst who adds additional security controls for their department's assets; the DBA who is a perfectionist and wants to secure data in their systems beyond what policy states; the user who reports any suspicious email they receive. These individuals are a part of the blue team. I want all of these people on my blue team—imagine if they weren't.

What are two core capabilities that a blue team should have?

Blue teams should have the ability to negotiate and communicate. Of course, technical skills in multiple specialization fields are needed, but this is all subjective based on the type of organization. A critical capability for a blue team is the ability to understand when something is not a priority to an organization and efforts should be focused elsewhere. It's important to understand when it is/is not worth the time, concentration, and effort for a security-related improvement. Unfortunately, if an organization is not security focused, then this can feel like an uphill battle.

Understanding when to accept a risk is extremely important, and communication is critical for any blue team, whether it be explaining the extent and impact of an incident or showing the value a tool/product will add to detection, response, or remediation capabilities. Communication is a core requirement when responding to an incident. It's important to make sure everyone is on the same page and understands the objectives and next steps. Additionally, communication is required throughout the entire incident response process. It's vital whether you are in the preparation, identification, containment, eradiation, recovery, or retrospective phases.

What are some of the key strengths of an incident response program?

The key strengths of an incident response program should be apparent during the preparation and retrospective phases. Within the incident response program, you should have clear and precise documentation. This documentation is defined in what many consider the preparation phase of an incident. The documentation should contain clear guidelines on the incident response processes, when and who to contact during an incident, and procedural references, which help the incident response team coordinate and respond effectively.

Another key strength of the incident response program is the retrospective phase. If the retrospective phase is properly conducted and followed through, then it should be continually updating, modifying, and adjusting the processes, which includes documentation. All of these changes and updates will feed back into the preparation phase. This means that the incident response plan documentation is never complete and is a living, breathing document that should be changed and reviewed continually.

> If the retrospective phase is properly conducted and followed through, then it should be continually updating, modifying, and adjusting the processes, which includes documentation.

If a team has these two phases down, then they will do well when the next incident occurs. They will know who, when, and what to do, even if the team shrinks, grows, or changes.

How can blue teamers learn, practice, and grow?

The best way for blue teamers to learn, practice, and grow is by feeding their curiosity. Many organizations treat, especially entry-level

> The best way for blue teamers to learn, practice, and grow is by feeding their curiosity.

analysts, as worker bees in a hive mentality. They want them to stare at a screen and do their job without deviating as much as possible. This approach leads to burnout, which can result in teams overlooking threats.

Companies need to identify the skills of their blue teamers and utilize them. Security professionals are natural tinkerers and want to understand how things work at a deep level. They don't just want to understand how to examine email headers; they want to understand how message transports work, how you can spoof headers, and how to set up an open SMTP relay, just like attackers do on a daily basis. Organizations need to foster and use this for their benefit. Instead of making an analyst look at your SIEM all day every day, the next time they ask if they can work on something that interests them, let them. Feed this energy and curiosity. If organizations shift to this mentality, analysts/teams will use that curiosity to help strengthen defenses.

In my experience, organizations that create an environment of experimentation are better off when it comes to securing their environment. I previously worked in higher education as a security analyst where my primary responsibilities were digital forensics and incident response. We were a small team, and if you have worked in the public sector, you know that we didn't have the fancy tools, unlimited logging, EDR, robust alerting, etc., because budget is restricted for security. So, we built our own tools like automated vulnerability tracking, reporting, account-ability, patching, and notification systems. We also automated our mundane tasks such as inspection of, reporting, analysis, and remediation of phishing emails. Using the skills of your blue team in this way ensures that your team understands the environment they are working with as well as instilling curiosity, which moves your team forward in terms of skill and maturity.

How do you reward good blue teaming work?
I believe that the best reward for anyone in a senior manage-ment position within a security team is to follow and practice the mantra of "Praise rolls down and blame rolls up." A manager, director, ISO, or CISO should always make sure that any accom-plishments, improvements, enhancements, etc., the team has made should always be credited to that individual/team. Any blame during (or after) an incident should not roll down; instead, it should roll up.

When it comes to a more concrete way to reward good blue teaming work, I highly recommend that anyone in a management position not blindly deny ideas brought by analysts. If management doesn't have time to work through the details, then ask the team to come back with a proof of concept (POC) all the while setting expectations that they still have their duties. Encouraging analysts and giving the opportunity to prove themselves shows that management cares about their career and wants them to succeed.

If you give credit where credit is due, when it comes to an analyst detecting a new threat or bubbling up an event, then they will know you trust them and believe in their abilities. If you are a senior member of the blue team, you should do the same, but if you deserve the credit, then make sure you get it. You're experienced, you're skilled, and you have been through things that others have not; you deserve that credit when it's warranted.

What are some core metrics that a blue team can use to build, measure, and maintain a successful information security program?

There are many different metrics you could or should track as part of your security program. Many of them are dependent on what your organization's mission is. For example, if you build, release, and sell your own products, your metrics may be focused on the response time for vulnerabilities reported to your team. You may also have metrics on static and dynamic analysis of your code base as well as the number of automated tests and performance of your tooling. If your product is a SaaS based, then you may also have metrics around the average security threats facing your application and your ability to respond to these threats.

Traditional security teams, in a security operations center (SOC) or a team of security analysts, will have different metrics. Depending on your security maturity, you should start to capture and track your exposure on a continuous basis. Use tools like Shodan.io or Nmap or your vulnerability management platform or all of them to build an exposure risk profile. Additionally, you *must* understand and track what data your company has, where it is, who has access to it, how they access it, and why individuals need access to it. Answering these questions for all data within your organization's purview is critical for a mature security program.

Organizations differ in their approach to security programs. Some focus on assets, systems, applications, etc., and some focus on data. I personally believe that having an understanding of the assets is needed, but your core focus should first and foremost be your data. Focus your efforts and defensive strategies on this data and focus your security team toward a data-centric security model instead of an asset-centric model.

Finally, the biggest metric you should have is showing your percentage of visibility versus all assets, applications, services, etc. To get to this metric, you should have a SIEM or some log aggregator (you do, don't you?). Begin by doing inventory on what is currently being sent to your SIEM. Whether this includes raw event logs, packet captures, product logs, or even just alerts from products, do an inventory and make sure it is updated any time a change is made. Next, focus on what security tools you have and whether those are being sent to your SIEM. If they are not, then figure out why and how to get them in there. Finally, gather a list of critical (or preferably all) assets or data locations.

Once you have these, begin by looking at all the data you are currently receiving in your SIEM and map this to a framework like MITRE ATT&CK. What visibility do you currently have? Begin creating models (using the same framework) for each additional product that you could add. Find the most critical items you want coverage of and add those to your SIEM. Continue to go through this process until you're satisfied with your coverage. Once you have this coverage, review them all and see whether any are redundant and could be removed. Or look at other products that may cover a majority of two or three you already have in place.

The goal of this metric is understanding gaps in detection capabilities. Once you have an understanding of those gaps, then look for opportunities to harden or restrict access to these systems, applications, data, etc.

Where would you start if you were the only information security staff member at a small to medium-sized business with a primitive security infrastructure?
Centralized logging, with visibility into all assets, applications, and services, and the logs related to how they are used, accessed, and authenticated to. Defining a baseline of normalcy is where I would start. Once you have this visibility and understand normal

user, system, application, services, etc., behavior, then you can build robust but flexible detection rules for any number of events and use cases.

Once this logging is achieved, assuming SSO is used, then I would ensure that I am part of any development, implementation, or purchasing of services, applications, or systems to ensure that security is not an afterthought and is part of the initial planning phases.

What is the most bang-for-your-buck security control?

Principle of least privilege (PoLP). Make sure that when designing, developing, or implementing services that your organization is following PoLP. PoLP requires understanding how a service will be used and who will need to use it. Once this is understood, then make sure that the product you are bringing into your organization has the ability to be configured using PoLP.

Has your organization implemented any deception technologies?

The organizations I have worked for have not implemented a deception product, but we have used the same concept with internally built tooling. For example, during my time at a previous organization we created and purposely exposed multiple mailbox credentials on multiple different sites (e.g., Pastebin). This was our attempt (before deception products existed really) to lure certain actors into our environment so we could monitor the activities in a controlled manner. This was both successful in some ways but futile in others. We ended up getting lots of activity such as sending of phishing emails from this account, syncing using SMTP/IMAP/ActiveSync to their local machines, etc. The problem was that we attracted more attackers than our intended audience.

At another organization, we deployed files that contained canary tokens to different file shares throughout our network. When they were opened, it would send us an alert of this activity. This is a great way to see who is snooping around on your network, but it can lead to false positives, especially if an employee is bored and just nosy.

Where should an organization use cryptography?

Everywhere and anywhere. An organization should encrypt every piece of communication on the network (in an ideal world) and all data in transit and at rest. You should implement or purchase a centralized certificate authority and use it everywhere. If you so happen to use Active Directory, you can implement Active Directory Certificate Services and deploy certificates to all workstations, servers, applications, and services. This means you can deploy certificates for RDP use, TPM chips and BitLocker encryption, authentication and encryption of web servers, PowerShell, code signing certificates, etc.

One advantage that many do not point out is that if everything is encrypted on your network using your certificates, then the outliers of nonencrypted communications or the use of external certificates becomes a lot more visible to your security team.

How do you approach data governance and other methods of reducing your data footprint?

This is a difficult question, but my approach would be to first understand or establish a data classification system. This requires that you understand your businesses focus areas and the types of data within the environment. I would then reach out to my business leaders and have them explain to me what they consider the most critical data within the environment from a business, compliance, and legal perspective.

Next, I would work with development, auditing, compliance, and IT teams to understand how the data is used, transferred, and stored. Once you have a firm grasp on the types of data and where it's stored, you can begin assessing the security controls around this data and making sure that you're taking input both from the business leaders as well as from operational views about the data in question.

This approach is for internal data, but you must also measure and assess your exposure externally. Scanning and some automation can help you determine what data is exposed externally, for example, open AWS S3 buckets or databases that are public that should not be. Having the understanding and the previous conversation can help when assessing external exposure.

What is your opinion on compliance?

Compliance is typically seen, from an analyst point of view, as a four-letter word. Honestly, I don't personally mind compliance when I think from the perspective of a potential customer or client as well as a user of a service/company. I want them to follow guidelines that protect my personal data, so I expect the same internally.

Compliance frameworks are constantly changing and expanding their scopes, which can be difficult to implement. Some frameworks, like DoD 6510, can be extremely stringent when it comes to reporting requirements, which can be burdensome. Others are extremely flexible in their definitions. So, I can understand both the frustrations and praises given for compliance frameworks.

Compliance has its place, especially when an incident occurs and you're required to have clear documentation, procedures, and reporting requirements. This is to ensure that your organization is following mandated best practices as well as any legal actions or recourse your organization must take.

Is there a framework that aligns the activities or functions performed by the blue team with regulatory compliance requirements?

There is no single framework that aligns blue teamwork with all compliance frameworks (that I'm aware of), but there are products and tools that facilitate this. I have a personal bias, but security, orchestration, automation, and response (SOAR) tools fit this model well.

Most SOAR products enable blue teams to define their business and operational procedures within a series of conditions and actions. These compliance requirements can be automated (to some extent) using these conditions and actions in the form a workflow or playbook. Additionally, any auditing requirement you may have will (should) be built into the SOAR platform of choice. Think of this as a play-by-play of every action (automated or manual) taken within the platform. SOAR platforms also enable you to generate or create reports for any requirements around reporting right within the platform itself.

I believe that SOAR will drive compliance requirements for many organizations, especially compliance frameworks that require highly detailed auditing trails. You can perform some of this through automation, but SOAR is different than automation. Being able to ingest, make a determination that is based on business and operational processes, and orchestrate the gathering or verification of events is where SOAR shines.

Again, I am biased as I currently work for a SOAR vendor, but if you can define a process on a whiteboard or piece of paper, then you can automate it with SOAR.

How do you engage all the different units of an organization to maximize defense?

There are multiple approaches to maximizing defense, but I have found that the best way is to create content that is relatable. One of my past positions on a security team included an awareness coordinator who was responsible for organizational outreach on behalf of our security team. This included awareness about relevant and topical threats facing our type of organization as well as even personal events (e.g., phishing attempts). This works really well when you are trying to communicate best practices.

Also, your security team should be relatable and have open lines of communication with different organizational meetings. At one largish organization, I was part of an incident response and digital forensics team, but I was also the president of our employee award committee (which gave out grants for employees to get training or go to events). Having this type of visibility and communication with individuals outside of my team enabled me to personally do my job better while also sharing the latest information from our security team.

Finally, the security team should do tailored or targeted presentations for different organizational units. You may talk about personal security when chatting with departmental administrators, or you may talk about phishing when talking with administrative staff; it all depends. Whatever you do, make sure that it's modern and topical, and throw in a few memes or inside jokes to show your humor and google some dad jokes if you need some inspiration.

What strategies do you use to communicate the threats you encounter to nontechnical decision-makers?

When communicating to nontechnical decision-makers about threats you encounter, I highly recommend showing the operational impact of those threats. For example, some zero-day comes out, and it impacts your organizational fleet. Showing the impact a threat has had on your organization division helps level the playing field. Most nontechnical decision-makers understand capacity planning, resource constraints, and productivity impact, so show how this event has impacted your team. You can do this by sharing hours spent on incident response, total number of FTE used, and the impact this may have had to normal operations like a project being delayed due to response efforts.

What recommendations do you have for managing nontechnical executives' expectations during a significant ongoing incident?

Clear lines of communication and setting of expectations are required. If you have created an incident response plan (IRP) properly, then you have reviewed and received sign-off from your executives. This means your IRP contains the process in which status updates will be given. If not, no worries—but as part of your retrospective, you should make sure that this is added to your IRP.

In reality, every event will be different, and every executive will have different expectations. Make sure you communicate the status of the ongoing incident clearly and try to not give an estimate on completion. If you have to give an estimate, then make sure all the caveats are there as well. Also, provide a precise time when you will provide an update and make sure you follow through exactly at the set time—no matter what.

A critical part of an incident response process is ensuring that all communications go to and from the incident commander. This individual is running the show; you can think of them as a quarterback. They announce the plays and talk to individual players on the incident response team, and those players relay information back to that quarterback, always making sure they are the source of truth for all communications. This individual then will work with either a PR or marketing department to ensure that all communications are the same and do not deviate.

While you want to keep communication to any media the same, you also want this same mentality with your executive team. Make sure you are communicating the truth but also a concise message. You do not want your executive team to be told by some individual on your team a different hypothesis or story. This will not go well for you and may result in them taking control of the situation themselves.

"In some sense, the blue team is comprised of the individuals whose core job responsibility is to ensure the security of the organization."

Twitter: @megan_roddie

Megan Roddie

43

Megan Roddie currently works as a cyberthreat researcher. With previous experience in the public sector and a current position in the private sector, she has a variety of experience in different types of environments. With a love for public speaking, she has spoken at DEF CON, multiple BSides events, and various other conferences around the world. Megan has a master's degree in digital forensics and holds several industry certifications.

How do you define a blue team?

Defining blue team is such a challenge because of the large scope of everyone involved in such operations. In some sense, the blue team is comprised of the individuals whose core job responsibility is to ensure the security of the organization. However, the team of security engineers, SOC analysts, and incident responders who may fall in this category could not be successful in their roles without the support of the entire organization, developers, network engineers, help desk, and more.

What are two core capabilities that a blue team should have?

Communication and management support. While not necessarily traditional "capabilities" from a technical/skill perspective, all the technology in the world isn't going to provide any value without the ability to coordinate within your team. Additionally, security is an often neglected or disliked department within organizations. We are seen as the "no" men, trying to make things more difficult with security controls.

> Without a management team that knows how to effectively communicate the team's needs and provide top cover, success in any projects is going to be challenging.

Without a management team that knows how to effectively communicate the team's needs and provide top cover, success in any projects is going to be challenging.

How can blue teamers learn, practice, and grow?

Hands-on, practical experience is the best, most efficient, and most fun method of learning, practicing, and growing. The newcomers I admire most and believe will achieve much throughout their careers are those who thirst for knowledge and respond by just trying things, asking questions, and making mistakes. The individuals who want to

> The newcomers I admire most and believe will achieve much throughout their careers are those who thirst for knowledge and respond by just trying things, asking questions, and making mistakes.

understand network traffic analysis just fire up Wireshark and start looking through packets. These are the people who are going to go places in their careers. Additionally, it's important for management to encourage employees to pursue interests and spend time learning new skills as opposed to locking them into their current skill set.

How do you reward good blue teaming work?

It's important to realize the stress and burnout that can result from working in cybersecurity, especially in a blue team role.

It's often a thankless job where you come into the light when something goes wrong but are rarely acknowledged when things are going right. Because of this, I believe there are two key things that can be done for blue teamers to reward that work. First, general acknowledgment of successes, a thank-you, or a note up the chain of command recognizing an employee can go a long way in assuring that the employee understands their value. Second, understand the need for mental health breaks. Especially coming off of a major project or incident, it is important that an employee is provided the opportunity to recover from the increased stress, whether that is a day off or providing the employee with a day for training/working on what they want.

What is the most bang-for-your-buck security control?

Logging. Often turning on logging in applications and operating systems provides no additional product costs, only project time and resources. While there are plenty of defensive technologies that can and should be implemented, there will likely always be a way into your organization. When it comes time to respond to such an incident, having no visibility over attack activity limits the blue team's ability to find root cause, contain and remediate the incident, and ultimately prevent repeat attacks.

What is your opinion on compliance?

While in theory compliance provides a method of ensuring organizations meet certain security standards, the number of breaches we are observing occurring in supposedly regulated industries is not supporting the effectiveness of these efforts. Even when punishment, such as fines, is enforced for noncompliance, we see many organizations cutting checks and moving on with their operations. Like many things in life, compliance is a great idea on paper but has not proven its effectiveness in practice.

Is there a framework that aligns the activities or functions performed by the blue team with regulatory compliance requirements?

The best and clearest framework I have worked with is the CIS Controls (albeit that's with a limited history in regulatory compliance). I think working with frameworks comes with pros and cons, and it really depends on the mindset that organizations approach them with. If an organization is being forced by regulation and simply doing the bare minimum to pass an inspection and then moving on, I don't think it's being leveraged properly. However, there are a couple positive uses for using such a framework.

First, for new organizations that need a starting point, such frameworks often provide good recommendations on implementing key security controls.

Second, executives like guidance such as frameworks to justify projects. Being able to map proposed projects to a well-known regulatory framework may provide justification that hesitant approval chains (that don't necessarily understand security) can follow.

How do you engage all the different units of an organization to maximize defense?

I believe one of the keys to engaging other units is to ensure there is continuous communication and relationship building. If you wait until you urgently need something from a team to first engage them, you are far less likely to have smooth interactions and willingness to assist than if you've got a pre-established relationship. Start building relationships with all units ASAP, regardless of whether you need their assistance right now or not. I've also seen the benefits of allowing cross-training.

In my current job, I've been given the opportunity to cross-train with multiple teams, and I feel that it has had a positive influence on the organization as a whole because I have the perspective of others instead of just my team's.

What recommendations do you have for managing nontechnical executives' expectations during a significant ongoing incident?

Establish expectations and communication protocols prior to incidents. The heat of an incident, with the stress facing all involved, makes communication so much more challenging. It's important to pre-establish how nontechnical executives will remain updated before the chaos starts. This means agreeing on how often the executives should expect updates and ensuring they understand that outside those update periods, the team's priority needs to be on working the incident without distraction.

Also, understanding what the executives expect from the updates, format, and content. This will make it easier for staff to efficiently prepare updates instead of an extensive back-and-forth trying to provide that content.

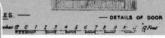

"Anyone who's actively working to keep networks safe from malicious actors qualifies as blue team in my book."

Twitter: @0xBanana • **Website:** 0xbanana.com

Jason Schorr

44 Jason Schorr has served as an information security professional for some of the largest technical companies in the world where he used his knowledge and experience to strengthen their security posture and minimize risk. He currently serves as chief operating officer for Spyglass Security. Most recently acting as project lead, he helped develop Data Drifter, a tool to analyze the contents of insecure cloud storage buckets. He lives in New York City with an amazing partner and their two beautiful girls.

How do you define a blue team?

We are all the defenders of the realm. Anyone who's actively working to keep networks safe from malicious actors qualifies as blue team in my book.

We as security practitioners see security from different viewpoints. It would be a shame to discount someone else or their experience because they "do something different," aren't "eyes on glass," or aren't "on the front lines." This does not mean they don't bring value to the table.

We can learn from each other; through that communal learning, we all become stronger.

How can blue teamers learn, practice, and grow?

There are so many skills needed for a well-rounded blue team practitioner. Since we live in a golden age for personal computing, every blue team practitioner needs their own personal lab. It doesn't have to be big, expensive, physical, or even persistent to be effective and provide an abundance of educational value.

Cloud computing costs are at an all-time low. You can spin up any configuration of systems and services and pay only for the time and resources you use. Single-board computing miniaturizes your lab and puts it in your pocket.

The most important needs for any practitioner? Motivation and dedication to learning.

> The most important needs for any practitioner? Motivation and dedication to learning.

What are some core metrics that a blue team can use to build, measure, and maintain a successful information security program?

Metrics play a key role in any security program, especially since we cannot improve what we do not measure. Quality metrics give us insights into how our organization is performing and can highlight key deficiencies.

Metrics focused around the state of the network are paramount to understanding attack surface, identifying potential footholds, and determining the overall health of systems and networks.

Some helpful metrics to collect about your security program's vulnerability management include the following:

- **Network and service coverage:** Don't assume vulnerability scans fully cover every system and service on the network. Full coverage depends on up-to-date asset inventories and usually authentication credentials to get detailed service information.

- **Vulnerability dwell time:** How long does a vulnerability exist before it is patched? The longer the dwell, the greater the organizational risk. When dealing with vulnerabilities in business-critical applications and servers, the impact is bigger and the more important this metric becomes.
- **Time to patch:** Once a patch for a security vulnerability is released from a vendor, how long does it take your organization to apply these updates to your assets before they're exploited by attackers?

Where would you start if you were the only information security staff member at a small to medium-sized business with a primitive security infrastructure?

The foundation of any good security program is good visibility. You can't defend what you can't see and don't know about. The first thing I would do is build an asset list, which is an enriched list of every piece of technology and software owned and operated by the business.

- Yes, this will take time.
- Yes, this will be a living document.
- Yes, this will be frustrating.
- Yes, this will be worth it.

Once you know the details about what you're defending, you can start planning the best ways of defending it.

What is the most bang-for-your-buck security control?

Host-based firewalls are the best bang-for-your-security-buck control.

Host-based firewalls are the best bang-for-your-security-buck control. Every modern operating system has one built in and can be configured before mass deployment.

If we cannot create a perimeter around our entire network, we must bring the perimeter down to individual network items. Some folks call this a *zero-trust* model.

Limiting ingress and egress network traffic will mitigate the majority of attacks from bad actors. In the event a compromise occurs, the chances of further exploitation, data exfiltration, or internal network propagation will be drastically reduced.

How do you approach data governance and other methods of reducing your data footprint?

First, take a big look at all your accounts, apps, devices, services, subscriptions, etc., and try to classify them in big buckets like "personal," "school," "work"—or whatever works best for you.

Now, start deleting those unused accounts, not just by removing an app (do this too) but by finding the "delete account" option buried under all that UI. Unsubscribe from unwanted and unused subscription services. Spend an afternoon cleaning up the files on your computer and properly backing them up.

Reducing our footprint depends on knowing what we have out there; once we have that, we can begin assessing specific risks and then work to minimize the impacts if something were to go wrong.

What is your opinion on compliance?

Compliance is a wonderful way to get companies to do the absolute barest minimum when it comes to securing their networks and keeping data safe.

What strategies do you use to communicate the threats you encounter to nontechnical decision-makers?

To communicate technical threats to nontechnical decision-makers, I begin the same way I would with anyone: by first working to understand their current perceptions. Security is a key part of every enterprise and organization, and while how we view security may be different, our desired end goal is the same: operational and business success.

> Security is a key part of every enterprise and organization, and while how we view security may be different, our desired end goal is the same: operational and business success.

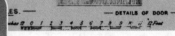

> "Often, the blue team is responsible for identifying risks, vulnerabilities, and threats, and for leading incident response or risk mitigation activities."

Twitter: @chrissistrunk • **Website:** www.linkedin.com/in/chrissistrunk

Chris Sistrunk

45

Chris Sistrunk is the technical manager on the Mandiant ICS/OT security consulting team at FireEye, focusing on protecting critical infrastructure. Before FireEye, Sistrunk was a senior engineer at Entergy, where he was a subject-matter expert for transmission and distribution SCADA systems.

Sistrunk was awarded Energy Sector Security Professional of the Year in 2014. He is a senior member of the IEEE and is a registered professional engineer in Louisiana. He founded BSidesJackson, cofounded the BEER-ISAC, and helped organize the ICS Village at DEF CON 22. He holds a BS in electrical engineering and an MS in engineering and technology management from Louisiana Tech University.

How do you define a blue team?

A blue team, simply put, is a group of people tasked with proactively defending/protecting a system or network from threats. Often, the blue team is responsible for identifying risks, vulnerabilities, and threats, and for leading incident response or risk mitigation activities.

What are two core capabilities that a blue team should have?

People and tools.

The people must have that curious mindset that seeks to find the unexpected. Also, blue teamers must be able to use, enhance, or create detection and response tools to find the unexpected. . .or more importantly. . .the threats.

What are some of the key strengths of an incident response program?

A strong incident response program includes the following:

- Key stakeholders from each part of the organization, critical third parties, vendors, etc.
- Mission and vision statement and who is responsible
- Core team with their responsibilities
- Tools (whether they are purchased or home-grown, tools are a must for data collection/review, forensics analysis, and rapidly detecting new threats)
- Visibility with logs and sensors
- Playbook for different types of threats (practice the plays annually)
- Industrial control systems/operational technology (with a unified plan that covers both IT and OT)
- Incident response metrics so that you can improve

Knowledge is the most powerful tool to operate and defend your system. Use that knowledge as an advantage over any threats.

These are awesome detailed references for incident response programs:

- **NIST Special Publication 800-61 Revision 2:** nvlpubs.nist.gov/nistpubs/SpecialPublications/NIST .SP.800-61r2.pdf
- **NIST Special Publication 800-82 Revision 2, Section 6.2.8 Incident Response:** nvlpubs.nist.gov/ nistpubs/SpecialPublications/NIST.SP.800-82r2.pdf

How can blue teamers learn, practice, and grow?
First is to learn by doing. Work with your blue team teammates on the key tasks.

Second is to get external training by going to conferences with a blue team track, watching videos on the Internet, or attending paid professional training courses.

Practicing is important, which goes back to on-the-job learning and tabletop exercises. Also, you can hone your skills with blue team challenges (capture the flags). Many are free! A great way to grow is to share what you've learned with your peers at work or by presenting at a conference, writing a blog, or releasing tools (privately or publicly).

How do you reward good blue teaming work?
If you're in a position of leadership, reward your blue team members by communicating their importance to key management.

Send them to advanced training or a conference they wanted to attend. Or take the team out for a dinner or some kind of team fun.

What are some core metrics that a blue team can use to build, measure, and maintain a successful information security program?
Like the saying goes, you can't manage what you don't measure. Showing on paper where your strengths and weaknesses are can guide you on head count, budget, and technology deployment decisions.

There are several good blogs and white papers for security operations center (SOC) staffing as well.

Here are some IR metrics references:

- **NIST SP-800-61 Rev2, Section 3.4.2, "Using Collected Incident Data":** nvlpubs.nist.gov/nistpubs/ SpecialPublications/NIST.SP.800-61r2.pdf
- **Mandiant's "Using Metrics to Mature Incident Response Capabilities":** www.nist.gov/system/files/ documents/2016/09/16/mandiant_rfi_response.pdf
- **SANS' "Common and Best Practices for Security Operations Centers":** www.sans.org/media/analyst- program/common-practices-security-operations-centers- results-2019-soc-survey-39060.pdf

Where would you start if you were the only information security staff member at a small to medium-sized business with a primitive security infrastructure?

I would start making backups of every critical system and then eventually every system. I would also make sure that anti-malware/antivirus is active with updated signatures.

As for building a secure network from the ground up, use a risk-based approach to security starting with asset inventory. You must know what you have, especially the most critical systems, to be able to protect what the business needs to operate.

What is the most bang-for-your-buck security control?

There are so many, but perhaps with the rise in destructive malware (ransomware and wipers) the best control could be up-to-date, working backups. The best way to prevent account compromise is multifactor authentication.

> The best way to prevent account compromise is multi-factor authentication.

For ICS, strong network segmentation/isolation is hard to do sometimes but very effective.

Has your organization implemented any deception technologies?

I am not sure about my organization, but I suppose honeypots and fake network segments are examples.

Where should an organization use cryptography?

An organization should use cryptography to keep the most sensitive or vulnerable data protected (things like customer/personal data, payment data, proprietary data, and backups of those data).

Also, laptops, smart devices (phones and tablets), and other mobile devices that can be lost/stolen should have encrypted disks. Protocols that go to the Internet or across network boundaries should be encrypted as well (such as VPNs, HTTPS, SFTP, etc.).

How do you approach data governance and other methods of reducing your data footprint?

I think data governance has its place in companies with sensitive data. Measuring compliance by frequent enough audits will help show how effective the governance policies and procedures are working.

What is your opinion on compliance?

It has been said that "compliance does not equal security." However, compliance can help an organization be better at security basics.

For instance, there is a marked difference in ICS security between power utilities having to meet NERC-CIP compliance than those companies/utilities with ICS where NERC-CIP does not apply.

Is there a framework that aligns the activities or functions performed by the blue team with regulatory compliance requirements?

Alternately, security does not equal compliance. I believe that the blue team should be out in front of compliance require-ments, because attackers and threats don't care if you're compliant or not.

With that said, it should be fairly easy for the blue team to show baselines and other things that compliance audits ask for.

How do you engage all the different units of an organization to maximize defense?

Operators and engineers aren't stupid; they just weren't taught cybersecurity in their training. Vice versa, IT folks should listen to the engineers.

With regard to compa-nies that have IT and ICS, I've been telling IT folks for many years to bring a box of donuts (or kolaches if in Texas) down to the plant operators or engineers to learn their pain points.

Then the IT folks will need to listen. Operators and engineers aren't stupid; they just weren't taught cybersecurity in their training. Vice versa, IT folks should listen to the engineers.

There's a reason they can't upgrade to Windows 10 tomorrow; maybe the vendor didn't support it when they bought it, or maybe it's because they have to wait to patch or upgrade only during an annual plant maintenance outage.

What strategies do you use to communicate the threats you encounter to nontechnical decision-makers?

Keep it simple, stupid (KISS). Executives may not understand MS08-067 or ETERNALBLUE, but they understand money and risk. "If we can't get XYZ$$$ security budget for this year, we may not be able to make _____ product anymore because our cyber risk is too high."

Do your homework. Dig up the evidence and build your case. Translate the security gaps into a strategy they understand. Don't be afraid to use a valid recent example to drive the point home.

Lastly, don't use fear, uncertainty, and doubt (FUD) as they will likely see through that.

What recommendations do you have for managing nontechnical executives' expectations during a significant ongoing incident?

The lead IR manager should have a daily executive summary prepared. It should contain the following:

- Business operations impacts (including which part of the core business functions are affected)
- Some details about the attack vector (stating how they got in; if that's not known, show the main tactics the attacker is using)
- Timeline (incident start, dwell time if known)
- Remediation (what has happened and the plan)
- Number of compromised systems and users
- Corporate communications updates (internal and external)
- Legal updates

> "Every employee has defensive responsibilities as part of their role, no matter what their main role might be. This means from the CEO to the mail room."

Twitter: @jaysonstreet • **Website:** JaysonEStreet.com

Jayson E. Street

46

Jayson E. Street* is an author of the Dissecting the Hack series, the DEF CON Groups Global Ambassador, and the VP of InfoSec for SphereNY. He has also spoken at DEF CON, DerbyCon, GRRCon, and several other "CONs" and colleges on a variety of InfoSec subjects.

How do you define a blue team?

Blue team, I believe, means anyone working for the company in a position that involves specific defensive functions. I designate it that way because every employee has defensive responsibilities as part of their role, no matter what their main role might be. This means from the CEO to the mail room. However, blue team designates those in information security such as the SOC, network security, DFIR, etc.

---

* He was a highly carbonated speaker who has partaken of pizza from Beijing to Brazil. He does not expect anybody to still be reading this far, but if they are, please note he was chosen as one of *Time*'s Persons of the Year for 2006.

What are two core capabilities that a blue team should have?

A comprehensive incident response skillset and established procedure for reacting to a breach.

While blue teams should have creating a defensive perimeter to prevent compromise as a top priority, in this day and age they should also be prepared just as equally if and most likely when a breach occurs. To think fortifications are what ultimately is going to protect you is not just outdated but foolhardy! We need to understand that our perimeter defense's main function is to act like a fireproof safe. Every one of those safes come with a rating on how long they can withstand a fire before the insides burn. The more you pay, the longer the safe can withstand the heat before it fails. That is the way your defenses work. The more you pay and implement should mean the longer your perimeter can withstand an attack before they breach it. This time is the window you have to detect them before that occurs, like the safe withstands the fire, which gives you a window to put the fire out or rescue the safe.

Also, a well-thought-out perimeter, while it may not withstand a prolonged attack, could also make the attacker become noisier, in their attack, which could lead to discovery.

The second capability is having amicable relationships with all other departments and a communication channel that is open and conducive to collaboration between other departments, especially those that the blue team will directly rely on when a breach occurs. If your only contact with the networking department or any other department for that matter is during a breach or other issue, they need be involved or they will be less likely to report or interact before a breach is apparent. They need to feel comfortable approaching you before an incident occurs. If employees see information security only as the enforcement arm of management or in other negative connotations, then they will work on avoiding any interactions with the blue team even when it's to their benefit to communicate with them.

What are some of the key strengths of an incident response program?

- It should have well-thought-out scenarios that cover as many potential incidents as they can envision as well as keeping room in their program for unforeseen scenarios too.

- It should have a solid response structure where everyone in every department knows their role if activated during a breach.
- Complete buy-in from management is always imperative.
- A program that fully understands the business units and their functions and processes. They will need to be accounted for during any incident even if they are not essential during the incident.

How can blue teamers learn, practice, and grow?

Unfortunately, for a majority of blue teamers, finding ways to grow, learn, and practice are things they will have to achieve and strive for on their own. It is a shame that more companies don't properly invest in their employees through continual education. It usually falls to the employee to fight to get paid training or to find ways to learn while on the job. Luckily, in this community, there are quite a few resources available for those wanting to learn and practice and improve their skills.

Ways for a blue teamer to learn while on the job is to actually shadow others in other departments to see how their processes work; this also helps to make InfoSec more approachable so when an incident occurs, it will not be the first interaction that the employee has with the team. Also, play several different IR games that are available, such as Oh Noes! and Backdoors & Breaches, which are two team-building games that can make learning how to handle certain issues fun.

How do you reward good blue teaming work?

With recognition, most blue teamers understand that the better they do, the less they will be seen. In a movie that involved the CIA, I remember a phrase an actor said about their job: "Our successes are secret; our failures are public." It is almost the same with a good security program: The more adept you become at keeping things secure, the less you are seen. So, it is a major thing when management recognizes the contribution the team makes to the overall company!

Another thing that some may say is the main way is simply by investing in your team through paying for continuing education such as certification training and allowing the team to attend conferences.

What are some core metrics that a blue team can use to build, measure, and maintain a successful information security program?

Metrics are vital for any successful program. All core metrics should be determined by every single team because each information security program must be tailored specifically to the company and assets they are protecting.

A few that I would recommend that should fit into any program would be first asset tracking of any device with an IP address that is connected to the network. It should be recorded when it is first added and when it is taken off of it. A patch management should have a metrics tracking component to it as well. Several generic metrics would be firewall changes, IDS/IPS alerts, proxy changes, unusual activity investigations, and the results of them.

Where would you start if you were the only information security staff member at a small to medium-sized business with a primitive security infrastructure?

Find out what you're protecting. First and foremost, you can't protect what you don't know exists. In a smaller company, it should be even easier to manage.

Also, realize that assets are only part of it. You need to know what makes your company profitable. What would negatively impact your company during a breach? Those are some questions that need to be asked as soon as possible.

Additionally, the ability to monitor inbound/outbound traffic is a foundational element in building a secure network from the ground up. It's hard to respond/contain a breach if you're not aware it is occurring. So, many current attacks depend on the internal source of the compromise to call out to the attacker to download the rest of the malicious payload or to connect to the command-and-control server. Instead of just monitoring the perimeter for suspicious inbound traffic, I believe at the least, equal time/resources should be spent monitoring internal activity and traffic.

What is the most bang-for-your-buck security control?

An educated workforce that fully understands and accepts their responsibility that an important role of their job also includes owning their part of keeping the company's assets secure.

Where should an organization use cryptography?

In all seriousness, everywhere it is possible that does not hinder the business model or negatively impact the overall budget of the InfoSec and networking teams. There is always a trade-off to have encryption, be it cost, speed, or manageability. Every individual should make their own informed decision on where and when it should be used. At the least, I highly recommend it for secure communications and every device hard drive that it is viable to implement on.

What is your opinion on compliance?

My opinion starts out with one relevant observation. It seems to me that every company I have seen in the news for being breached was "PCI compliant." I find that odd that everyone seems to be compliant until they aren't. It's a case of Schrodinger's security program! Instead of a company striving to be compliant so they can pass certifications or regulations, maybe we should strive to be secure and with the success of that realize that compliance and regulations will be one of the byproducts of it!

Is there a framework that aligns the activities or functions performed by the blue team with regulatory compliance requirements?

I don't believe a framework is best in this capacity. Though if a framework is necessary, it should be the one your team created specifically for your business model while taking into account your threat model. After those factors are taken into account, then compliance should be factored in. Otherwise, you will end up creating a mashup of different parts of frameworks that you think will work best for your company when a more complete and comprehensive one could have been created internally.

How do you engage all the different units of an organization to maximize defense?

From the first day of orientation, *every* employee should be introduced and educated in their responsibilities as it pertains to information security. That should be also constantly reinforced throughout the year. This is achieved via a comprehensive security awareness program. If they don't feel that security is part of their responsibility or something that won't impact their employment in a negative way, then you really don't have a security program! You have a lot of best intentions! It's like having bought a parachute from a person on the corner and then using it without inspecting it. Yeah, it might work fine, but the other person involved in your plans doesn't really have any issues no matter if it works or not!

What strategies do you use to communicate the threats you encounter to nontechnical decision-makers?

Very simply, by talking like I'm trying to educate someone wanting to learn, not trying to impress or intimidate them to get what I know I need! These people are not idiots; they are just uninformed, and it is part of your responsibilities to make sure they are fully informed and educated on the risk and implications plus the possible ramifications on what responses are taken. You need to explain using the least amount of technical jargon possible, and every single term you do use should be immediately followed by the layperson's definition of it. If an executive doesn't fully understand the risk they are facing, then they may not feel comfortable taking the proper actions to remedy the situation.

What recommendations do you have for managing nontechnical executives' expectations during a significant ongoing incident?

Establish a trusted relationship with the entire management structure of the company before any incident has occurred. Involve management in security awareness training and understand their roles in keeping the company secure. Deliver the metrics you are collecting at least on a monthly basis and make sure they understand what they mean. You will create a trust with them that pays dividends when an incident occurs. You will not have to manage their expectations because they will already know your capabilities and have faith that you are doing what is required. They will expect you to inform them what is occurring and what is needed from them. They will trust you to provide in a way they understand so they can make informed decisions.

> "A blue team is responsible for what's going on over the wire and on endpoints *now*."

Twitter: @mtanji • **Website:** www.linkedin.com/in/mtanji

Michael Tanji

47

Michael has spent nearly 30 years in a wide variety of roles in the computer security and intelligence fields. He has held front-line, managerial, and executive roles in the military, government, and commercial markets. Michael has cofounded, held C-level roles, or played a significant role in the formation and operation of multiple security startups, and he has been exceedingly lucky in that he's won more than he's lost.

How do you define a blue team?

Real-time defensive operations, secure coding, security engineering, policy. . .all that's great and important, but in each of those spaces they have the benefit of time, or at least the benefit of *some* time. A blue team doesn't have that luxury. A blue team is responsible for what's going on over the wire and on endpoints *now*. There is no pause button; there is no asking for an extension of a deadline.

What are two core capabilities that a blue team should have?

Awareness and curiosity. You have to know what you're trying to defend and protect. Everything else starts with that. What's the point of investing in security technology or services if you don't know what it's supposed to be focused on?

Curiosity is something that the people on the team need to have. It is an essential trait that anyone in any security role—defense or offense—needs to have. Without a sense of curiosity and its cousin tenacity, you're just staring at screens waiting for something to happen, which of course is the exact opposite of what you should be doing.

> Curiosity is something that the people on the team need to have.

What are some of the key strengths of an incident response program?

A good IR program needs to be clearly understood and work-able by everyone who will be called upon to participate in the corresponding activities. If you draw on staff outside of security (as you should), roles and responsibilities need to be well defined, and the language used should be unambiguous to all parties.

All of this needs to be tested regularly so that kinks can be worked out and people have a sense of what it's going to be like when the real thing happens (the real thing is rarely like an exercise, but some practice beats no practice). An after-action report should be developed after every real incident so that new developments or unforeseen issues can be addressed and incorporated into the program. A good IR program is the definition of a living document.

How can blue teamers learn, practice, and grow?

- **Read:** Read like your job depends on it. Read as diverse a set of content as you can. It won't take long for you to figure out what the most reliable and timely sources are for security-related content. Once you've got that sorted, start looking for input from sources of business content or what-ever industry you're in. Develop a working knowledge of the organization you're supporting and how they do business. Pick up a history book. *The Lessons of History* by the Durants is a quick, high-level read that can get you started.

The Cuckoo's Egg by Stoll is a short course in the history of our field; it's as current and accurate today as when it was written in the mid-1980s.

- **Train:** If you don't have a training budget, take advantage of free resources like Cybrary (www.cybrary.it). A whole lot of vendors and service providers make free or limited-capability versions of their tools available. Use them to get familiar with new technologies and methodologies. You may not get to use them in your current position, but it can only enhance your understanding and prepare you for what comes next.
- **Write:** None of us is Shakespeare, but the exercise of writing about your issues, your victories, and your discoveries (with permission if necessary) does two things: It helps you focus your thoughts (clarity is key), and it opens up lines of communication between others in the space. Someone somewhere has had the same problem you do and has an answer. Someone else needs to know they are not alone dealing with these issues. Engage with others and become part of the community. This is not a function of trying to become "the famous so and so" or the dreaded cybersecurity "rock star." It's equal parts learning and giving back.

How do you reward good blue teaming work?

Well, we're assuming a lot if we think that the organization has established clear and achievable goals and measures of success for the blue team, along with a reward system and career path. I don't know too many outfits that have done that. The mission is too often "stop evil **** from happening," which is why so many blue teams are considered wastes, cost centers, and having come up short. But if we assume good metrics have been established and those metrics are met, the best thing you can do is an after-action report of what went on during the evaluation period or incident and identify those things that would have made things go better/faster and invest in that. Show those who are protecting you that you care, that you value what they do, and that you respect their efforts and want to

> Show those who are protecting you that you care, that you value what they do, and that you respect their efforts and want to provide them with the tools they need to do better.

provide them with the tools they need to do better. Executives will bend over backward to get the latest and best tools for finance, marketing, etc., but for some reason security is expected to pull miracles from thin air.

What are some core metrics that a blue team can use to build, measure, and maintain a successful information security program?

Every industry or organization is going to have different specific things that they care about, but there are a few metrics that I'd consider "universal." Speed is one. How much faster can you detect malicious activity now versus when you started? How quickly can you get an impacted box back into operation? In the face of a novel situation, how quickly can you assemble the right people and make a decision?

Another is influence. Are you rarely talking to executives, or are you a CISO where the *C* actually means something? Your ability to communicate at the right levels in order to get things done is as important as any technology.

I don't know how to describe this beyond the word *communication*. Is security talked about as often as operations or finance or the supply chain? When the rank and file have questions, do they freely and readily come to you? When they accidentally do something wrong, do they come to you? You don't see a lot of communication in organizations where security is viewed as a police function and response a form of punishment.

Where would you start if you were the only information security staff member at a small to medium-sized business with a primitive security infrastructure?

It all goes back to awareness. What am I responsible for? What am I protecting? From that base all things grow. From that base I know what I've got, including what native capabilities I have (e.g., all OSs are recent and have FDE capabilities) and what critical issues I have (e.g., 90 percent of the OSs are past end-of-life). When you know what you have, you know what you lack, and you can communicate those shortcomings and your plan for remedying them to echelons above. You can back up your request with data. That's 50 percent of it.

> You can back up your request with data. That's 50 percent of it.

The other 50 percent is a frank and open discussion with the CEO about how they really feel about security and what they expect from you. You are getting nothing done without their full and public support. There is what they have to say for optics, and there is what they do in order to achieve their goals. You have to be aligned with the latter if you're going to succeed. This inevitably means compromise on your part. You have to be okay with imperfection because nobody *wants* security; they're *obliged* to have it for myriad reasons.

What is the most bang-for-your-buck security control?

2FA. It is increasingly available and increasingly free. Done properly and comprehensively, it takes a whole class of attacks off the table. There is a contingent that loves to point out the shortcomings of 2FA, particularly over SMS, but something is still better than nothing, and the theorized threat model of most of those saying "2FA is broken" isn't the threat model of most of the rest of the computer-using world.

Has your organization implemented any deception technologies?

As a former intelligence officer, I have particularly strong opinions about the co-opting of terms like *deception* in the cybersecurity realm. To me, a deception operation means something very specific, and simulated fake endpoints acting as triggers don't quite make the cut. That and elaborate deception schemes feed into this pernicious drive in some quarters to get customers to pay for people's spy-versus-spy fantasies. I understand the arguments, but I've yet to run into a client who wanted to extend pwnage because they wanted to develop a deep understanding of threat actors. People want to get back to work.

Now, the effectiveness of deception methodology is hard to dispute. Go back to Cliff Stoll and *The Cuckoo's Egg*, and you see how powerful such efforts can be. I prefer deception efforts to function as an "early warning" mechanism. A lot of people start with a good idea like a sensor and then try to be all things to all men. I mean, who doesn't need another pane of glass to look at? Warning that evil is present should be sufficient. If you have a deception tool, you've got other tools that can help; you don't need yet another.

Where should an organization use cryptography?

I'm not entirely sure most organizations should get too heavily invested in cryptography. I know math nerds reading this are getting out their torches and pitchforks, but hear me out. If you, as an organization, don't know where all your data is, who controls it, and who has access to it, getting on the crypto bandwagon is probably the last thing you should do.

> If you, as an organization, don't know where all your data is, who controls it, and who has access to it, getting on the crypto bandwagon is probably the last thing you should do.

If you want to do crypto, do your homework first. The best-case scenario is that your data resides in or with someone who actually understands crypto and how to implement it and they've got the baton. Let them run with it because they can afford the specific nerds required to do crypto right; you probably cannot.

Having said that, everyone ought to understand what native crypto capabilities are available to them via various means and implement them. Just HTTPS already.

How do you approach data governance and other methods of reducing your data footprint?

We really need to break ourselves of the notion that because we can store everything we should. I remember my first 100 MB hard drive; it was expensive as hell, and I thought I'd never need another.

> I'm not going to belabor the hazards of ransomware, but data-nappers can't lock up what doesn't exist.

Today we think nothing of storing all the music, all the movies, all the books, and all the pictures because storage is beyond cheap and plentiful. But all that data is a risk. I'm not going to belabor the hazards of ransomware, but data-nappers can't lock up what doesn't exist. It is more grunt work, but it is essential in this day and age. Where is your data? Who controls it? Who has access to it? How do you determine what to keep and what you can delete? How often and how comprehensively do you back it up? Where do you keep those backups? It's grunt work, but it's vital if you ever hope to exercise some level of control.

What is your opinion on compliance?

Compliance gets a bad rap because too many people conflate compliance with security. Compliance establishes where you're at relative to a standard. If you're starting from zero and go through a compliance exercise—even if you're noncompliant in many ways (or all the ways)—you're in better shape than where you were before because you know where you stand. Decision-makers need to understand, though, that security is a continuous process, not a binary state. Compliance is basically "showing up." If you want to succeed, you've got to do more.

Is there a framework that aligns the activities or functions performed by the blue team with regulatory compliance requirements?

Off the top of my head I'm not sure this is a thing in any formal or widely accepted form. It would probably not be too much heavy lifting to do a crosswalk between something like NIST or CIS and map it to something like HIPPA and so on, depending on the standards that apply to your business. I'd be willing to bet more than one person has done this internally to their own firm; it's a matter of getting them to share.

How do you engage all the different units of an organization to maximize defense?

Everything starts with the CEO. Your plans for organizational defense have to be explained, the purpose and value have to be clear, and you need their affirmative acknowledgment that they agree, approve, and want it to happen. They need to personally communicate that message to his executive team and the workforce. With that backing, you will have the support you need to get everyone on board with efforts to move forward. This is not to say there will not be pushback, because inevitably what you want to do is going to run smack-dab into the face of how the company makes money, but you'll get engagement, which is more than half the battle.

What strategies do you use to communicate the threats you encounter to nontechnical decision-makers?

You have to use the vocabulary of your audience and understand what they care about. This is why I say you need to read so much and understand who you're working for. You have to demonstrate what I call "domain respect" because they are not going to bother to understand security. Read a malware report from any AV vendor; most say "may result in the execution of arbitrary code." What does that mean to someone who bends metal for a living? Manages a fleet of trucks? Tracks the productivity of 100 people on an assembly line? "May allow someone to interrupt your ability to make money" is a crude example of how to do it better, but you get the gist.

I used to run the warning system the DOD used to alert military commands, and most of the rest of the government, to cyberthreats from nation-states and nonstate actors. The warning business has its own vocabulary, as does the CNO business, so to a degree there was little we could do to adjust our message without being noncompliant with the established methodology (yeah, bureaucracy!). But you could almost always find an analog between disciplines that would make things more understandable to a wider audience. You could also include comments or supplementary input that would expound upon the mandatory so that you could make your points relevant to the audience.

What recommendations do you have for managing nontechnical executives' expectations during a significant ongoing incident?

The ideal situation is that you've developed and promulgated policies and procedures related to security in general and incidents in particular before an incident, and you've had a chance to practice at least once. If you're not dealing with an ideal situation, then do two things: Embed people from the rest of the organization in the response team (some organizations call this a CSIRT). Let them be the liaisons to other parts of the business.

The second thing is to make expectations clear from the get-go: You have a process, you're going to follow that process to the best of your ability, and it includes touchpoints and opportunities to communicate the state of things. Trust that we know what we're doing and will keep you informed. You standing over our shoulders is not going to help; it will in fact hinder us and prolong the pain. The delivery of this message by the CEO would be supremely helpful.

"The unsung heroes of blue teams are the engineering departments that spend countless hours trouble-shooting and installing network appliances and testing security logging, not to mention ruined holidays when a critical security appliance goes down to ensure 99.9 percent uptime for responders."

Twitter: @iHeartMalware • **Website:** www.linkedin.com/in/ronnietokazowski

Ronnie Tokazowski

48 Ronnie Tokazowski, aka iHeartMalware, is a senior threat researcher with Agari who specializes in BEC intelligence. Ronnie also has experience reverse engineering APT malware and finds enjoyment by messing with threat actors.

How do you define a blue team?

When asked about what the definition of what a blue teamer is, the first role that comes to mind is incident response. While this is partially true that a blue teamer is an incident responder, there are a lot of other moving parts behind the scenes. The unsung heroes of blue teams are the engineering departments that spend countless hours troubleshooting and installing network appliances and testing security logging, not to mention ruined holidays when a critical security appliance goes down to ensure 99.9 percent uptime for responders.

A blue team is all of these things working together as one, with responders analyzing the logs and data to protect the company, while providing intelligence and feedback to engineering teams to help mitigate the threats. While one can exist without the other, knowing and mitigating the known threat helps everyone to succeed.

What are two core capabilities that a blue team should have?

The two core capabilities that I look for in a blue teamer aren't technical, like some may think. The two most important capabilities are having a positive attitude and being eager and willing to learn. Hacks constantly evolve with new techniques to bypass protections, and as a defender, you need to understand this and be able to quickly adapt.

When things do hit the fan, it's important to keep a level head and a positive attitude, as you are better equipped to articulate needs and details during an incident. Everyone needs to work together, because at the end of the day you're fighting the same fight. Leave that toxicity at the door, because it will only make a stressful situation 10 times worse.

Becoming a blue teamer isn't something to be taken lightly, as you are forever chasing moving targets. Throughout your career, you're going to see real zero-day exploits, think outside the box to create mitigations with security tools when budgets are tight, and find yourself in situations where you're learning some niche technology that you don't like, because it was purchased years before. An education in information security can get you there, but it doesn't really hit home until you're 2 weeks and 1,000 compromised devices into an incident with a CEO breathing down your neck, asking "Why isn't this fixed yet? This is costing the company X thousands of dollars per hour in downtime."

What are some of the key strengths of an incident response program?

Documentation, documentation, documentation. Without having processes and procedures written down, steps get missed to human error, and these mistakes always happen at the worst possible moments. By having the documentation written, processes become repeatable, and you can train junior analysts.

How can blue teamers learn, practice, and grow?

One of the best ways that blue teamers can grow, practice, and learn is to collaborate with each other! Security conferences can be a great way to find individuals who are working in your field, and that doesn't mean you have to go to DEF CON. There are plenty of smaller/local meetups, so find one in your area, get off your computer, and go talk to people!

Another thing that will help you learn is to pick up a scripting language, as this will help you automate repetitive tasks to focus on the more important ones. If you run the same five commands on the terminal, throw it into a Python script. You may only save yourself two minutes every time that script runs, but that two minutes saved multiple times a day across a team of 20 analysts equates to a ton of time saved over a year. Seriously, script the repetitive tasks out.

How do you reward good blue teaming work?

Growing up in North Carolina, the answer to a multitude of problems is simple: chatting over food. While it may seem small, something like ordering pizzas to the office to talk over lunch goes a long way for team building, especially when multiple teams are involved. For rewarding blue teamers, offering training in an area that *they* are interested in (not necessarily what *you* want them to take) goes a long way, too. People obviously like more money, but this can be a double-edged sword when a team is struggling to work together. Ensuring that employees are happy goes a long way for the health and productivity of the team.

What are some core metrics that a blue team can use to build, measure, and maintain a successful information security program?

When it comes to metrics, ask leadership what type of information they want. Do they want to know how many incidents happened, how much money was saved, or how much money was lost during an incident? Provide it. If some questions aren't able to be answered, try to get as close to the question as possible so leadership has visibility into how the security program is operating. Not only does providing the information up front help build trust, but it also helps show supporting evidence when head count needs to be increased.

What is your opinion on compliance?

When it comes to compliance, this can be a double-edged sword. For organizations that are starting to take security seriously, it helps give a good benchmark on where to start. The problem is that some organizations see compliance and security as a checkbox, and if all those boxes are checked, the company must be secure. This is the incorrect approach, as hackers constantly evolve to bypass these protections.

Security and compliance should be a race to ensuring that devices are protected, not just a simple checkbox because you need it for a contract.

What strategies do you use to communicate the threats you encounter to nontechnical decision-makers?

As a hacker and reverse engineer, the hardest lesson I've had to learn over the years is to stop talking nerdy, unless your executives ask. Yes, that encryption algorithm that you spent 10 hours breaking on a Saturday night fueled by caffeine is cool, but at the end of the day you have to provide metrics, such as dollars saved, earned, or lost, and what it means in the context of business operations. To the business, blue teamers provide protection to the company to help mitigate the risks associated with cybersecurity events.

To articulate your needs, here's the secret formula. You need to mathematically explain why something is important, why it needs to be done, what risks will be mitigated, and what the costs with each step will be. If the protections are able to offset the costs of the threat, making the business justification is pretty straightforward. If you're able to save the business money, that's an even bigger win! But make sure you have trackable metrics to support your claims, because if you can't back up what you're saying, your request will probably be denied.

Or to reword this for the techy crowd reading this: "Provide metrics and hashes or it won't happen."

What recommendations do you have for managing nontechnical executives' expectations during a significant ongoing incident?

First, incidents are stressful for everyone, and providing timely updates to management and key decision-makers is extremely important. By providing constant updates, the spread of rumors is limited, depending on the sensitivity around the incident.

In some cases, an incident can span days or even weeks, depending on how widespread the problem is. In cases like this, provide daily metrics and updates, and keep details to the facts (not speculations) about an incident. If you have to provide detail and theories about an incident, make it clear beyond a reasonable doubt that it's a theory that can change at a later date. It's okay to say that you don't know something, but it's usually a good idea to provide a time frame on when the question might be answered.

"The blue team defends the organization's networks, endpoints, data, and all digital assets against cyber threats."

Twitter: @ashleytolb • **Website:** www.linkedin.com/in/ashleytolbert

Ashley Tolbert

49

Ashley is currently a senior security engineer at Netflix focusing on crisis management and incident response; she has also worked for the Department of Energy and Stanford University Linear Accelerator Center (SLAC). Her diverse background includes researching compromises of electrical SMART grids at NASA's Jet Propulsion Lab. Ashley holds an MS in information security from Carnegie Mellon University and a BS in software engineering from Auburn University. She currently sits on the Board of Women in Security and Privacy (WISP). When not defending cyberspace, she's running outside, discovering new music like Afrobeats, or traveling to be inspired.

How do you define a blue team?

I define the blue team as the incident response and defense function at any organization—those responding to cyberattacks and cyber crisis. Many organizations customize their recipe of which "ingredients" are baked into their blue team; it could include a tier 1 SOC, detection team, networking team, threat intelligence, forensics, etc. Smaller organizations may have a subset or all functions baked into one team, while larger organizations are often large enough to staff these functions separately. The blue team defends the organization's networks, endpoints, data, and all digital assets against cyber threats. When not in defense, the blue team is practicing a response or play—much like a basketball team runs through a play—strengthening their technical armor and coordinated defense. Blue teamers are constantly in a state of training asking, "How do we reduce our time to resolve incidents? What skillsets, playbooks, or tools are needed to do so?"

What are two core capabilities that a blue team should have? What are some of the key strengths of an incident response program?

Two core capabilities that a blue team should have are the ability to do the following:

- Investigate and analyze incidents effectively, gathering any information resources relevant or needed
- Drive resolution for incidents efficiently

The following are key strengths that make these capabilities possible:

- **Having the right team with a complementary set of skills:** It's imperative that members of the blue team have unique skills that strengthen the team's overall defense against adversaries and attacks.
- **Predictability of process (i.e., having a complete and practiced incident response plan and playbook):** During an incident should not be the first time the blue team sees the incident response plan or playbooks. They should be practiced and fine-tuned regularly, leveraging tabletops and exercises. The plan should guide the team in identifying severity of the incident, isolating the attack, containing the attack, eradicating the incident cause, remediating, and doing any post-incident actions.
- **Having the right tooling and quick access to it:** Having access to tools or logs that prove valuable for incident analysis is imperative. These tools are often used to retrieve information such as NetFlow or authentication logs for investigations.

How can blue teamers learn, practice, and grow?

CTFs are an invaluable resource for learning, practicing, and growing blue team skills. Spending time red teaming is a great method to strengthen your attacker mindset; it allows you to deploy attack tactics that you will defend against. Books like *The Blue Teamer's Manual* and *Intelligence Drive Incident Response* are practical resources that I keep handy. Start digging into system hardening. Windows or Linux are great starters. Utilize MITRE ATT&CK to catch up on common adversary tactics and techniques; then, review the DeTT&CT framework to learn how a blue team would defend against such attacks such as reading and compare data log source quality, visibility coverage, detection coverage, and threat actor behaviors.

Other skills to develop are analytical mindset and familiarity with response. For developing an analytical mindset, *Psychology of Intelligence Analysis* is a book often recommended to blue teamers. It covers concepts such as memory, biases, and how we humans often distort data with our biases. We come with our own assumptions, and it recommends mechanisms for seeing data purely and then analyzing with an unassuming mindset.

To familiarize oneself with response, I recommend studying crisis management and large accidents. Studying cases of large-scale incidents (both cyber and non-cyber-related) such as Stuxnet or the BP oil spill—and the handling thereof—tremendously improves your scope and variety of incident response knowledge. Studying crisis responders' actions, such as law enforcement during a crisis, can aid in understanding nuances in crisis response tone, communication strategy, and remediation actions. You may consider how these actions can be inserted into your program for improvement. Every organization is different and calls for a customized incident response program.Lastly, practice your incident response playbook over and over. Tabletop fun scenarios with your team and compare your response against your playbook.

> Every organization is different and calls for a customized incident response program.

**What are some core metrics that a blue team can use
to build, measure, and maintain a successful
information security program?**

Core metrics should be actionable and valuables—data that
drives continuous improvement. Measuring the mean time it
takes to assemble the incident response team and triage the
incident is a core metric. Measuring the average time the team
needs to resolve incidents is helping in measuring the team's
overall effectiveness. Other metrics such as incident trends—
are particular incident types increasing or decreasing in
occurrence?—are key indicators that post-incident hardening
may be lacking.

Cost per incident is valuable in knowing how much of the
company's costs are consumed by security incidents. This
cost may consist of both detection and response costs.
The number of false positive detections rendered for
response and the number of alerts reported by users versus
your detection system are telling in determining whether
your detection strategy and mechanisms are valuable.
Overwhelming false positives will erode the team's confidence
in alerts altogether and slow down response time. To be an
effective IR team, the team cannot waste time investigating
large volumes of alerts that are miniscule in impact or irrel-
evant. Another interesting metric is the amount of time
between a compromise occurrence and its discovery within
your ecosystem.

**Where would you start if you were the only
information security staff member at a small to
medium-sized business with a primitive security
infrastructure?**

If you're small to medium-sized, that means you're already
overseeing a number of endpoints that likely require some
hardening. I'd start with training your employees (people
security) on security awareness and the engineers on secure
coding. Patching and encrypting all endpoints, enforcing a
password policy, implementing an email security tool, enabling
multifactor authentication on critical data systems, enabling
logging/detecting via a security information and event management (SIEM) if possible, and ensuring valuable assets are behind

VPN all make up the security-from-the-ground-up starter packer for me. Next on the agenda are encrypting all sensitive data in transit in our ecosystem, implementing host-based intrusion detection systems, using a vulnerability scanner to check for unpatched systems and known vulnerabilities, and ensuring a business continuity plan is documented. Open source hardening and detection tools are a great resource for small businesses with limited funds.

What is the most bang-for-your-buck security control?

A firewall and an intrusion detection system. Once logging from both systems is ingested into a SIEM, logs from your network, from your web servers, from scanners, etc., can all be analyzed alongside firewall or IDS alerts and used for investigations.

Where should an organization use cryptography?

Organizations should encrypt or hash credentials stored in your ecosystem as well as sensitive, confidential, or financial data such as PI or PCI. Encrypting user desktops and laptops is essential. Your organization should be using an SSL certificate to encrypt data in transit on your site.

> Encrypting user desktops and laptops is essential.

How do you approach data governance and other methods of reducing your data footprint? What is your opinion on compliance?

Data governance is essential to cybersecurity. Here are some strong steps: classifying data types and associated risks with each data type, implementing access control and data manipulation guidelines based on risks, implementing data loss prevention software and data security controls, and considering a centralized data model.

Knowing the security classification of your data informs which security controls are needed. Understanding which data needs protecting is a key step to defending against threats. Data governance is the process that helps us to assign resources appropriately to the most at-risk data in our environment.

How do you engage all the different units of an organization to maximize defense?

Tabletops and general security awareness are two concepts that can bring together many different units of an organization to band together on defense. Tabletops assist in conveying shared security responsibility to multiple teams at once. Responding to a live-simulated security incident is a useful opportunity to remind other units of the value in putting security first, for all teams.

> Responding to a live-simulated security incident is a useful opportunity to remind other units of the value in putting security first, for all teams.

What strategies do you use to communicate the threats you encounter to nontechnical decision-makers?

As an incident commander, a goal during significant incidents is to relay information on the current status of an incident, its risk and severity level, and any organizational/operational impact to executive leaders as fast and regularly as possible. Different incidents call for varied notification needs. Significant incidents will always likely call for high-level executive updates. Relaying timely information that clearly states data or services at risk and what will be done to eradicate the cause of the incident, with an estimated time to resolve it, helps to manage and alleviate concerns.

To communicate threats to nontechnical decision-makers, I lean out of the technical impact of the threat and more into the data loss, value loss, financial loss, or legal liability of a threat as well as its projected operational impact, should it actualize. I try to relate threats to the specific function of decision-makers if possible. Learning how to analogize threat information and convey it in a way that highlights holistic risk across the company is helpful in driving alignment risk severity and residual risk.

> I try to relate threats to the specific function of decision-makers if possible.

"To me, a blue teamer is essentially an 'all-around defender,' a security professional who is versatile and possesses an arsenal of skills that are critical to protect an organization from a wide variety of threats."

Twitter: @aboutsecurity • **Website:** aboutsecurity.io

Ismael Valenzuela

50

Since he founded one of the first IT security consultancies in Spain, Ismael Valenzuela has participated as a security professional in numerous projects across the globe over the past 20 years. Prior to his current role as senior principal engineer at McAfee, Ismael led the delivery of SOC, IR, and forensics services for the Foundstone Services team within Intel globally.

Ismael is a SANS Certified Instructor and coauthor of the CyberDefense and Blue Team Operations course, SANS SEC530: Defensible Security Architecture, and holds many professional certifications, including the highly regarded GIAC Security Expert (GSE #132).

How do you define a blue team?

Let me start by defining what I picture in my head when I think of the blue teamer. To me, a blue teamer is essentially an "all-around defender," a security professional who is versatile and possesses an arsenal of skills that are critical to protect an organization from a wide variety of threats. Let's be honest, a lot of blue teams out there are composed of a great, single team of one (does it sound familiar?). That's one of the reasons why blue teaming is hard: It usually requires wearing many hats, as you are probably in charge of cloud security, endpoint security, network security, application security, and all things cyber.

The practice of blue teaming, therefore, includes not only the designing and building of defensible security architectures but also the ongoing operations, hardening, monitoring, and in many cases responding when these systems get compromised too. Does it sound like a lot? Well, it surely is, but that's why blue teaming is probably the most rewarding role you can take in this field. It represents the essence of why companies invest in information security capabilities; it is an essential function that allows organizations to manage risk and mitigate the impact of cyberattacks.

What are two core capabilities that a blue team should have?

Only two? Okay, challenge accepted.

I'd say the first one would be the ability to think red and act blue. Mitigating every risk is simply impossible; that's why one of the most important things that blue teams have to do is to learn to prioritize. Every single day you will have many more things that you can possibly do. So, as you start your day, should you invest your time on tuning these SIEM rules that are too noisy? Should you work on your new incident response collection script? Conduct a data discovery exercise to figure out who's keeping unauthorized records on their laptops? Or, would you rather go hunting for the newest and greatest APT on the network? How do you prioritize?

> Mitigating every risk is simply impossible; that's why one of the most important things that blue teams have to do is to learn to prioritize.

The answer requires you to think like an attacker (red) while acting like a defender (blue). For example, thinking red would mean asking, "What are the threats that are likely to cause an impact on my organization?" Acting blue, on the other side, will require an understanding of how the different layers of networks, infrastructure, applications, data, and business architectures deal with those threats, and knowing what are the technical and nontechnical countermeasures that will help you defend against them. Adopting this mindset will keep you on track and help you to concentrate on higher-value tasks.

The second would be the ability to balance a strategic and tactical vision. As a blue teamer, you'll find yourself down in the weeds many times: investigating a threat, parsing logs, carving artifacts out of memory, analyzing network traffic, or setting up a bunch of docker containers to rehearse an attacker's technique in a lab. But a good blue teamer realizes that security is probably not the core business of her organization. Therefore, they can also see the bigger picture, the strategic one, and can zoom in and zoom out depending on what is required or the hat they are wearing at that time. This skill is paramount and can be built over time by developing critical thinking and investigative skills that come from analyzing, hypothesizing, synthesizing, and reporting.

For example, when you see an evidence of an attacker's activities, you would analyze them by breaking down the activity into its different components to understand better how they behave. You would take your analysis a step further now by hypothesizing over the tools used and possibly even the motivation of the attacker, looking for evidence that would prove or disprove your hypothesis. Finally, you would report your findings, synthesizing what you found and reporting it in a way that would be understandable to the business and decision-makers. In many cases, you would be responsible for presenting these results too, so being able to speak this "strategic" language, the language of the business, would set you apart from those who can "only" speak bits and bytes (although speaking hex is still pretty cool, don't take me wrong).

What are some of the key strengths of an incident response program?

There is no doubt that one of the key strengths of an incident response program resides in the ability to "stop the bleeding." However, we have to realize that this is one of the six phases of IR only: *containment*. But how about the other five: preparation, identification, eradication, recovery, and lessons learned? Unfortunately, I still see many organizations that are constantly putting out fires, responding, containing, and eradicating incidents every single day while paying very little attention to why these incidents are happening in the first place.

This was the case with one of the customers I consulted for several years ago. With almost 100,000 systems supporting critical operations across one of the largest cities in the United States, they would spend many cycles dealing with repeated infections, reporting them on a weekly basis on different committees, documenting minutes of meetings, colleting metrics, and re-imaging boxes, but when I asked, "Has anybody done any analysis on *why* these machines got infected in the first place?" I got a "Well, we are not sure of that." It is like going to the doctor when you have been feeling sick for a while, only to get prescribed some drugs that will treat the symptom rather than looking at why you are sick in the first place or what the underlying problem is. Likewise, without strong root-cause analysis that stems from advanced IR capabilities such as intrusion analysis and digital forensics, organizations are doomed to continue getting sick, repeating the same mistakes that result in security breaches, over and over again.

How can blue teamers learn, practice, and grow?

I'm a big fan of home labs, as this is one of the cheapest and most effective ways of getting hands-on training without breaking things in production. I know playing with things in production can be more fun, but let's admit it, playing Russian roulette is not for everyone and can be a career-limiting move too.

I've been doing this for years, since early in my career, focusing on practicing those skills that I knew I was weaker on and implementing something that years later I learned was called *deliberate practice* (tim.blog/2016/10/06/the-art-and-science-of-learning-anything-faster/). For example, I remember taking Security 503 (www.sans.org/course/intrusion-detection-in-depth), a SANS class on network intrusion analysis, more than 12 years ago and thinking, "Wow, there's so much more I need to learn on traffic analysis and intrusion detection!"

So, I started rebuilding my home network in a way that would allow me to capture all the outbound traffic so I could practice all the cool tcpdump tricks I was learning (who doesn't love bit masking and BPF filters?), as well as practicing more with advanced Snort configurations and rules. My new interest on this field led me to introduce a network security monitoring (NSM) sensor in the environment I was working with back then.

When management saw the value coming out of this POC, I was allowed to deploy a larger network of sensors, and in no time, I was able to have full visibility and advanced detection capabilities across all the organization. My new hobby at home turned into an opportunity for career growth at work. Who knew that years later I would end up teaching this same class on traffic analysis to hundreds of students?

Home labs are fun, and today's virtualization technologies make it easier and cheaper than ever, so make good use of that. Build your security systems from scratch, learn the inner workings of the operating systems, harden them, break them, analyze the logs, capture and analyze traffic, experiment with Docker containers, and share your experiences in a blog, where others can benefit from your learning experience.

> **Please, don't be afraid to learn on the job.**

Please, don't be afraid to learn on the job. Every day there's an opportunity to learn, practice, and grow in whatever you are doing; you just need to identify these opportunities and embrace them. In the end, nobody knows everything, and if you did already, think about how boring that would be!

How do you reward good blue teaming work?
We all want recognition. It's human nature. Of course, recognition in the form of a well-deserved salary and bonuses is important. But when these basic needs are met, there is another type of reward that can be as important if not more in some cases.

One way of rewarding your blue teamers is by giving them an opportunity to grow, such as by having them attend conferences and trainings. I have the opportunity to speak and teach internationally at many conferences, and I feel privileged for that, as it represents a great opportunity to extend my network of fellow blue teamers and learn from their experience. So, this is something I encourage everyone to do to reward your blue team. Many of these conferences offer cyber-defense ranges and exercises where they can also get hands-on experience playing as teams. Of course, not everybody can travel, but there are still many training programs that will offer remote online programs too.

But let's take this idea a step further. Something that has always worked well for me when managing blue teams has been to encourage participation in events by submitting to their call for papers (CFPs). This can be an amazing and unforgettable learning experience for the team. If somebody is too new in the team and is intimidated by the thought of speaking in public, encourage them to submit with a more experienced co-worker. Or, why not provide practical help and mentoring by offering to submit with her? I've had the opportunity to do that many times over the years, and it's a rewarding experience.

> Something that has always worked well for me when managing blue teams has been to encourage participation in events by submitting to their call for papers (CFPs).

Even when that's not possible, there are many opportunities to reward good blue teamwork. For example, if somebody did a fantastic job during an investigation, encourage them to present their findings of their work during next month's "lunch and learn" so everybody can benefit from it. A few sincere words of appreciation or small gift cards can also go a long way in feeling appreciated and a valued member of the team. It doesn't take that much!

What are some core metrics that a blue team can use to build, measure, and maintain a successful information security program?

Metrics are the holy grail of security. We're on an eternal quest to find the perfect metrics, but we can't simply find them!

Part of the problem is that we spend too much time thinking about metrics and coming up with complicated formulas in Excel spreadsheets (yes, the spreadsheet of doom), and we forget that metrics aren't the solution. Metrics can never be the goal. Metrics are just a means to an end or, simply put, a communication tool. The best metrics are simply those that allow you to achieve *your* goal, regardless what formula is behind it. If these metrics allow you to communicate progress, convey value of your security program, and help you to get management support, then those are great metrics!

> The best metrics are simply those that allow you to achieve *your* goal, regardless what formula is behind it.

Of course, it's tempting to choose metrics just because the numbers are available to you or simply because the tool of choice provides you with that number, without putting too much thinking into what's the real value of it. A good example of a "bad metric" would be number of incidents per day/month/<insert whatever time range here>.

Let's say you had 30 incidents two months ago, 20 last month, and finally 10 this month. Sounds great, right? But what's the message you're trying to convey with it? Is it really good that you have fewer incidents, or could it possibly mean that you have little visibility to new attacks and therefore you are not seeing them?

Now, think about an organization that's setting up a new blue team and invests in the right people, by training them and providing them with the right tools that support the right processes. Part of that means instrumenting the network and endpoints for visibility and detection of attack tactics such as command and control. What would you expect to happen over the first few months this new program is established? The number of incidents will definitely go up. And that's good! It means you have visibility where you had blind spots before. Over time, as you react to those incidents and address root cause, the number of incidents will progressively go down, and this metric will start to have less and less value. Other more strategic metrics related to the quality of the detection content and the number of improvements in the security posture of the organization will become more relevant.

So, in summary, set your strategic and tactical goals for your program, establish your baseline to identify where you start, and measure progress as you strive to achieve your goals. Be ready to adjust your metrics as your program evolves and matures and as your organization goes through acquisitions, mergers, new changes in technology, new products or services, and so on. Business goals change and so should your metrics. Did I answer your question? Probably not! But that was intentional!

Where would you start if you were the only information security staff member at a small to medium-sized business with a primitive security infrastructure?

An all-around-defender should always start by finding out what the crown jewels of the organization are and by learning more of the culture where they work so they can be an effective communicator. We can't simply protect everything, despite what many people may think, so prioritizing is key. Whether large or small, every organization has critical products and services that the business can't live without, and these are what you need to focus on.

> We can't simply protect everything, despite what many people may think, so prioritizing is key.

Once you have found what it is that you need to protect, think about the threats you need to defend the organization against, and find where these crown jewels are located across your network before your adversaries do. Of course, not all the threats are related to exfiltration of data, so you'll need to consider things like ransomware and other threats that can impact and disrupt business operations. To keep it simple and relevant, start with threats related to incidents the business has already suffered in the past or that similar organizations in the same vertical have suffered. Small organizations might not be worried about nation-states, but at least they should consider ransomware and other crimeware attacks.

Once you've completed the discovery phase, you're ready to define a 30-, 60-, and 90-day plan, following the TTP0 model (blog.ismaelvalenzuela.com/2018/11/01/getting-secops-foundations-right-with-techniques-tactics-and-procedures-zero-ttp0).

In this model, you'd choose one project at a time and work in agile-like short cycles to achieve a specific goal. For example, one of the most foundational elements in building a secure network from the ground up is establishing visibility. Without visibility, it is hard to detect and investigate threats, and without these capabilities, it's difficult to justify and obtain the support needed to improve the security infrastructure. To get started, during the first 30 days, in addition to completing your discovery exercise, you'd like to start deploying

> Without visibility, it is hard to detect and investigate threats, and without these capabilities, it's difficult to justify and obtain the support needed to improve the security infrastructure.

some network and endpoint-based capabilities to monitor identified critical assets as well as some basic incident response plans related to those assets. You'd also start automating some of the most common actions such as creating tickets or data acquisition scripts to gather basic forensic evidence from suspicious systems. You'd complete your 30-day goal by measuring what your time to notify and time to remediate are at that point, establishing your initial baseline.

After that, and during the first 60 days, you will focus on monitoring critical and high alerts only, refining your incident response plans as you follow them, creating awareness among management by leveraging the lessons learned from your IR activities, and measuring time to investigate and time to recovery.

Finally, you'll complete your initial 90-day cycle analyzing and communicating lessons learned from your IR activities, identifying points of improvement, and transforming your program based on how those results align to business goals.

These short-cycle programs, in my experience, work pretty well, not only for larger organizations but also for small to medium-sized businesses where you need to show value quickly.

What is the most bang-for-your-buck security control?
I know it's going to sound boring, but the inventory of assets has been the number-one control in the CIS Top 20 for many years for a reason (www.cisecurity.org/controls/cis-controls-list). In the end, you can't protect what you don't know you have! Trust me, it sounds easier than what it really is. The best (or worst) thing is. . .you'll never be done with this project. It's something you'll have to do continuously. On the active side, Nmap or any other sort of network scanner is probably your best ally. Automating your scans is definitely the way to go by exporting data into a platform like Elastic Stack, for example, to add indexing, searching, and reporting capabilities.

But active asset inventory has its limitations; that's why it's important to complement it with passive techniques. For that purpose, I'm a big fan of Zeek (formerly known as Bro) to generate NetFlow-like data on any network segment in order to discover devices that generate traffic along with their IP and physical addresses and to discover other elements that can be used to fingerprint the device-like user agents and service banners. This data can be also fed into the same Elastic engine to complement the data obtained through active scans.

Can I add one more control? Probably my favorite control ever is a proxy. Proxies are simply amazing. Deployed as forward or reverse proxies, these technologies allow you to broker connections, breaking them into two so they can be inspected, controlling the flow of the data, and allowing or blocking it based on application-specific policies. For example, forward proxies are great to protect outbound traffic to the Internet and can be deployed both on-site and off-site, for example, in the cloud, while reverse proxies can protect a number of web servers against common web application attacks with some WAF and load balancing type of capabilities. But while they're great prevention devices, most people underestimate the value proxies provide for detection and threat hunting! If you don't believe me, get the latest report of the top 20 connections that were allowed outbound from your network going to suspicious domains and inspect those endpoints. If you look carefully, I guarantee you'll find evidence of attacks that bypassed your prevention technologies and compromised these systems. Happy hunting!

Has your organization implemented any deception technologies?

I've had great success over the years using deception technology to detect things that are pretty hard to spot otherwise, especially tactics like lateral movement. There are few things that can provide more value to detect the presence of an attacker once it's in the internal network than well-placed tripwires and red herrings, for example in the form of honey tokens. However, I have to admit that I've *always* had a hard time convincing companies that this was a necessary element in a defensible security architecture. The reason is that legal, and sometimes even HR, doesn't like the word *deception* at all. In fact, the conversation is typically over as soon as you drop that word in a corporate environment. The reason? Some believe that deception involves enticing somebody to hack into a system, essentially to commit a crime, and no legal team will ever allow you to do that on their systems. The solution? I'll share a little secret that has worked great for me on multiple occasions. I call it Ismael's mental Jedi trick! Ready?

The key is to change the way you present it. Yes, marketing matters! Instead of saying you're going to implement a honeypot or any other sort of deception technology, say you'll deploy "early warning systems." I remember I was consulting for a large customer that wouldn't allow me to deploy honeypots under any circumstance. After they suffered an incident, they asked me to come up with a solution to augment their visibility and detection capabilities for lateral movement. I went back to them with a proposal to deploy early warning systems, using virtualization and open source technologies. The project was accepted without any issues! All we changed was the name. As I always say, the industry uses marketing against us. It's time for us, blue teamers, to use marketing to our advantage.

> As I always say, the industry uses marketing against us. It's time for us, blue teamers, to use marketing to our advantage.

Where should an organization use cryptography?
Encryption can be a powerful weapon to have on your toolbelt, but it can hurt you badly if you are not careful.

Encryption is a great tool to provide privacy to users, but it can put blinders to your enterprise layer 7 inspection technologies. Many companies have made big investments in next-gen firewalls, IPSs, IDSs, application proxies, and other types of layer 7 inspection tools to realize that these systems are now 90 percent ineffective, as 90 percent of their traffic is TLS encrypted. To put these systems back into the game, you should employ some TLS inspection or TLS offloading to man-in-the-middle connections that need to be inspected to protect your organization, such as HTTPS traffic going outbound. Politics and privacy directives might prevent you from fully implementing these controls, but at the least you should have a conversation with management around this to assess the risk.

On the other hand, encryption should be used when sensitive traffic traverses an untrusted zone. In the old perimeter-based security, we would consider the LAN trusted, so we would only encrypt traffic from remote systems to our VPN concentrator and leave it unencrypted throughout our internal segments for desktop-to-desktop communications. It's pretty clear that this model doesn't work anymore, as pretty much every device should be treated as untrusted, and potentially hostile, which is the philosophy behind the "zero-trust" model (www.sans.org/webcasts/zero-trust-architecture-108795). Therefore, balance is needed, especially when considering encryption in motion. Whenever possible, architect for visibility. Even when privacy directives win, make sure you have the required visibility by levering NetFlow data for analytics.

With data at rest, encryption should always be considered as an essential control to mitigate the impact of data theft. But realize that this is essentially a physical control only and that it'll be more effective when used on devices that are subject to be lost or stolen, such as laptops, portable drives, phones, tables, etc. In addition to that, full-disk encryption on workstations or servers can prevent attackers from using hacking tools like Kon-Boot (kon-boot.com) to boot up these systems and bypass authentication.

How do you approach data governance and other methods of reducing your data footprint?

I always try to follow a practical approach to blue teaming, and with data governance it is no different. To me, data governance starts with knowing where the data you care about resides. Trust me, assume it's never in the places it should be! To do this, especially in small to medium environments where buying an enterprise data discovery or DLP solution wasn't an option for me, I had to be creative. I've successfully used the awesome Yara engine (virustotal.github.io/yara) for this purpose throughout the years, with customized rules, to search for specific data sitting at rest across thousands of endpoints, including searching recursively through directories in disk and even inside memory processes. My open source rastrea2r project (github.com/rastrea2r/rastrea2r) offers a portable implementation of this idea that can be used for threat-hunting purposes, for searching for IOCs, or for data discovery purposes as well.

Once you have found where it is, data governance is also about classifying the data. Again, data classification is not the most thrilling project you'll get to do as a blue teamer, but there's a reason why it's been used within the military for so many years: It simply works! While many don't know it, Microsoft Windows allows you implement file classification automatically through the File Classification Infrastructure (FCI) that's likely to be included with the licensing you already have (techcommunity .microsoft.com/t5/storage-at-microsoft/file-classification-infrastructure-fci-classification-and-policy/ba-p/423879). This will allow you to set up rules that automatically classify files based on various factors, such as location or content, and can be managed through PowerShell.

Finally, data governance requires enforcement of these policies across all your systems. Again, many organizations will find it useful to leverage things they already have in their environment, or tools they may already have paid for, like Microsoft's Dynamic Access Control (DAC); see technet.microsoft .com/en-us/library/dn408191(v=ws.11).aspx. This can be used to enforce conditional access based on users and devices, but it also allows you to reduce attack surface by implementing time-based restrictions. For example, why would user Bob have access to this piece of data on a Sunday afternoon, or on a Monday at 3 a.m.? Together with FCI, DAC can also allow you to automatically delete or remove data that has expired based on conditions like X days since creation, modified, last access, or other properties.

What is your opinion on compliance?

To me, compliance is not security but rather a subset of it. Being compliant is necessary and, I'd say, even a critical component, but it's not nearly enough to provide an effective defense. I know many blue teamers who have developed this aversion toward compliance, and I don't blame them, as many organizations have seemed to believe that information security is as simple as crossing off a list of controls in a checklist. The truth is, compliance can help you, if you know how to leverage it.

> The truth is, compliance can help you, if you know how to leverage it.

For example, compliance often provides the budget that you need to implement effective security. To do that, go beyond the controls and think about the security principles that are involved. For example, doing regular vulnerability assessments can make you compliant, but it's focusing on the threats and mitigating impact that will really make the process effective. The tools you need to achieve the latter might be the same you need to be compliant. The difference is the mindset with which you approach the problem and how you implement it. When in doubt, as I always say, think red—think as an attacker— to act blue.

Remember, compliance is not the goal, but it can be useful if you use it strategically. Besides, being compliant won't make you secure, but if you make the right decisions, designing, building, and maintaining defensible security architectures, chances are, you'll be compliant as well.

Is there a framework that aligns the activities or functions performed by the blue team with regulatory compliance requirements?

I don't think there's a single framework or model that works for everybody. First, any framework or model is always going to be simplified representations of a much more complex reality. Second, no organization has the same culture, and other aspects like the country in which the company operates make a big difference.

Having said that, and after many years of experience consulting for companies all over the globe, I'll admit that I'm a big fan of the ISO 27000 series and of the NIST Cyber Security Framework. I personally like to use the ISO 27001 as a risk-driven framework to establish an Information Security Management System (ISMS) to then use the ISO 27002 controls and the NIST CSF at a more tactical level to map technical controls. In the end, to me, these are just communication tools. It's like metrics: Use whatever will help you to get the work done. For some organizations, especially in the United States, that will be easier following frameworks created by U.S. organizations like NIST, DISA, MITRE, and so on. On the other hand, frameworks and models published by the ISO or ENISA might be more popular in Europe. These are means to an end, so choose whatever will help you to get the support from upper management to implement your security program.

How do you engage all the different units of an organization to maximize defense?

A big part of getting the support from all business units is to explain to them why they should care and getting them involved early in the process. Typically, nobody likes to be sent a policy that they haven't been consulted on and are expected to comply to it, especially if this is going to create more burden on on them and their team.

A strategy that has worked very well for me across different continents, projects, and employers has been to organize training sessions with all involved business units. Everybody loves free training, especially if it's on something relevant to their day-to-day work and will help them to be better at their job. As you train these business units, think about what you need to communicate and do it succinctly. Use engaging and relevant stories to explain what the threats are, and give them the opportunity to participate, sharing their opinion and experience on the matter. As you do that, you'll achieve various goals.

> Everybody loves free training, especially if it's on something relevant to their day-to-day work and will help them to be better at their job.

- You end up developing a relationship with them that will help improve communications going forward.
- They end up understanding why security matters to them and why they should care about it.

This allows you to understand better the business you are trying to protect, why they work in a specific way, and why you may need to be adaptable.

What strategies do you use to communicate the threats you encounter to nontechnical decision-makers?

It all comes down to the language we use. Let's face it, many of us are geeks at the core. We love to play with our sniffers, write our scripts, dissect hexadecimal payloads, and analyze memory dumps, but that doesn't translate well to those who need to make strategic business decisions.

One of the most powerful questions I often ask myself before I present something to an executive is, what is the problem I'm trying to fix, and why should this person care? Once you have figured out what the goal is, focus on how to convey the message next and how you format that message matters. Ask yourself, in what type of format do these executives consume data on a regular basis? I've found that infographics is a powerful way of conveying data and one that execs are familiar with. Some online services offer low-cost or even free templates that can be used for this purpose. Also, think in terms of stories. When talking about this, I often refer to one of my favorite books and to one of the forefathers of blue teaming, Cliff Stoll's *The Cuckoo's Egg* (www.amazon.com/Cuckoos-Egg-Tracking-Computer-Espionage/dp/1416507787). In a presentation that he recently gave (blog.ismaelvalenzuela.com/2018/10/11/intelligence-driven-defense-successfully-embedding-cyber-threat-intel-in-security-operations), he said this:

Raw data can be dry, but when presented in the form of a story that illustrates the cost of acting versus the cost of nonacting, it can help you drive your point home.

"I thought all I had to do was show the data and people would understand. It doesn't work. You have to tell a story."

—Cliff Stoll

What recommendations do you have for managing nontechnical executives' expectations during a significant ongoing incident?

First, it's important to understand that the best time to manage expectations is not when the house is on fire and everybody is running around in the middle of a crisis. As with physical disasters, proper incident command is paramount, and this is always better planned in advance. When there is weak or inadequate planning, communication problems are guaranteed to appear during the handling of the incident.

If this is not possible, there's a few points that are important to communicate as soon as possible.

- It's all about managing risk. Executive and business unit cooperation will be critical to ensure rapid containment and mitigation of the impact. Make sure they understand their responsibility to make the IR plan successful and that the response is coordinated to avoid further damage.

- Define the chain of command, nonambiguously, with the proper handover. Remember that decision-making should be business-driven, not technical-driven, with a focus on understanding the impact, not fixing it right away. Senior leadership should help to balance investigative efforts with impact assessment.
- Ensure the business understands that a proper response requires a proper scoping. A response will not be effective without a *complete* understanding of the total threat. Improper scoping and misread signals usually lead to partial remediation, which can lead to disaster.
- Consider long-duration responses or long-term recovery. If it's some sort of targeted attack, the attacker won't go to cry in a corner, even if the attack is successfully contained and eradicated. Make sure the business understands that it's likely that the attacker will come back.
- Public relations, legal, and compliance impacts are often not considered. Don't overlook these or any other notification requirements. These should not be deferred as a post-incident issue.
- Communicate frequently through executive and technical briefings depending on your audience. A consistent and effective communication process is critical. Regular incident status meetings should be required, and incident status details should be documented in a secure out-of-band location. All critical teams must be in a communication chain, and don't forget that the communication of sensitive information must be tightly controlled at all times.

Finally, don't be quick to jump into conclusions. Use the Analysis of Competing Hypothesis (ACH) model (www.sans.org/cyber-security-summit/archives/file/summit-archive-1496695240.pdf) to conduct your investigative efforts, and make sure you always get down to the root cause of the incident to continue improving your security posture.

"I tend to think of the blue team as the entire security organization within a company, from the trenches to the CISO."

Twitter: @davevenable • **Website:** www.linkedin.com/in/dvenable

Dave Venable

51

Dave Venable is a former intelligence professional with the U.S. National Security Agency with extensive experience in computer network exploitation, information operations, and cryptography. Dave has developed and managed several U.S. national-level projects in support of global anti-terrorism operations and the Global War on Terror, in addition to providing security advisory services to Global 500 companies.

Dave is a regular speaker and author on information security and is the vice president of cybersecurity at Masergy. Dave also serves on the Cyber Security Advisory Council of Southern Methodist University, where he also teaches security.

How do you define a blue team?
I tend to think of the blue team as the entire security organization within a company, from the trenches to the CISO. Granted, the IR team is probably the forefront of the blue team in most people's minds, but as long as you're focused on the company's security, you're on the blue team.

That said, I distinguish between security roles and IT roles, even if those IT roles might some security functions. In fact, I don't view cybersecurity as an IT specialization but rather as a security specialization. Coming from my background in the intelligence community, we see a wide variety of security specializations: physical, communications, and so on. Cyber is one more area of focus within that realm.

The analogy I always like to use is looking at a building's security: You have security guards, people monitoring alarm systems, testing security controls, auditing them, and so on. These are security roles. On the other hand, there are the people who work in building maintenance. These are not security roles, even though they might change locks or install some of the wiring for alarm systems. I often hear cybersecurity viewed as a specialization within IT, but this is as flawed as viewing building security as a specialization within building maintenance. They are very different fields altogether.

What are two core capabilities that a blue team should have?

The ability to detect an incident and the ability to respond to an incident.

What are some of the key strengths of an incident response program?

Obviously, the technical abilities to detect and respond to an incident are key, but one key strength that enables that ability is for the security team to effectively work across the company and collaborate closely with every organization within the company. This often comes down to building and maintaining relationships, and it's much easier to do this before an incident than during one.

How can blue teamers learn, practice, and grow?

Get a wide variety of experience throughout your career. Be sure to work on different types of projects, with different people, and in different environments. Each organization or company typically has its own way of doing things, and it is always good to learn these ways but also to experience other perspectives from a variety of vantage points. This diversity of perceptions will provide more insight later in your career and enable you to understand, empathize, and help the people you will lead in the future. This includes spending time working on the offensive side of security as well. I encourage anyone on a blue team to spend some time in their career—or at least on the side—doing offensive security work so that they can understand an attacker's mindset.

How do you reward good blue teaming work?
In the ways that every employee cares about: time off, bonuses, and salary increases. In addition to that, I'm always happy to send the team members who set themselves apart with their work to more advanced training and task them with higher-priority projects.

What are some core metrics that a blue team can use to build, measure, and maintain a successful information security program?
This could be an entire book by itself, but this is really one of the most key aspects to a security program. As the saying goes, what's measured matters. However, you want to keep it simple enough that the nonsecurity experts on the executive leadership team and the board of directors can understand.

I recommend using no more than five metrics at that level and then use the Capability Maturity Model (CMM) to track maturity in these areas. I've developed a simple maturity model that can be downloaded at davevenable.com/maturity. This tracks the maturity of the security program across the following:

- Policy
- Technology
- Human factors
- Risk and vulnerability management
- Support

It includes descriptions of the company's capabilities, maturity, and even budget across different areas.

Where would you start if you were the only information security staff member at a small to medium-sized business with a primitive security infrastructure?
I would first want to understand the business objectives for the next three years and then translate that into security requirements, which I would then prioritize in accordance with the

priorities of the business objectives, the current state of the security program, and which controls could accomplish the most for the least spend in terms of effort, time, and money.

What is the most bang-for-your-buck security control?
I'll list four.

- **Multifactor authentication:** This one is obvious. Phishing to get access to user accounts is the primary way attacks are occurring today.
- **Password managers to prevent password reuse:** This is the same rationale as the previous one.
- **Deception technology:** This is low cost and has almost zero false positives.
- **24/7 SOC monitoring as a service:** This is more expensive than the other three, but outsourcing 24/7 monitoring is far less expensive than building a 24/7 SOC, staffing it, and keeping qualified individuals. Be sure to have sensors in place to detect traffic across the internal network.

Has your organization implemented any deception technologies?
I'm a fan of deception technology because it's inexpensive, it's easy to maintain (or even forget about), and it has an extremely low false positive rate. It's one of the first things I like to implement in any new environment.

Where should an organization use cryptography?
Anywhere it can. After some of the revelations around the PRISM program, where internal communications at large companies were being monitored, I like to recommend using encryption on as much as possible, both in transit and at rest.

What is your opinion on compliance?
Compliance is a double-edged sword. If you rely on it too much, or even worse, conflate compliance with security, it can be your downfall. Look at how many major data breaches occurred in organizations that were compliant with security frameworks in recent years.

However, few things are as useful as compliance to drive support, buy-in, and funding for your security program. It's a great justification for security, especially in organizations that don't yet understand the value. Use it to your advantage, but don't mistake it for the goal.

Is there a framework that aligns the activities or functions performed by the blue team with regulatory compliance requirements?

In terms of the overall security program, there are countless frameworks to do this. I prefer to select the target framework (something like ISO 27002, a subset of NIST 800-53, or similar) and then look at the controls within that framework that are mapped to the Critical Security Controls. I then prioritize those controls based on the real-world risk faced by the organization as well as the effort and cost involved in implementing mitigation. This provides a fairly objective way of looking at which controls should be implemented first.

How do you engage all the different units of an organization to maximize defense?

In my experience, the key to this is developing and maintaining relationships with the leaders of the different units *before* an incident occurs. I prefer to try to be consultative, rather than directive, and make sure the leadership understands we're there to make their jobs easier.

What strategies do you use to communicate the threats you encounter to nontechnical decision-makers?

Never exaggerate. Understand that sometimes businesses need to accept risks. If you're ever viewed as exaggerating risk, your credibility will be lost when it matters most. Always try to be down-to-earth and reasonable, and I always like to come up with a metaphor firmly rooted in the physical world when explaining cyber threats.

What recommendations do you have for managing nontechnical executives' expectations during a significant ongoing incident?

Be transparent with them about what's happening and update them often enough that they don't feel like they're having to ask for updates, but not so often that they get tired of receiving your emails. This can be a tough balance sometimes. If you're not sure about something, don't update them until you are.

"Some blue teams want to be exclusionary. My management style is radically inclusive. If you want to help, welcome to the team!"

Website: www.linkedin.com/in/robertwa

Robert "TProphet" Walker

52 Robert Walker is a senior security architect. After spending 13 years at Microsoft (three of them in Beijing) and founding PCPursuit, whose work was featured on the front page of the *New York Times*, he was drawn to the unique challenge of public-sector information security. Robert's combination of business, management, information security, and deep IT expertise makes him a trusted voice across business and technology teams. In his personal life, Robert has visited all seven continents and is working toward membership in the Traveler's Century Club.

How do you define a blue team?

To me, it's simple: If you're playing defense, you're on the blue team, even if it isn't your primary job. Even red teams temporarily become part of the blue team when they provide a read-out and after-action report, because their entire job is to help make the blue team better.

Some blue teams want to be exclusionary. My management style is radically inclusive. If you want to help, welcome to the team!

What are two core capabilities that a blue team should have?

- **Influence:** Everything a blue team does starts and ends with people. Blue teams can't defend everything on their own. They need to be highly influential with business and technology teams throughout the organization and ensure that InfoSec is always part of the conversation.
- **Insight:** The most effective blue teamers are able to rapidly synthesize information from disparate sources and quickly spot what is most important. This level of insight typically comes from experience, but a fresh set of eyes can also be amazing!

What are some of the key strengths of an incident response program?

It's always better to not have incidents in the first place. Good information security hygiene is good IT hygiene, and this should be diligently practiced.

Incident response is a specialized area, so it may be entirely appropriate to contract for these services. However, the right time to be looking for a contractor *isn't* in the middle of an incident. Have a quality firm on retainer.

Having a *current* and *tested* incident response plan is an absolutely essential success factor. Unfortunately, most organizations don't invest appropriately here.

- A good plan will clearly define who is in command, where the command is physically located, and who owns which functional areas. If your plan contains nothing else, at least have this!
- The plan shouldn't be on your SharePoint and only there, because it won't be accessible if ransomware just ate your SharePoint server. An old-fashioned printout is a good option. Update it every time you test your plan.

An incident response team's ability to quickly respond is highly dependent upon accurate documentation. Most systems, however, are poorly documented.

- Current, up-to-date artifacts detailing reference architecture and system and network components are essential.
- An accurate, up-to-date asset inventory (servers, virtual machines, containers, cloud instances, network devices, backups, etc.) with *current* escalation contacts is critical. You don't want to be paying a specialized incident response contractor to be running around your data center scanning barcodes into Excel and trying to figure out who owns the crusty old server that has a "Do not *ever* power off!" sticky note.
- An inventory of system and service accounts in use and permissions assigned (this allows incident responders to spot unauthorized modifications more easily).

How can blue teamers learn, practice, and grow?
The best blue teamers are intrinsically motivated. What's the best way to grow? Find something in the field you have a burning desire to make better and then go do it! Help other people: Volunteer, give conference talks, lead workshops. The more you pay it forward, the more people will pay it forward with you.

How do you specifically *not* get better and grow? Going through certification programs and adding a bunch of letters to the end of your name or getting a master's degree in cyber something. It's like being a cook versus a chef: Anyone can go to cooking school and learn how to follow a recipe, but chefs have innate talent.

How do you reward good blue teaming work?
Being on the blue team is a uniquely underappreciated role because the better blue teams are at their job, the less visible they will often be to the rest of the business. The best way to reward a blue team for good work is to trust them, listen to them, consider them a strategic partner in the business, and, where possible, follow their recommendations. This means a great deal more to them than a $5 Starbucks gift card ever could.

Pay your blue team a fair salary without making them interview and get another offer first. Just track midpoint or higher for market and automatically match it annually. Yes, I know that salary compression was an HR module of your MBA, but InfoSec people are wise

Pay your blue team a fair salary without making them interview and get another offer first.

to that. It's a small, tight-knit community where engineers regularly talk to their peers. When their salary falls below market, they'll just leave rather than play games.

What are some core metrics that a blue team can use to build, measure, and maintain a successful information security program?

The answer is very much "it depends." Start with your threat model, and consider the risk factors that are the most important. Priority stack those, and build your instrumentation to measure accordingly.

Businesses like to have quantitative measures for everything. However, not everything in information security is easily quantifiable. You can't always wait for data to make decisions, and every organization will have blind spots. It's important for data to be *an* element in the decision-making process but not the *only* element.

That being said, unpatched systems, misconfigurations, and compromised accounts are at the root of most security breaches. Having clear accountability around unpatched systems can help to drive the conversation around mitigation. The same goes for account maintenance and configuration management.

Where would you start if you were the only information security staff member at a small to medium-sized business with a primitive security infrastructure?

I'd start with the development and test organizations and work with them on implementing a secure development lifecycle (SDLC). Good reference architecture, sane development patterns, and (most importantly) modern frameworks can paper over a lot of security cracks. The more that potential security issues can be pushed upstream and mitigated in design and code, the easier and cheaper those mitigations generally are.

What is the most bang-for-your-buck security control?

Patching on schedule with no excuses. Patches are extensively tested by vendors, and in any given organization, it's highly unusual for a patch to cause any issues (remember, a patch has to have a bug *and* the bug has to create a blocking impact for it to cause any real problems). More than half of breaches start with an unpatched system. In most organizations, this is far and away the best/cheapest security ROI. Yes, there's an occasional bug—but that's why rollback capability exists. You have that, right?

Where should an organization use cryptography?

Everywhere. But seriously, *everywhere*. Here's why: You should assume that any given component of any given information system in your enterprise could be breached. An architecture that takes a layered approach to information storage and retrieval, with encryption at every stage, can still protect sensitive data even if an individual component is breached. It used to be *much* harder to build things this way, but modern tooling and frameworks often have built-in encryption capabilities. This is where pushing security upstream into architecture and development patterns and closely partnering with development teams can really pay off.

How do you approach data governance and other methods of reducing your data footprint?

There should be a healthy tension between product management teams, who will want to collect any data that might be potentially useful, and security teams, who should want to collect as little data as possible. This is a negotiation, and where it typically ends up is collecting *only* the data for which a specific, current business justification exists.

What is your opinion on compliance?

It's a useful tool but is often conflated with security, and the two are not the same thing.

Is there a framework that aligns the activities or functions performed by the blue team with regulatory compliance requirements?

Sure, it's possible that you can find a framework that accommodates both fish and bicycles, but would it be useful or accomplish anything? To me, compliance and security are separate business functions. They are loosely aligned, and security reviews can even serve as a useful gate in the deployment pipeline to ensure compliance requirements are also met, but the two activities run on parallel tracks and should involve separate staff. After all, compliance regulates the activities of security teams, too!

How do you engage all the different units of an organization to maximize defense?

"Speak softly and carry a big stick." Security leadership starts from the top, so to get traction, obtaining executive sponsorship should be a priority; this is my approach. If you understand the tools and decision-making processes used in the executive suite, you'll be better prepared to leverage them. It's important not to just get a general statement of support, but to be integrated in the organization's reporting processes at the executive level, right down to the weekly dashboards they review. Nobody wants to be the block on any initiative with top-level executive visibility, and everyone wants the opportunity to be the hero on initiatives with executive visibility. It totally changes the conversation.

> Security leadership starts from the top, so to get traction, obtaining executive sponsorship should be a priority; this is my approach.

It's not easy to remain a top-level item for executive visibility. To get there, you need to be seen as a strategic partner of the business, representing a key business area that regularly requires executive-level review.

What strategies do you use to communicate the threats you encounter to nontechnical decision-makers?

Information security decisions, to business decision-makers, are primarily risk decisions. They're assessed and rated using risk frameworks. One key problem is that executives will often try to apply a *project* risk framework to *information security* risks. This will almost always cram the risks into a lower category than they should be. Using a more appropriate framework (such as FAIR) and ensuring that the business has the appropriate context for the decision are good strategies.

The skills I learned in my MBA really help in communicating effectively with executives because I understand the *business* context in which they're thinking, and I can speak their language. While I don't recommend that you run out and get an MBA, I do recommend you review the course work (which you can do for free) and learn some of the tools and techniques.

I'm never emotional—*ever*. My job is to ensure the business has appropriate context for the decisions it is making. Certainly, I have recommendations, but I don't always get what I want. Business decision-makers aren't wrong or stupid to prioritize other things; when decisions get to the level where I operate (and where every security professional should want to operate), they just aren't always easy or obvious. Perfect isn't the enemy of the good, so as long as a risk is logged, the business fully understands it, and the business accepts it, I feel like I have done a good job—even if a security initiative is delayed.

What recommendations do you have for managing nontechnical executives' expectations during a significant ongoing incident?

The first and most important thing is to build trust and establish command. It's really easy for people in the business to panic and start going off in different directions. Leadership should do the following:

- Acknowledge the incident
- Explain that an action plan is in development
- Let people know when they'll hear next

Always have a battle speech ready: "The good news is that this is only a computer incident. Nobody died. Statistically, the odds are in our favor. We have the best people in the organization working on this, we're working the plan, and the sun will come up tomorrow."

Be sure that the business priorities are fully understood and get a sense of the trade-offs that the business is willing to accept.

Help executives understand what the risks probably are, what the risks probably are not, and which are unknown. Be sure they understand that incidents are fast-moving and early information isn't always correct, so they should be prepared that information may change based on the facts that are discovered. Executives generally appreciate candor and transparency.

It's likely that executives will ask key business questions and ask for a confidence level regarding impact. It's fair to say "it's too early to know" in some areas, as long as you don't deflect *everything*. In the background, they'll have a business analyst using this information to build a model and simulate outcomes so they can try to understand best-case/worst-case scenarios.

If a legal situation is potentially involved, be sure that your organization's general counsel is engaged and executives are fully aware. It's usually a good idea to involve legal in the first few meetings, because in a fast-moving incident, evidence requiring their review can potentially surface.

Make sure that executives know what is important for them to do, what isn't helpful right now, where and how often you'll provide status, and whom to contact for information.

Activate the incident response plan, and free up all contingency funding required.

Activate contractor resources (on retainer) as needed.

Be clear that right now it doesn't matter who or what is to blame. No time should be spent on this; it's time that can be better spent solving the problem. There will be a post-mortem later.

If you say, "We need a steady supply of pizza to the SOC," that can *totally* happen! Seriously, don't be shy to ask for anything that an executive assistant can make happen to keep your team fueled, on-site, and productive.

Understand that executives are managing a lot of constituencies too—the board, potentially media, customers, and other stakeholders. They're under a lot of pressure, so do respect that.

Every one of these constituencies wants to know exactly what happened, the full details of the impact, and your next steps. At the beginning of an incident, this also happens to be exactly what you don't know.

Make sure executives know how they'll get updates and on what cadence. You'll likely need a more frequent cadence at the beginning as facts are uncovered, but negotiate for as infrequent a cadence as possible to keep your team focused on solving the problem versus providing status.

Project management teams from all over the organization will swarm on the incident response team looking for constant status updates if this isn't specifically stopped, and in so doing, they'll absorb a lot of engineering time. Executives can help by centralizing all reporting, and this is a specific ask you should make.

> "The blue team is not responsible for actually implementing secure configuration controls (that's the job of systems admins), but they do make the recommendations for configuration changes that systems admins may have missed."

Twitter: @MalwareJake • **Website:** www.renditioninfosec.com

Jake Williams

53 Jake Williams is an accomplished InfoSec professional with almost two decades of industry experience. After spending more than a decade in the U.S. intelligence community performing various missions in offensive and defensive cyber, Jake founded Rendition Infosec where he leads a team of professionals performing adversary emulation, incident response, malware reverse engineering, forensics, and exploit development.

How do you define a blue team?

A blue team is the core of an organization's defensive cybersecurity mission. The blue team is not responsible for actually implementing secure configuration controls (that's the job of systems admins), but they do make the recommendations for configuration changes that systems admins may have missed.

Additionally, the blue team helps inform strategy for the SOC on the specific threats they'll need to detect. While the SOC is generally in charge of writing their own correlation rules, the blue team ensures that the proper log sources are available for the correlations.

What are two core capabilities that a blue team should have?

It's hard to limit this to just two, but if we're playing "Blue Team Survivor," the two capabilities I wouldn't vote off the island are indicator sweeps and full network security monitoring (including east-west NetFlow coverage).

The ability to perform indicator of compromise (IOC) sweeps is absolutely critical to any blue team operation. This is a critical capability to enable threat hunting operations. Network security monitoring (NSM) solutions are often deployed with only north-south (internal to external) coverage. While this is how all deployments should begin, east-west (internal network communications) is a tremendous enabler for finding insider threats and attackers in the network.

What are some of the key strengths of an incident response program?

Beyond the obvious answer of "being ready to get an attacker out of the network," I view an incident response program as a decision support tool. The incident response program arms decision-makers with the data they need to answer queries from customers and regulators when an incident occurs. The existence of a program (and to some extent the maturity of the program) shows that the organization has a commitment to security and is prepared to deal with incidents.

How can blue teamers learn, practice, and grow?

Network, network, network. That's the biggest thing. In any organization, it's easy to get tunnel vision. Attend webinars, go to conferences, and learn what others are doing. The worst thing a blue team can do is expend resources planning for the threats of yesterday rather than dealing with the threats of today. People in the community share an amazing amount of information about what they are doing, how they are hunting, etc. Blue teamers can tap into this knowledge through networking and become a force multiplier for their organization.

How do you reward good blue teaming work?

This one is hard, but we try to highlight team wins (e.g., finding an attacker during threat hunting) whenever possible.

The reality is that blue team work isn't sexy (not in the traditional way red team work is), and people often contribute to a win without being the "face" of the win. To help with this, we celebrate as a team and communicate how well the whole team did to ensure the win.

What are some core metrics that a blue team can use to build, measure, and maintain a successful information security program?

Blue team metrics are hard to measure. In the context of a threat hunting program, you can emphasize any threats detected. However, the danger here is that when threats aren't detected, the program seems to have less value. We instead recommend measuring the number of assets scanned for threats to demonstrate that activity is happening regardless of a detection.

On the incident response side, we try to show improvement in the incident response program. Any time we can answer a question to stakeholders that we couldn't answer 12 months ago, we highlight that fact to give tangible examples of improvement in the program.

Where would you start if you were the only information security staff member at a small to medium-sized business with a primitive security infrastructure?

The one foundational element in building security from the ground up is visibility. The quickest way to get visibility is to deploy a SIEM, but that's not in the budget for many small shops. In that case, I recommend prioritizing logging and retention. Repurpose a legacy server or workstation and fill up the drive bays. Then deploy Winlogbeat or a syslog forwarder on critical servers to get logs to the makeshift SIEM. The SOF-ELK distribution is a great way to search through this data (though you won't confuse it for a commercial SIEM without significant tuning).

The thing you can do immediately to make your life easier down the road is to increase the event log size on all workstations and servers. Most devices have tons of free space, and no investigator ever has said, "What will I do with all these logs?!" Turn on process auditing too and your investigations will be like reading a book.

What is the most bang-for-your-buck security control?

This depends a lot on the maturity of the security program. If the program is relatively immature and doesn't have a SIEM, that's my first step. If teams already have a SIEM, they need to quickly implement EDR. After that, I'm looking for NetFlow and DNS monitoring. All of these are great additions to any security program and will provide excellent value to the blue team but can also be used to troubleshoot IT operations problems. Highlighting the use of security tools to detect and respond to operations issues is a great way to get buy-in from IT (and in some cases get them to share some of the financial burden of deploying the tools).

Has your organization implemented any deception technologies?

We use deception technologies both in our network and in customer networks. Deception technologies are a great enabler, but they should always be thought of as a secondary detection technology. Too often, CISOs chase the latest buzzwords rather than making more sensible decisions about security controls. Deception technologies should only be thought of as a safety net to be used when primary detection technologies have failed.

How do you approach data governance and other methods of reducing your data footprint?

While data is obviously a detection enabler, it can also be a liability if the organization is breached. After all, an attacker can't steal data you don't have. We recommend working with legal counsel to establish a risk-based data retention policy for security data. Data is needed to answer questions about incidents that have just been detected. However, too much data becomes a liability. We always recommend that organizations examine other breaches that have been publicly announced and adjust data retention to what they need to answer questions to stakeholders and regulators during an incident. My golden rule of data retention, though, is this: If you can't articulate how data will be used to answer questions during an incident, don't retain it.

What is your opinion on compliance?

Ugh, the C word. Compliance is important, as are compliance frameworks. But compliance gets a bad name in security because too many organizations consider compliance to be synonymous with security. Showing compliance with a framework is a positive step toward actual security, but we should never think achieving compliance means that the organization is secure. We always remind customers that compliance is a *minimum* standard and then remind them that they wouldn't want open-heart surgery from a doctor who bragged, "Pick me, I met the minimum educational standards!"

Is there a framework that aligns the activities or functions performed by the blue team with regulatory compliance requirements?

I'm a big fan of the CIS 20 Critical Security Controls (CSCs) as a way to prioritize deployment of security controls. However, many organizations need to align with NIST CSF, PCI, or other frameworks that are far less risk-based. I always recommend organizations look at the free crosswalk between the CSCs and other frameworks from James and Keli Tarala (www.auditscripts. com/download/2742).

How do you engage all the different units of an organization to maximize defense?

This really starts at the top with a culture shift that security is everyone's job. The biggest impact for involving those outside of the security team in defensive tasks is when systems administrators are brought into the security mindset. This isn't us versus them. The reality is that no competent systems admin has ever said, "I'll deploy this in a way that will get hacked later." Cybersecurity professionals curious about why this keeps happening may find the answer in behavioral economics.

Most job descriptions for systems administrators discuss availability of systems without addressing security. When presented with the choice of "Make it work insecurely now" or "Figure out how to do it securely, even though we are in the middle of an outage," most will choose the former since it addresses the singular thing they are rated on. Job descriptions need to be changed for systems administrators in most cases.

What strategies do you use to communicate the threats you encounter to nontechnical decision-makers?

I always use analogies to explain threats by comparing the cyber threat to a risk in the business they are in. All analogies are lossy, meaning there is definitely a loss of fidelity in the quality of the communication when using an analogy. However, this is worthwhile since the amount of information retained by the receiving party is usually greater when an analogy is used. The thing that doesn't work is using technical jargon and asking, "Did you understand that?" People have a natural tendency to confirm they understood information they may not truly have to avoid looking inadequate in front of their peers.

It's probably worth it to read a few business books too. Most of your decision-makers have a business degree, and most degree programs have the same reading list (give or take). I find that most executives have read *Good to Great*, and I can use stories from that as anchors for analogies.

What recommendations do you have for managing nontechnical executives' expectations during a significant ongoing incident?

I always go in explaining that major incidents take significant time to resolve, and this won't play out immediately. I always analogize to crime shows like *CSI: Cyber* and note that while LL Cool J can investigate an incident and pistol whip a suspect in an hour, I cannot. I then usually note that if they want that service, then

> I always analogize to crime shows like *CSI: Cyber* and note that while LL Cool J can investigate an incident and pistol whip a suspect in an hour, I cannot.

perhaps they should call in Ted Danson. That usually gets a laugh (even during a stressful time) and gets everyone level set on the fact that we have a hard road ahead of us with the investigation.

The other thing we always do is to be clear in our reporting when the next communication will occur and what they should expect from that communication. If you send a morning status report but then don't send anything else, by 2 p.m. you can bet questions will be coming from decision-makers. But if you tell them that the next scheduled communication will occur at 4 p.m. and will include assessments about lateral movement from the NetFlow data we received at 7 a.m., they're far more likely to wait patiently (in our experience).

"In short, the blue team defends organizations through various controls and responds to malicious activity, working to keep an organization as protected as possible while having the knowledge to respond to worse-case scenarios for a proper containment and recovery."

Twitter: @rej_ex • **Website:** www.linkedin.com/in/blueteam

Robert Willis

54

Robert Willis is a security consultant at 1337 Inc. He has a BS in management and certifications in IT and security from Stanford University, USAF, DHS, CompTIA, EC-Council, ELS, and various other organizations. He began his journey into programming and hacking in the late 1990s on AOL. Robert is also currently enlisted in the Texas State Guard, working in cybersecurity at Camp Mabry in Austin, Texas. Robert recently received the Texas Medal of Merit for his cyber work.

How do you define a blue team?
Blue teamers are security professionals who prepare and protect organizations from malicious actors. There are many different roles blue teamers can specialize in, from managing proactive defense measures to responding to incidents—all the way through the identification and recovery process. In short, the blue team defends organizations through various controls and responds to malicious activity, working to keep an organization as protected as possible while having the knowledge to

respond to worse-case scenarios for a proper containment and recovery.

What are two core capabilities that a blue team should have?

Hardening systems, maintaining the security stack, analyzing traffic, and being able to respond and recover from malicious activity are some of the core functions of a blue team. The blue team is an organization's defenders; they must maintain their security program to be proactive against possible threats while being able to remediate issues.

Blue teamers should regularly patch systems, maintain a properly set up (and tested) security stack for protection and detection, and be able to analyze traffic, while being prepared to respond to malicious activity with a proper response. After an incident, lessons learned should always be added to a program that's regularly tested.

What are some of the key strengths of an incident response program?

A couple key strengths to having an incident response program are reducing confusion and downtime when an incident occurs. If an organization is abiding by recommended practices with their program, it will be tested annually and incorporate lessons learned to continue making it more effective and efficient. Individuals will know their roles and what is expected of them prior to an actual event, which will make the recovery process more streamlined in terms of task and team management.

How can blue teamers learn, practice, and grow?

Researching certification paths from industry-recognized organizations is a really intelligent way to learn. Although some people argue that certifications don't prove real-world knowledge and experience, the materials you study from give a great amount of exposure to subjects that will enable one who wants to go further "down the rabbit hole" to practice deeper on their own. Over the years, many of my successful friends have set their goals for learning by what certifications they wanted to go after. It's a great way to put together a self-study syllabus.

Many websites offer labs for blue teamers to practice in. There are many great resources available for free or low cost online.

I've found a good way to grow skills is to surround yourself with others who are also passionate about InfoSec. Attend conferences, get on Twitter, and follow people in the industry (both red teamers and blue teamers) who post newly discovered products and vulnerabilities. Reading open conversations about what's being seen in the field offers a great wealth of knowledge. There's always something new to learn; the industry continues to greatly expand in terms of products, practitioners, compliance needs, and organizations seeking to become more secure.

How do you reward good blue teaming work?

Good work should be rewarded the same way it is across any industry: with incentives. I think this is a management question and could be asked as, "How do you keep employees happy, especially when they are in such demand?" Incentives should include things like time off and receiving pay raises. I would say that incentives should include things such as going to conferences (fully paid) and InfoSec training and certifications, but these are things that companies should already be providing to their employees. Incentives should be things that aren't already expected to be provided; that's how you lose employees.

What are some core metrics that a blue team can use to build, measure, and maintain a successful information security program?

Metrics should be specific, measurable, attainable, repeatable, and time-dependent (SMART). For metrics it's important to have a baseline to analyze against. Metrics can involve everything from measuring improvements to processes to tracking remediations made to systems. Testing response plans and phishing test outcomes can help provide information on improvements.

Where would you start if you were the only information security staff member at a small to medium-sized business with a primitive security infrastructure?

The infrastructure would obviously need to be brought to a good maturity level if it's currently in a primitive state. At small to medium-sized businesses, it's important to build a security program (I like using the NIST Cybersecurity Framework) to create proper secure system engineering guidelines. Not only would this help map what needs to be done in an organization to current best practices (if you're building policy against an accepted framework), but it also takes care of many issues that can arise from not having set policies or guidelines as the company grows.

In many real-world instances, the biggest threats can be an employee who wasn't properly trained who ends up accidentally compromising their organization. Make sure the infrastructure's security is set up abiding by policy, but also make sure that individuals aren't going to do something with their current access that would make a security practitioner facepalm. It isn't enough to set up a firewall, IDS/IPS, SIEM, and DLP if an individual who already has access is the biggest threat.

What is the most bang-for-your-buck security control?

Patching is free and stops lots of issues. It isn't a surprise that there's a Patch Tuesday and then the next day is Exploit Wednesday, where newly released vulnerability information is used against targets. I have been called in on some very large incident responses that could have been easily avoided if systems were patched.

I would also say that it's cheap for smaller companies to have backups. I've seen a few companies get hit hard with ransomware, and their recovery would have been much better for them if they had backups.

Has your organization implemented any deception technologies?

This is definitely a honeypot question—a honeypot being a decoy setup to lure attackers in. I've worked with honeypots, and they are great to gather data from to understand what methods and traffic an attacker is creating, but it's important to make sure that setting up a honeypot is actually necessary for the client's current maturity level. I say this because a honeypot can be something a possible client asks for, but in many cases I find that a client's current network may be so immature that they need to concentrate on fixing their own issues before setting up a decoy. A vulnerable decoy would just be one of many vulnerable machines on a network to choose from at that point.

If you're a mature organization, a honeypot is great to gather and analyze information from to see what actual attackers are attempting to do (and how they are attempting to do it). This information can be used in briefings with the blue team and to pinpoint activity to specifically look for (especially if the attacker is attempting advanced tactics to be undetected).

Where should an organization use cryptography?

An organization should first build a data classification policy to identify and classify different types of data. This should help the organization understand what type of data is most sensitive and begin taking measures to protect that data first, working from the most to the least sensitive data. You should look at how data is being accessed/used (data at rest versus data in transit) and current visibility of data (for example, public-facing data). All PII and sensitive data should be encrypted. In fact, organizations should try to encrypt as much data as possible; some data may not seem sensitive to some people but can be used by attackers in many different ways.

How do you approach data governance and other methods of reducing your data footprint?

The approach to data governance falls many times on what regulations or compliance an organization must meet. Requirements help to clearly define the scope of needs.

There are many things that can be done to reduce a data footprint. This includes getting rid of unneeded duplicate content and archiving (or deleting) older data that is no longer needed. Organizations can also use third parties to store and handle data. I see this a lot with credit card processing and storage when it's put onto a third-party processor—it eliminates lots of headaches.

What is your opinion on compliance?

Being compliant doesn't mean you're secure. Also, in the field I find that many organizations are not compliant yet still say they are, especially when it comes to HIPAA (be afraid, be very afraid). It's the most confusing thing ever.

I trust certain compliances that have to be verified by a specific body with auditors who must meet requirements (PCI DSS and SOC2 are great), but others are a complete mess because many organizations attempt to put mapping to compliance on their general IT staff—who don't specialize or fully understand security or the language of security—and it almost always ends up being a complete mess, especially when self-assessments are completed in-house with pure confusion.

Unfortunately, it's no longer a shock when an organization doing many millions of dollars a year (or more) is a complete dumpster fire and not compliant with many things they claim to be.

Is there a framework that aligns the activities or functions performed by the blue team with regulatory compliance requirements?

There are different frameworks that can closely align with regulatory compliance requirements, but many have to be used as more of a "skeletal" structure for a security program eventually being expanded for specific regulatory requirements—depending on which one is looking to be met.

When building a security program, I like to use the NIST Cybersecurity Framework and then build off of it to meet specific requirements. There are other frameworks that have crosswalks to multiple compliance needs, a popular one being HITRUST.

> When building a security program, I like to use the NIST Cybersecurity Framework and then build off of it to meet specific requirements.

Some negatives associated with frameworks with too many crosswalks is that they can be too clunky for many organizations' needs, which is why I like to understand what regulatory compliances need to be met. I then know exactly what additions I need to add to a framework like NIST, without too much overkill.

How do you engage all the different units of an organization to maximize defense?

All employees need security training. From executives to human resources, everyone needs to understand possible threats, especially when it comes to social engineering and handling data properly. It's important to maximize defense outside of the security department by having all employees understand what they need to be aware of in their own daily activities, which could include the possibility of being phished to giving out too much information.

What strategies do you use to communicate the threats you encounter to nontechnical decision-makers?

As a consultant, I find that it's important to give positive feedback with the bad, while outlining exactly what an organization needs to build a better security posture. You can't get technical with nontechnical decision-makers because you will lose them. Even if they nod their head and say they know what you are talking about, there's a good chance they don't.

In a world where many businesses are only seeking to increase security because they're forced to for legal reasons (or because they have a large partner who is requiring them to meet certain standards), it's important to relate why something must be done for these reasons. Businesses generally don't want to spend money with security unless they are forced to if the possibility of losing deals and money is part of the fallout of doing nothing.

What recommendations do you have for managing nontechnical executives' expectations during a significant ongoing incident?

Don't create fear, uncertainty, and doubt (FUD), and be very specific with outlining benchmarks that don't include over-promising. Most executives' goals in an incident revolve around trying to minimize as much business interruption as possible, which translates to minimizing as much monetary loss as possible. Be realistic with recovery times because the information you give will get distributed internally to other executives, and if you're over-promising, you by default are making the executive over-promise, and you can get them thrown under the bus.

Get the Whole *Tribe of Hackers* Series!

The book that started it all, *Tribe of Hackers: Cybersecurity Advice from the Best Hackers in the World* is your guide to joining the ranks of hundreds of thousands of cybersecurity professionals around the world. Wherever you are in your cybersecurity career, *Tribe of Hackers* offers the practical know-how, industry perspectives, and technical insight you need to succeed in the rapidly growing information security market. It includes inspiring interviews from 70 security experts, including Lesley Carhart, Ming Chow, Bruce Potter, Robert M. Lee, and Jayson E. Street. ISBN: 9781119643371

The Tribe of Hackers team is back with a new guide with insights from dozens of the world's leading Red Team security specialists. With their deep knowledge of system vulnerabilities and innovative solutions for correcting security flaws, Red Team hackers are in high demand. *Tribe of Hackers Red Team: Tribal Knowledge from the Best in Offensive Cybersecurity* dives deep into penetration testing and ethical hacking with interviews from specialists including David Kennedy, Rob Fuller, and Georgia Weidman. ISBN: 9781119643326

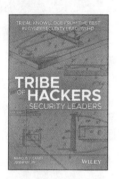

The Tribe of Hackers series continues, sharing what CISSPs, CISOs, and other security leaders need to know to build solid cybersecurity teams and keep organizations secure. Dozens of experts and influential security specialists reveal their best strategies for building, leading, and managing information security within organizations. *Tribe of Hackers Security Leaders: Tribal Knowledge from the best in Cybersecurity Leadership* looks at organizational security impact with Mike Chapple, Kimber Dowsett, Andrew Hay, Tanya Janca, Rafał Łoś, Tracy Z. Maleeff (@InfoSecSherpa), Ray [REDACTED], Khalil Sehnaoui, and many others. ISBN: 9781119643777

The Tribe of Hackers team is back. This new guide is packed with insights on blue team issues from the biggest names in cybersecurity. Inside, dozens of the world's leading Blue Team security specialists show you how to harden systems against real and simulated breaches and attacks. You'll discover the latest strategies for blocking even the most advanced red-team attacks and preventing costly losses. The experts share their hard-earned wisdom, revealing what works and what doesn't in the real world of cybersecurity. ISBN: 9781119643418